To Lissy

July 1945

THE HOUSE THAT BERRY BUILT

BY THE SAME AUTHOR

Published by
WARD, LOCK & CO., LTD.

THE "BERRY" BOOKS

THE BROTHER OF DAPHNE
THE COURTS OF IDLENESS
BERRY AND CO.
JONAH AND CO.
ADÈLE AND CO.
AND BERRY CAME TOO
THE HOUSE THAT BERRY
  BUILT

THE "CHANDOS" BOOKS

BLIND CORNER
PERISHABLE GOODS
BLOOD ROYAL
FIRE BELOW
SHE FELL AMONG THIEVES
AN EYE FOR A TOOTH

OTHER VOLUMES

THE STOLEN MARCH
THIS PUBLICAN
ANTHONY LYVEDEN
VALERIE FRENCH
SAFE CUSTODY
STORM MUSIC
AND FIVE WERE FOOLISH
AS OTHER MEN ARE
MAIDEN STAKES
SHE PAINTED HER FACE
GALE WARNING
SHOAL WATER
PERIOD STUFF

THE HOUSE THAT BERRY BUILT

BY

DORNFORD YATES

WARD, LOCK & CO., LIMITED
LONDON AND MELBOURNE

First published . January 1945
Reprinted . . . January 1945
Reprinted . . . March 1945

THE TYPOGRAPHY OF THIS BOOK
CONFORMS TO THE
AUTHORIZED ECONOMY STANDARD.

MADE IN ENGLAND
Printed in Great Britain by Butler & Tanner Ltd., Frome and London

*To the memory of my beloved terrier,
Tumble, to whom I owe so much.*

CONTENTS

THE HOUSE THAT BERRY BUILT

CHAPTER I

IN WHICH WE REMOVE TO THE HILLS, AND BERRY PULLS HIS WEIGHT

STANDING by Berry's shoulder, I threw a glance round the chamber I knew so well.

The book-lined walls, the chiselled mantelpiece; the original, elegant ceiling; the three, fair windows, whose upper lights were badged with coats of arms; the built-in reader's stall, the little pulpit-staircase; the rugs and the summer cretonnes, the polished furniture; the tulips peering out of their Lowestoft bowls—I looked upon these things and found them valuable. So, I knew, did the others, but their eyes were upon the ground. Daphne was sitting back in an easy chair: Jill was perched on its arm—her hand, I knew, was in Daphne's, holding it tight: Jonah was standing behind them, grave-faced with folded arms.

Lord Atlas looked at Berry, sitting behind the carved table, pencil in hand.

"As I see it, Major Pleydell, the exact position is this. When you and your cousins inherited White Ladies, the cost of maintaining the place as your father and his brother had maintained it was less than three thousand a year. To-day it is nearly eight thousand—eight thousand pounds."

Berry nodded.

"That's right," he said. "Very nearly three times as much. The average cost of maintenance for the last three years was seven thousand eight hundred and sixty pounds. That's sparing no expense: but we never have spared expense where White Ladies was concerned."

"Your books show that." Lord Atlas cleared his throat. "And now the time has come when you and your cousins are really no longer able to find this very large sum."

"I'm afraid that's so. But I think that I should say this—

that that sum does not include the salary of a controller or
bailiff. My cousin, Captain Pleydell, and I have always done
that work."

" What would that come to ? "

Berry shrugged his shoulders and looked at me.

" I think," said I, " that a capable, faithful man would deserve
six hundred a year and to live rent-free."

" Shall we say eight thousand five hundred ? "

" Yes," said Berry, " I think that that would be right."

" Very well. In these circumstances, you and your cousins
are willing to make White Ladies over to the nation, as it stands,
with its gardens and park, to be used as an official retreat for the
Secretary of State for Foreign Affairs, on condition that I endow
it in perpetuity by handing to the trustees, of which you will
be one, a capital sum which will bring in, free of tax, eight
thousand five hundred a year."

" Yes."

" You stipulate that, except for maintenance and repair, the
property shall never be touched, and that the four principal
servants shall remain—the butler, as groom of the chambers ;
the house-keeper and head-gardener in their respective offices,
and the chauffeur at the lodge."

" Yes. Unless and until they may desire to retire upon
pension, for which we shall be responsible."

There was a little silence.

Then—

" D'you think," said my sister, " there should be a little
margin ? I mean, we can't see ahead ; and if prices go on
rising . . ."

Lord Atlas smiled.

" I think Mrs. Pleydell is right. My idea was to transfer a
sum which will bring in ten thousand a year—any surplus to be
placed to reserve."

" That's very handsome of you."

Lord Atlas inclined his head.

" I think the word ' handsome ' must be reserved for you. I
have a great deal more money than I can spend. But you are
giving away your very beautiful home."

*   *   *   *   *

In May, 1937, the Deeds had been signed and sealed.

This was, we hoped, the last of our misfortunes, for Fate had been rough with us for several years. More. Apart from calamities in which we had no say, we had been repeatedly confronted with the unpalatable task of choosing the lesser evil. In this, I think we succeeded ; but the exercise was one of which we were growing tired. Of the more personal blows, I shall say nothing. Suffice it that we, who had been seven, were back to five ; and when Jonah suggested that we should go right away and seek distraction in the heart of the Pyrenees, Jill spoke for us all by flinging her arms round his neck.

*　　　*　　　*　　　*　　　*

" This place," said Berry, " ministers to the mind. You can't get away from that. When we left England, my soul was over at the knees. Now—well, I can't say it's leaping like a ram, but it is no longer decrepit."

" That," said I, " is the mountains. I've always——"

" No laxatives, please," said Berry. " Once before——"

Protests from Daphne and Jill abbreviated the insult.

" You really are filthy," said Daphne. " I don't know about your soul ; but your mind——"

" I know," said her husband. " It's like a dunghill—a thing that steams in the sun. But rich fruit burgeons thereon. That's Nature. Take the melons you gur-nash twice a day. If you were to visit their birth-place——"

" It isn't true," shrieked Jill. " They're most carefully grown in gardens near Angoulême. Katrine told me——"

" Farms, not gardens," said Berry. " I always give full marks to the fellow who thought of that. ' Farm ' sounds so warm and homely. It, so to speak, draws the sting. Oh, and talking of sewage . . ."

When order had been restored—

" The point," said Berry, " which I was endeavouring to make was that we are no better than a lot of mugs. We reside in a hired villa at Pau—a house which has been not only constructed, but furnished in the worst of taste : it might be all right for a blind man who was bed-ridden, but it doesn't exactly subscribe to the well-being of anyone whose eyes and whose hams still function normally."

" That," said Jonah, " is undeniable."

" Very well.   On four days out of five, with one consent, we drive a matter of thirty miles, in order to spend the day in this vicinity.   Unless we are to fast until we get back, we must either take our lunch with us or pay a considerable sum of money for the privilege of eating a collation, as inferior as it is pretentious, in some inconveniently situated hotel.   We, therefore, take our lunch with us.   After a discussion which is invariably character- ized by great bitterness, we select some high place upon which we can eat undisturbed, and we then proceed to lug hampers, cushions, rugs, sunshades, thermoi and two buckets of beer upon ice up a gradient that the Gadarene swine would have refused. We then devour this parody of a meal in attitudes not only of extreme discomfort but calculated to embarrass the entrails— a solemn thought.   No sooner have we satisfied our cravings than we are faced with the fascinating duty of employing scraps of grease-paper to smear from our platters the traces of our feast, of burying the treasure thus won, and of sousing in some ravening torrent the cups and glasses which we are to use for tea. These are then embalmed in anybody's napkin and restored to their hamper, which, though obviously containing less than when we started, has to be held together because it will not shut. After an hour or so of diversion, the same bestial rites are observed, in order that we may have tea : and by the time that function is over, if we are to sit down to dinner clothed and in our right minds, it is time to pack the car and drive our thirty odd miles back to the poisonous habitation in which we take our rest.

" Now, it's hardly credible, but, as I have said, we do this four days out of five.   With one consent.   And we do it four days out of five, because we enjoy this neighbourhood.   Well, even blue-based baboons do better than that.   Where the sugar- cane is sweetest, there their caravan rests."   He addressed his wife.   " What about that villa you spoke of ? "

" ' Spoke of ' ! " said Daphne indignantly.   " Jill and I were all for it : but you turned it down."

" I admit," said Berry, " that my enthusiasm was not marked.

The 'usual offices' were so, er, unusual. But, in the light of what I've suffered in the last ten days, I've been doing division sums. Two into five won't go : but if——''

" That's more than enough," said Daphne. " Does this mean that, if it's still going, you're ready to take that house ? ''

" I'd consider it," said Berry. " The thought of consuming my lunch sitting down in a chair . . ."

My sister rose to her feet.

" Come on, Boy," she said. " If it hasn't gone, we'll take it. And that will be that."

I followed my sister across the sloping meadow, handed her down the bank and into the Rolls.

As I let in the clutch—

" The bedrooms will do," she observed, " but downstairs is rather bare. We'll have to get some chairs and a sofa, or Berry will throw in his hand. We can always sell them again at the end of our time."

" That was in my mind," I said thoughtfully. " Then again, there's the hot-water system. . . . Oh, and what about ice ? Will they deliver up here ? ''

" Now don't say you're going to rat."

" I'm not, indeed," I declared. " I'd put up with quite a lot to be staying up here. But your husband has large ideas ; and when he declares that he is prepared to reduce them, you may be perfectly sure that any such reduction will be effected at somebody else's expense. Take the ice, for instance. He'll have his ice all right, even if it's got to be fetched. But *he* won't fetch it. Then, again, he'll take all the hot water every day."

" I don't care," said Daphne. " We may have to rough it a bit, but at the present moment I'd rather have a caravan here than a castle anywhere else. Berry's perfectly right. This district is curiously healing. I don't know why."

I made no reply. The thought of sharing a caravan with my brother-in-law was precluding speech.

The villa for which we were bound was a modest house, five minutes' walk from Lally, by the side of the mountain road that climbed to the hamlet of Besse. Had it been built upon the same mountainside—but ten minutes' walk from Lally, instead of five, its site would have been incomparable, commanding mountains and valleys and league-long forests, laced with the flash of falls : but, though its view was restricted to the meadows which sloped to Lally and the woods in which that village was sunk, the outlook was very pleasing and the house was retired enough to be very quiet. It had been well built, and there were plenty of rooms, but the furniture was scanty and most austere. Still, a little, natural terrace, shaded by sweet-smelling limes, made a most charming pleasance upon which we could lunch and dine, and I would have suffered a much less convenient lodging for the pleasure of sleeping beneath the topless hills.

Well as we knew the mountains, the fifty square miles about Lally had always been for us the sweetest patch of all in a lovely quilt. Every kind of beauty lay in that zone—a rarer beauty than we could find elsewhere. I sometimes think that the fact of the matter was this—that thereabouts the ' close-up ' never belied the promise the prospect made. Any way, the tract drew us, as a magnet draws steel : and if ever we went else-where, we always were disappointed, because our surroundings fell short of the very lovely standard which Lally's neighbour-hood set.

As we flicked through Lally, I saw a caravan standing beside the petrol-pump. It was not a true caravan : it was something between a caravan and a car. For a couple, that way inclined, it looked a good thing to me. The owner, in shirt and shorts, was standing beside the vehicle, watching the petrol gauge. He did not look round as we passed, but his profile was vaguely familiar. I felt as though I had seen him somewhere before. Then we swung to the left, and down the narrow way to the old, stone bridge. Two minutes later, we reached the Villa Bel Air.

As we made to enter the hall—

" Madame," said the hostess, " will excuse the state of the place. The workmen are in possession, and workmen know no law."

" Workmen ? " said my sister.

The good woman spread out her hands.

" Electricians and plumbers, Madame. But they have almost done. They instal an electric heater to furnish baths. A refrigerator also."

Daphne cried out.

"But that is marvellous. When I was here three weeks ago . . ."

"Madame, what will you ? Indeed, it was Madame who taught me. To let a villa to-day, one must be up to date. The initial expense is fearful ; but . . ."

We arranged to take possession in two days' time.

* * * * *

For five people to take up residence at a villa, which stands some twenty-five miles from the nearest town, necessitates preparation, even in France : and when that villa is very simply found, odd stuff must be hired or purchased, if the tenants are to enjoy their occupation.

At breakfast the following morning, the final arrangements were made.

"The chairs and the sofa," said Berry, "will be my concern."

The rest of us stopped eating.

"Touch of the sun," said Jonah. "He ought to have stayed in bed."

Daphne stared upon her husband.

"D'you mean to say," she said, "that you're going to pull your weight ? "

Berry frowned upon a slice of cold ham.

"Lesser souls," he observed, "can select glass and napery, size up housemaids or order a packet of Vim : but to discover a comfortable chair in the Department of the Basses Pyrénées calls for a brilliance of intellect very seldom encountered and never recognized. Not that I relish the prospect of entering the premises of the average French upholsterer : what you can see from the pavement is quite bad enough for the heart : but there's a good deal at stake. The blessing and the curse are set before us this day. If we choose the curse, for the next two months those exquisite post-prandial periods which French cooking alone can induce, will be defiled. More. It's a matter of health. Nothing is so calculated to turn the stomach as to spend two hours after dinner writhing upon a squab which has been so framed as to call into play muscles which nobody but a rowing Blue knows that he has."

"Well, don't spend too much," said Daphne. "We can sell

which the auctioneer agreed was a proper price.   Over the second brandy, he told me not to come in till he lighted a cigarette. . . .

" Well, all went according to plan.   The stuff was put up at three, and the dealers got round.   They'd made a ring, of course. . . .   I stood at the back, watching.   The bidding rose to twenty, and there it hung.   The auctioneer tried to raise it, without success.   I saw the dealers laughing and moving away. Then the auctioneer struck a match and I nodded my head. ' Twenty-one pounds,' he snapped, and knocked them down. Before the ring had recovered, he was selling a bust of Flora, which was short of one ear.

" And there you are.   When I gave his clerk the cheque, he gave me the dealers' names, so that when we want to sell, we've only to let them know."

" Of course," said Daphne, " one of these days you'll be prosecuted."

" Nonsense," said Berry.   " It was a business deal.   For once the wicked were routed, and the righteous came into their own. What about transport, Jonah ? "

" That's all right," said my cousin.   " I've got a small furni-ture-van.   We can go round by Violet and pick them up."

" What about the covers ? " said Daphne.   " They'll have to go and be cleaned."

" Don't be silly," said Berry.   " You don't clean morocco leather.   You use a damp cloth and a chammy, to bring it up."

As soon as she could speak—

" And they're not in ribbons ? " said Daphne.

" A little rubbed," said Berry.   " But I didn't see any holes."

" And you paid twenty-one pounds for a three-piece suite ? You and that auctioneer ought to be in jail."

" All right," said Berry.   " Don't you sit on them.   Don't be involved in my iniquity."   He laughed wildly.   " I achieve the impossible, I secure our sanity for two months to come, only to be branded——"

" Good God ! " said Jonah suddenly, and lowered *The Times.*

" What is it ? " said everyone.

" Old Rowley's been murdered."

" Murdered ? " breathed Daphne.   " Old Rowley ? "

" Murdered," said Jonah.

All of us sat very still.

Sir Steuart Rowley was more than a King's Bench Judge. He was a great gentleman. He had the spirit and the manners of another and finer age ; and though our acquaintance was slight, we set great store by it. He had always dined at White Ladies, when he was at Brooch on Assize, and had seemed to enjoy his visits as much as had we. Little more than a year ago, his work at Brooch being done, he had spent the week-end with us, and it was the very great interest which he had shown in our home that had encouraged us to name him as one of White Ladies' Trustees. That was two months ago. To our delight, he had consented and had been appointed to act.

And now he was dead—murdered.

" What a filthy shame," cried Jill. " And he was so nice and so gentle in every way."

Jonah sighed.

" Someone doesn't seem to have thought so. Chloroformed and then strangled—with a piece of flexible cord."

" Good God ! "

" Found by the servants in the morning, dead in his chair."

" What a shocking thing," said my sister. " Have they any idea who did it ? "

" If they have, it doesn't say so. But that doesn't mean a thing."

" And his wife ? Oh, no. She's dead. What a merciful thing. Wasn't she John Shapely's widow ? "

" That's right. She died last year. The murder was done at Dewlap, the Shapelys' place."

" Shapely," said I. " That's who it was—his stepson. He was taking in petrol at Lally yesterday afternoon."

" That caravan ? " said my sister.

" That's right," said I. " I knew I knew him, but I couldn't put a name to his face."

" Which way was he going ? " said Jonah.

" Towards the Col de Fer."

" Then he doesn't know what's occurred. I mean, to-day is Thursday, and poor old Rowley was murdered on Monday night."

" They can call him on the wireless," said Jill.

"I didn't notice an aerial on the van. D'you think we should——"

"No," said Jonah. "Sooner or later he'll hear. And he can't do any good. It isn't as if his mother was still alive."

"But what an alibi!" said Berry.

"Yes, it lets him out," said Jonah. "But I hope they get the swine. Both on and off the Bench, Old Rowley was one of the best."

That night we listened to the news.

Sure enough, the call was made.

"Before I read the news, here is an S O S. Will Fergus Colin Shapely, believed to be touring in the Pyrenees, return home at once, as his presence is urgently required?"

*   *   *   *   *

However slight, a move is a hectic business, and we were all down the next morning by half-past eight. All, of course, except Berry. Half-past nine was his hour, though the heavens fell.

Jonah had found and had purchased an excellent run-about car. Again, our luck had come in, for, if we had had our choice, this was the make and the model which we would have owned. A brand new, four-cylinder Andret—a black saloon, and a very good bargain indeed at one hundred and fifty pounds. It had, of course, been ordered by somebody else, but he had grown sick of waiting and had purchased another car : so this one was free when Jonah walked into the shop.

And almost everything else was only awaiting collection by Jonah's van.

"I suggest," said my cousin, "that Berry and I should shepherd the furniture-van. When we've picked up the stuff here in Pau, we can drive to Violet and take in the nests for rest. And thence to Lally. We should be there about one."

"That's all right," said Daphne. "The servants are leaving at nine and should get there at half-past ten. They're taking some food with them, so they can give you lunch. Monique's not coming, so she will stay and clear up. The inventory here should be finished by twelve o'clock. Thérèse will attend to that, but I must have a car this morning—I've two or three things to get. Then we can lunch in the town, and Boy can drive us to Lally. We ought to be there by three."

" You bring Therèse with you ? "

" Yes. Did you wire for Carson ? "

" I did," said Jonah. " He'll be here to-morrow morning."

" Thank heaven for that," said Daphne. " With Therèse and Carson behind me, I could face the end of the world. No crisis fazes them. They just get down to things."

This was most true. Therèse was Daphne's maid—had been her personal maid for several years. And Carson was Jonah's servant. I have yet to learn what Carson could not do.

" Well, we'll take the Andret," said Jonah, " and you can have the Rolls. That'll work out very well, for the van will do about twenty and, because our engine is new we shall have to go slow."

So it fell out—except that, as I had expected, Daphne and Jill, between them, were not prepared to leave Pau until half past four.

Forty-five minutes later I brought the Rolls to rest in the drive of the Villa Bel Air.

Berry was at ease on the terrace—in two of the really excellent garden-chairs. By his side, a very large mug had contained some beer.

" Up to time, as usual," he murmured. " Or did you say three o'clock ? Ah, there's Therèse. Therèse, did you get that silk ? "

" Yes, indeed, Monsieur. And it is very fine. I purchased a metre, as Monsieur told me to do."

" What silk ? " said Daphne.

" In her spare time," said Berry, " Therèse is going to make me some ties. Dress ties. The ones I am wearing, she says, are unworthy of me."

" But it is true, Madame. All that Monsieur has is above reproach—excepting only his ties for evening wear. The merchant who sold him them was a man without conscience. A robber. There, I have said it. That Monsieur should be arrayed in stuff that Eugène would reject ! "

" Oh, it's outrageous," said Berry. " But there you are. If you have a lamb for a master——"

" Monsieur exaggerates. Not altogether a lamb."

"Half lamb, half archangel. Oh, and here's our water coming."

"Water?" said Jill. "What water?"

"Our water," said Berry, pointing.

Up the hill towards us was moving a donkey-cart. In this was wedged a gigantic, covered bucket, such as the French employ in the washing of clothes.

"You see," said Berry, "you can't drink the water here. At least, you can if you like; but if you do, you probably won't drink it long. It's quite all right for washing, but Eugène won't use it for cooking: he says it isn't safe."

"My God," said Daphne. "D'you mean to say——"

"Twice a day," said Berry, "that patient beast of burden will bring us the Lally water, that we may live. It's all arranged—at two francs fifty a voyage. Eugène and Jonah did it—and I approved their deed."

"But that rill at the back of the house!"

"Oh, that's still there," said Berry. "I wouldn't be without it for worlds. I count upon its babble to send me to sleep. But the trouble seems to be that we reside at its foot and not at its head. Eugène is a countryman and he's reconnoitred its source. It's quite all right for lavatories. By the time it gets to us, it's used to them."

"But what about washing?" screamed Jill.

"Well, I'm told it won't stain," said Berry, "unless they're dipping the sheep at the farm above. Besides, we can strain it for ticks."

"Where's Jonah?" said Daphne. "I don't believe——"

A shriek from Thérèse cut short the dialogue.

Daphne and Jill and I made for the hall.

Weak and helpless with laughter, Thérèse was leaning against the sitting-room door.

"What is it?" demanded Daphne.

By a stupendous effort, Thérèse controlled her mirth.

"Madame must excuse me," she said. "I am well accustomed to Monsieur, but not to this. Madame has not seen her *salon*."

With that, she opened the door. . . .

Jonah was in his shirt-sleeves, lovingly polishing a truly mountainous chair. Beyond this stood its fellow, another sumptuous product of the upholsterer's art. And against the wall on the left stood the very largest sofa that I have ever seen. It was just under twelve feet long by four feet wide. Had it stood in a banqueting-hall, its astounding proportions would have occasioned remark ; in a sitting-room twenty-two feet by seventeen . . .

I began to yell with laughter.

Then Jill broke down, and, finally, Daphne herself.

" It can't be true," she wailed. " We're imagining things."

Jonah looked round, pipe in mouth.

" You wouldn't say that," he observed, " if you'd helped to get it in. It took six of us to do it. We brought it in by the window—it wouldn't go through the door. And look at these chairs. Upon my soul, I give your husband best. These three bits together are worth two hundred and fifty to any London Club."

" But look at the room," wept Jill. " It's like a Pullman car."

" A sitting-room," said Jonah, " should justify its name. Besides, there'll be room for a table, in case we want to write."

Berry appeared at a window.

" Am I commended," he said. " Or am I reviled ? Not that I care two hoots of a b-bicycle b-bell. But, just as a matter of interest . . ."

" Darling," said Daphne. " Words fail me. The monuments are stupendous. Just at the moment I feel a little bit dazed. I mean, when you first come in . . ."

" I know what you mean," said her husband. " You see they're there. The room's a shade small, of course. But do sit down on them. Try the Chesterfield first."

My sister did as he said.

She settled herself in a corner and closed her eyes.

After a moment or two—

" You win," she said. " I never thought to live in a show-room. But comfort like this is too rare. I won't give it up."

Jill sank into a chair, and had to be helped to her feet. Finally, I sat down. I can only say that, once you had taken your seat, you were most reluctant to rise. It was rather like leaving a bath on a snowy day.

" You see ? " said Berry.

" I do, indeed," I said.   " And I give you best.   I've never seen anything like them in all my life."

My brother-in-law shrugged his shoulders.

" I struck while the iron was hot, but the point is the iron was there.   And not only there, but hot.   And that is a combination of circumstances with which I have not been faced for several years.   In a word, it looks as though our luck was beginning to turn."

" God send you're right," said Jonah.

" I believe he is," said I.

With that in my mind, I put some champagne upon ice. After all, the girls were tired.

CHAPTER II

IN WHICH JILL AND I NOTICE A MEADOW, AND BERRY'S CONFIDENCE IS MISPLACED

I WAS down the next morning by seven o'clock, and a quarter of an hour later Cousin Jill and I were climbing the mountain-side.

We moved through the lynchet-meadows directly above Bel Air, keeping to the side of the rill and going straight up.   (I call them lynchet-meadows, for lack of a better term.   In fact, they were larger than lynchets, and had the shape that meadows always have ; so that, while a series of lynchets resembles a mighty stairway cut on a mountainside, these meadows resembled a flight of broad, irregular steps, the treads of which were sloping, after the way of a ramp.   In every case their risers were piled stone walls : and these retained the soil, keeping the ' step ' above from gradually slipping on to the ' step ' below.)   In the meadows the going was easy, steep as they were ; but the piled stone walls were higher than they appeared, and more than once I found that the easiest way to help Jill was to set her upon my shoulder and let her scramble from there to the meadow above. For Jill is a feather-weight.

As I jōined her in the third meadow, she slid a bare arm through mine.

"You're very sweet to me, Boy."

"Rot," said I. "I've always looked after you."

"I know. All my life. You all have."

"We happen to love you," I said. "There's only one Jill."

She caught my hand and brushed it against her face.

As we came to the next stone wall, she gripped my wrist.

". . . Sh. There's a lizard. A great, big fellow, Boy. He's lying there, watching us with his big, bright eyes."

"Where?" I breathed. "I can't see him."

"You see that brown stone . . . ? Well, two o'clock from there—about seven feet off."

At last I saw the monster—a full ten inches in length, of a lovely, apple-green colour, brooching a boulder of granite, six feet away.

Lizards are timid things, though the larger are bolder than the small. Had I not seen what followed, I would not have thought it could be done.

Very slowly my cousin approached, to put a small hand on the stone in front of the lizard's nose. And he never moved. Then she talked to him as an equal. She said that we were his friends, that we liked the sunshine, as he did, and wished him well. And, after a little, he looked very hard at me, and set a foot on her wrist. One minute later, he was lying along her bare arm.

Jill never moved or touched him : but in her sweet way she spoke to him very kindly and talked to him exactly as she might have talked to me. And I will swear that that lizard understood. With a sense which we have not got, he read the heart that prompted the pretty words. But that is Jill's way. She is completely natural with man and beast : natural as the dawn and the sunshine and the shadows which great trees throw : natural as falling water and the lisp of the wind in the forest and the silence which sundown brings. And nature calls to nature, as deep to deep. So when she said we must be going, the lizard ran up to her shoulder : and there he turned, to run back, down her arm and on to his wall.

Jill looked at me, over her shoulder—and the light in her great, gray eyes was not of this world.

" Now wasn't that sweet of him ?   He knew I wanted him to do it : and so he did it—to give me pleasure, Boy."

" I know how he felt," said I.

" Oh, you're full of pretty sayings this morning.   But wasn't it fine ? "

" My sweet," said I, " I could give it another name."

Jill blew me a kiss—and climbed the wall on her own.

By eight o'clock we had gained the little road which we had set out to reach.

I must make this clear.

We were upon the side of the mountain which men call Evergreen.   It bears this name, for snow will never lie there for more than a very few hours.   For roughly half its height, Evergreen Mountain is served by a mountain road.   This rises from the Columbine Torrent which washes the mountain's base and it strikes the first stroke of a zigzag from Lally to Besse.   That first stroke of the zigzag is roughly one mile long ; and it is pretty steep, for Lally lies five hundred feet below the hamlet of Besse.   At Besse the road turns right in a hairpin bend, to strike the second stroke of the zigzag from Besse to Loup.   Our little villa, Bel Air, stood upon the first stroke of the zigzag and close to its base.   By moving straight up through the meadows we had met the second stroke of the zigzag, halfway between Besse and Loup.

We were now six hundred feet higher than we had been at Bel Air and were commanding a prospect which will not go into words.

I know fine promenades.   The famous boulevard of Pau commands a magnificent view—one of the finest in Europe, the guide-books say.   But much of the two-stroke zigzag that climbs from Lally to Besse and from Besse to Loup commands the fairest prospects I ever saw.   They are not ethereal.   They do not induce reflection upon the world to come.   But Nature, in all her glory, is there arrayed as she was in the golden age, when the gods came down from heaven, because they found earth so fair.

The sun was lighting Lally and the length of the valley below.

The mountain-tops stood up, clean-cut and glowing against the deep-blue sky. Beneath them, the mantle of forest was glancing green and gay—a magic cloak of foliage, shot all with light. Beneath this, again, the tilted, emerald meadows glittered like watered lawns. And an exquisite reef of cloud was floating on the breast of a mountain, midway between base and summit, a crow's mile from where we stood—a foolish virgin, caught in her gentle duty of shedding her being upon the grateful earth.

I pointed to the Niobe cloud.

"The last of the water-ladies. Now we know why the meadows are always green."

My cousin nodded.

"I like to be up against Nature and see the way she works. And we can do that up here. Oh, Boy, I'm so glad we came."

"So 'm I," said I, and meant it.

We turned west, down the road, and headed for Besse.

Until we came to the hamlet, we had the world to ourselves, for the herdsmen had already gone by and the shepherds were up on the hills : but the hamlet was busy enough, and everyone smiled upon Jill and gave us good day. Then we passed out of Besse and round to the left, to enter the stroke of the zigzag close to whose foot stood Bel Air.

We were half way down this limb—ten minutes' walk from Lally and ten minutes' walk from Besse—when I glanced away from the valley and up to my left.

"My word," I said, thinking aloud. "But what a site for a house ! "

Though I say it, it was a good place. Though the ground rose more sharply later, the first two lynchet-meadows were none too steep. To the left, a lively rill fell down in leaps and scurries, to brawl through a culvert hidden beneath the road. To the right, some sixty yards up, a bluff rose out of the meadows—a cornice of rock and bracken, neighboured by stripling oaks. This seemed to swell out of the mountain in the most graceful way—a gentle reminder that the hills were older than the meadows and were not the work of men's hands. At the foot of the bluff, the rock seemed to overhang, almost as if there was a grotto . . .

There was a grotto.

We left the road and slanted across the meadows, to find a

dripping well that was sunk in the base of the cliff : tiny ferns made it an arras, and trees hung down their branches to give it shade, and cushions of little, wild blossoms that I had never seen were overlaying its ledges and turning such water as fed them into a delicate fringe.

Jill was entranced—and had gone in over her ankles before I could draw her back : for the elegant meadow, below the foot of the bluff—it was as pretty a field as I ever saw—was watered day and night by the dripping well. Indeed, where it came to the road, an old stone trough had been let into its wall, to receive the surplus water and hold it for thirsty beasts. An ass was drinking there, as I helped my fair cousin down.

Regardless of her condition, she led the way back up the road and surveyed the site.

" Boy, it's ideal."

I sighed.

" I think it is," I said. " And if anyone is mug enough to build there, he'll have to cart all his water for nearly a mile."

" But the rill ? "

" Will be half its size in August : and though Berry was putting it high, it isn't drinking water. You can't get away from that."

" And the dripping well ? I'm sure that's pure, and I don't believe it dries up."

" I agree. If you piped its burden across and then pumped it up, you might get enough to wash your face twice a day. There's nothing doing, sweetheart. It's one of those pretty dreams that one has to put up on the shelf ; for a house without water to waste is a desolate place. It is the one thing that matters—water, I mean. Life is not worth living, if you've got to think before you turn on a tap."

With her eyes on the lovely site—

" I suppose you're right," said Jill. " But it does seem meant."

*　　　*　　　*　　　*　　　*

Breakfast beneath the limes was most agreeable.

My walk had made me hungry, and I was the only one eating when Berry appeared.

His resigned expression insisted that something was wrong.

" Darling," said Daphne, " I'm sure you had a good night."

" Superb," said her husband. " I was lulled to sleep by the waters over the earth. I wish I could go back to bed and have it again." He glanced at the flawless heaven before he took his seat. " But all that good is undone. I suppose they haven't connected the bath to the refrigerator by mistake. I mean, that would explain it."

" Five baths off the heater," said Jonah, " is asking rather a lot."

" I only want one bath," said Berry, selecting a piece of toast. " Just a little dash of warm water, in which to immerse my trunk. This morning there was nothing to choose between the taps. And this blasted rill is snow-broth. It goes clean through you. My large intestine's quite numb."

" Are you suggesting," said his wife, " that we should give up our baths ? "

" Certainly not," said Berry. " I will have my women clean."

When order had been restored—

" They'll have to boil me water," said Berry. " Boil it in a large vessel and carry it up when I call. Therèse can see about it.'

" I won't have Therèse lugging buckets of boiling water about the place."

" I don't care who does it," said Berry, " so long as it's done. After all, what does it mean ? Four or five buckets of water, twice a day."

" Don't be a fool," said Daphne. " Eugène has his work cut out to cook our food on that stove. He can't boil bathing-pools."

" I see," said her husband, coldly, " no need for blasphemy."

" I think it's clear," said Jonah, " that we should have a supplementary supply. I suggest a power-plug in the bathroom, and, plugged into that, a hot plate. On this, a vast receptacle, such as a *lessiveuse*, can constantly stand. In the morning, as in the evening, the water will be boiling—or very near. Electricity's dirt cheap here, so why not instal the thing ? Carson can do it this evening. We can get the stuff in Pau. I've got to go into Pau, to pick Carson up. I can get a plate and a plug and the rest of the stuff. And Carson can instal the contraption this afternoon."

" ' The Gordian knot of it,' " said Berry, " ' he will unloose.' And how does the b-bather transfer the b-boiling water from the receptacle to the b-bath ? "

" By means of a saucepan," said Jonah. " Don't spill it upon your feet."

" I think," said Berry, " Therèse should prepare my bath. I mean, I'm not used to ladling molten lead. And, if any did miscarry—well, think of the waste. And what are we doing to-day ? A stroll towards Besse would suit me down to the socks."

Jill cupped her chin in her palms.

" You're coming down to the torrent—the Columbine. Boy's going in with Jonah, and Daphne's got letters to write. So you must come."

" My sweet," said Berry, " we can see the swine from the bridge. From that convenient——"

" It's much bigger, lower down, because of the falls. Besides, a bridge is like tourists. I want to stand by its side. I've always wanted to, but we've never had time."

My brother-in-law swallowed.

" Don't you think," he said, " the first day we'd better stick to the roads ? "

" No," said Jill. " Besides, we must get into training. To-morrow we're going up Evergreen. Right to the top. Therèse says there's quite a good path, if you don't look down."

As soon as he could speak—

" What, up this mountain ? " cried Berry. He laughed wildly. " You must be mad. Besides, my doctors wouldn't hear of it. And I wish you wouldn't say these things. I was going to have a third egg, but I don't seem to fancy it now."

I put in my oar.

" Up and down Evergreen is considered an afternoon's stroll. But I've heard that, once you're up there, you can walk to the Col de Fer. All the way . . . on the mountain-tops. I don't know how true it is. Of course, that's a day's excursion."

" What's the matter with you," said Berry. " This isn't The Psalms. You can't go prancing about a lot of mountain-tops. They're not meant to be pranced on. They're meant to be surveyed."

" I shan't rest till we've done it," said Jill. " D'you really mean that we don't have to come down ? "

" So I'm told," said I. " Beautiful going, they say—like an English heath."

" But how gorgeous ! " said Berry. " Well, you go on and do it : and I'll come up to the Col and meet you by road. I can pilot the ambulance—for those who finish the stretch. The vultures'll look after the others. Remember that day we saw them helping a sheep ? "

" You filthy brute," said Daphne.

" As a punishment," said I, " he shall bear the beer. I'll get a rucksack to-day. Once it's adjusted, they say you don't feel the weight. Besides, it leaves the hands free for carrying other things."

Berry appeared to be communing with himself.

Ten minutes later, I was by Jonah's side, and the Rolls was whipping through Lally and heading for Pau.

*   *   *   *   *

We had picked up Carson and had done our odd jobs in the town before midday : so we drove to the *Place Royale* and berthed the car. Then we sat down beneath the chestnuts and ordered some beer.

As I lighted a cigarette—

" Hullo," said Jonah, " there's Shapely. He looks as though he had heard."

I looked up, to see the fellow whom I had seen in Lally by the side of his caravan. But now he was well turned out. His suit was gray, and I saw that his tie was black. He was standing still on the other side of the *Place*, as though he had just come out of the Hôtel de France. His underlip caught in his teeth, he gave the impression of a man confronted with duties he does not like, who is seeking to make up his mind how best to begin.

" D'you think we should speak to him ? "

" Not unless he sees us," said Jonah. " We hardly know the man—and we like him less."

Here Shapely looked up and saw us.

As he crossed the *Place*, we stood up.

"Hullo," he said. "Thank God for a face I know. Can I sit down with you?"

"Of course," said Jonah. "Is beer all right for you?"

"Please," said Shapely. And then, "I assume you know."

"Saw it in *The Times*," said Jonah. "We're all most awfully sorry. I take it you've only just heard."

"Last night," said Shapely. "At Argéles. I'm roving, you know, with a van. I was going on up the Tourmalet. But I happened to pick up a paper, and there it was."

"You were called on the wireless," I said.

"I know. I never heard it. I drove into Pau this morning, shoved the van in a garage and went to the Bank. A sheaf of wires there, of course, and a letter from Joan, my sister, telling me all she knows. Funeral's to-day, at Woking."

"Yes, I saw that," said Jonah. "Not your fault you're not there."

Shapely shrugged his shoulders.

"I can't get away even now. There isn't a train till six."

"You've missed," said I, "a lot of unpleasantness."

"That's very true," said Shapely. "All the same, I ought to be there—as a matter of form." He drank and set down his glass. "I'm not knocked out, you know. Old R. was—well, nothing to me. In fact, we didn't get on, or I shouldn't be here. But he had no relatives, and so it's up to me to do what I can."

"What can you do?" said Jonah.

Shapely crossed and uncrossed his legs.

"I really don't know," he said. "But the murder was done in my home, and Old R. was my stepfather."

"And you were in France. You can do nothing, Shapely. Even if you had been there, you couldn't have done very much. The matter's out of your hands. You may, of course, have some suggestion to make."

"Regarding the identity of the murderer?"

"Yes."

Shapely shook his head.

"You may know more than I do. I haven't seen a paper, except the one last night. But as soon as I read the news, I assumed it was a crime of revenge. Old R. was 'a hanging judge,' and he fairly weighed out time. There must have been plenty of felons who wanted to do him in."

"He was always just," said my cousin. "It is the unjust judge that gets under the criminal's skin. But we know nothing at all. The police are holding their tongues."

Shapely pulled out a letter and found a place in its text.

"This is what Joan says," he said, and began to read.

"*. . . Old R. was found by Still*—that's the butler—*at seven a.m. Still had come in, as usual, to open the room. The French windows were still wide open, and the reading-lamp was burning beside his chair. Poor Old R. was in the chair, dead and cold—with a length of flexible cord tied round his neck. The cord had been cut from the other standard lamp. The doctor says he knew nothing, because he had been chloroformed first. The pad of gauze and wool had been burned on the hearth. As far as I know, they found no finger-prints. When the brute had done it, he went to the coach-house and took the family car. You know, the Humber Snipe. Nobody heard him. The car was found at Hampstead that morning at eight o'clock. Abandoned, of course. We can place the time of the murder, more or less, for I said good night to Old R. at half-past ten, and you know he always goes up at a quarter to twelve. Always. So it must have been between those times. One Chief Inspector Falcon has taken charge of the case. He is a gentleman and extremely nice. I should say he was very efficient, but he gives nothing away. The crime was clearly studied. I mean the man must have watched and have got to know his ways—how he sat with the windows open and all alone. And he knew how to pick a lock, for the coach-house door wasn't forced. D'you think it could have been, say, a burglar, whom he had sent down? I mean, he had no enemies, and nothing at all was touched.*"

"Not very logical, that; but you see what she means." Shapely folded the letter and put it away.

"Thanks very much," said Jonah. "And Falcon's a very good man. Quite the best at the Yard, at the moment." He wrinkled his nose. "There doesn't seem much to go on, except the theft of the car."

"How does that help?" said Shapely.

" It goes to suggest that the murderer knew his way round. I don't believe it's a felon. You see, if it was, the police would have got him by now. The very first thing they would do would be to check up on all men whom poor Old Rowley had sentenced, who had been lately released. And that would be too easy. Every one would be placed in twenty-four hours. It looks much more like some servant who'd been dismissed, or——"

" Good God ! " said Shapely.

Both of us looked at him.

" Got a line ? " said Jonah.

Shapley frowned.

" Yes and no," he said. " If you'll forgive me, I'd like to leave it there."

" Of course," said Jonah, rising. " And we must be getting along. We're staying up in the mountains, and we've got to get back to lunch."

" Where's that ? " said Shapely.

" Just outside Lally," said I. " A lovely spot."

" You're telling me," said Shapely. " I passed through Lally on Tuesday, *en route* for the Col de Fer." He glanced at the Pyrenees. " My God, I hate leaving it all."

" You'll have to come back," said I, " to collect your van."

" One day, I suppose."

" Well, *au revoir*," said I. " Sorry we can't do more than say how sorry we are."

" You have done more. Being able to talk like this has done me a lot of good. See you again some day."

We took our leave.

As we ran out of Pau—

" He's got his eye on someone," said Jonah.

" A dismissed servant," said I. " You rang that bell."

" Looks like it," said Jonah. " And I'm going to write to Falcon. I'm not so sure that Shapely will spill the beans. He didn't like Old Rowley—he says as much : and he may have liked some servant Old Rowley fired."

" In which case, he may decide to hold his tongue ? "

" Exactly. And that's all wrong. Likes and dislikes shouldn't enter a show like this. It was a barbarous crime. Old Rowley was a great public servant and, begging Shapely's pardon, a very nice man."

There was a little silence, which I presently broke.

" I didn't know you knew Falcon."

" You know him, too," said Jonah. " Ascot two years ago. We brought him back to Cock Feathers."

" My God, was that Falcon ? " said I. " You said he was at the Bar."

" I know," said my cousin. " But that was Falcon all right. And he was a barrister, before he went to the police." He addressed the back of the car. " He's a good man, isn't he, Carson ? "

" A very good man, sir," said Carson.

" You remember Sir Steuart Rowley ? "

" Perfectly, sir. At White Ladies, more than once."

" That was his stepson, Mr. Shapely. He's only just heard the news."

" Was it indeed, sir ? The one they were asking for ? "

" That's right. Remember this road ? "

" Indeed I do, sir. A bend a mile ahead and under a bridge."

" Good for you," said Jonah, and lifted his foot. " Eighty-six. There's not much wrong with this car."

*　　*　　*　　*　　*

As we took our seats for lunch—

" Did Jill show you the site ? " I said.

My brother-in-law nodded.

" Very delectable," he said. " You'd want five thousand slaves to prepare the ground and another five thousand to haul the materials there. It's the sort of venture that would have appealed to Cheops. Now the field on the left——"

" Commands the graveyard," said I.

" What if it does ? " said Berry. " I rather believe in the contemplation of death. You're—well, more prepared then."

Jill began to shake with laughter, and Daphne covered her mouth.

Returning to Berry, I noticed that he had changed his coat—and tie.

When I looked at Jonah, I saw him close his left eye.

" And how," said I, " is the Columbine ? "

Berry accepted a piece of toast.

" You will oblige me," he said, " by not naming that open sewer."

I raised my eyebrows.

" I always thought——"

" I can think of nothing," said Berry, violently, " of less value or interest than any of your rooted beliefs. I have described that treacherous torrent as an open sewer. It's one of those things that should be heard, but not seen, and never, never approached. As a matter of fact, it ought to be filled up." He sat back and looked round malevolently. " This morning I declared my intuition that we should stick to the roads. Was my faithful instinct honoured ? No. Instead I was persuaded to take what was called a path. . . . Of course I was brought up on the Bible. When they say ' a path ' there, they mean a path—a small, but decent way for the sole of the foot. Just because half a dozen drunks have staggered the same way down a mountainside, that doesn't make a path. It was in the course of my efforts to remain upright that I found the souvenir. One moment, it wasn't there : the next, the toe-cap of one of the finest shoes I have ever put on was enshrined in a sardine-tin, which appeared to have been opened less in sorrow than in anger, by means of a cross-cut saw. . . . Of course, the shoe is finished. Damned well done in. Years of boning and polishing just chucked away—because we didn't keep to the road. I might have been playing soccer with a ball of barbed wire. By the time I'd got the tin off, the toe-cap was fringed." He covered his eyes. " Well, it was no good going back : the damage was done. I screamed whenever I saw it. So we came to the brink of the water which was our goal. Having attained our end, I proposed to rest a little, as well to fortify myself for the return journey as to recover from the shock which the devastation of a museum-piece is apt to provoke. Had I had a harp with me, I should have hung it up in a tree. But that gray-eyed siren said ' No.' Possessed of some evil spirit, she determined to cross the flood."

" Be fair," said Jill. " The path led down to a row of stepping-stones. And another path ran up from the other side. I naturally——"

"It all depends," said Berry, "on the definition of a stepping-stone. Personally, I should define it as a stone so stablished, either by nature or art, that whoso sets foot upon it may do so in the confidence that it will not only receive and maintain his weight, but will neither rock, sway, shudder or otherwise betray him. To-day such confidence would have been—was misplaced. From some filthy and mis-shapen conception of gallantry, I insisted on proving the uninviting series of boulders before she crossed. I can't say that I relished the prospect. The water was clearly excited—not to say, vexed. The stepping-stones (*sic*) were, of course, opposing its will, and the fury with which it squeezed between them argued an intolerance which would have made a lumber-jack think. On the right-hand side was a pool of which an offensive-looking trout and the remains of what appeared to be a blood-pudding were the only occupants.

"Apparently you shouldn't use the third stepping-stone. . . . I mean, the habitués don't. At least, that was what the peasant who helped me out said. Out of the pool, I mean. He said that the third stepping-stone was not too good. 'Not too good.' If he'd said that it was so poised that the slightest pressure upon it would cause it to tilt like a balance, he'd have been nearer the mark. And there you have this country. The approach of a *soi-disant* path from either side issues a direct invitation to step upon those stones. That invitation is a vile and treacherous snare, for anyone who sets foot upon the third stone must inevitably be cast into the draught. There's hospitality for you! There's Cretian charity!"

"What happened to the trout?" said Jonah.

With starting eyes—

"That," said Berry, "is what worries me. I brought up quite a lot of the blood-pudding, which, of course, was all to the good, but I couldn't find the trout anywhere. I do so hope he's all right. I mean, I don't mind my suit being ruined, I didn't mind tripping two and a half miles uphill, carrying top weight and soaked to the skin, or having to explain my condition to every peasant I met—they're a dull lot about here. If I meet a man who has obviously been submerged, I don't ask him if he's wet."

He turned upon Jill. " Yes, you'll never get over that, will you ? Every time they asked me, you screamed and yelled with laughter until the sheep looked round."

Jill was clinging to my shoulder.

" Boy, I nearly died. We met eight altogether, and everyone asked the same. They asked if he was wet. And he said no, it was sweat—that all his life he'd perspired very freely indeed and that walking uphill was apt to open his pores. And all the t-time the water was dripping out of his coat. If you could have seen their faces ! "

" As a matter of fact," said Berry, " the exercise saved my life. The chill of that snow-broth has to be felt to be believed. By the time I got back I was sweating. But that's by the way. I'm through with these country strolls. They're too exacting. And expensive. That coat I had on——"

" Thérèse will save it," said Daphne. " So long as you haven't caught cold . . . But you must be more careful next time."

" ' Careful ' ? " screamed Berry. " I tell you, I was betrayed. And I never wanted to do it. I was badgered into approaching the—The Leper's Delight. Badgered, betrayed and b-bitched— that's the poisonous order of my undoing. That's how I spend my first morning in the lap of the Pyrénées. Any suggestions for this afternoon ? "

" Sleep for you," said his wife. " I want to see this site."

" So you shall," said I. " It's window-shopping, of course. But I'd like to hear what you think."

Jonah came, too. They surveyed it from every angle and found it extremely good. But its lack of water confined it to the realm of dreams. About that, no one could argue.

" It's a pity," said Jonah, setting a match to his pipe. " A house built there would be incomparable. Facing full south, with this air and outlook and surroundings, it would diminish most homesteads that I have seen. And talk about landscape— gardening—you'd never be through."

" It's tantalizing," said Daphne. " I'm ripe for an ivory tower."

" I know," said my cousin. " Never mind. Plenty of fish in the sea. I'm told that château by Brace has a first-class spring."

My sister wrinkled her nose.

" I'm not mad about Brace," she said.   " Any way we're all of us fools.   Who wants to buy or build ? "

" We've never lived in hired houses."

" I know.   It can't be helped."

" As a matter of fact," said Jonah, " to build a house just now would do us a lot of good.   It's a primitive instinct, of course : but it's none the worse for that."

CHAPTER III

IN WHICH WE CAST OUR BREAD UPON THE WATERS, AND FIND IT IN TWO DAYS' TIME

THE summer days went by, and the country about us tightened the spell it had cast.   If ever we drove down to Pau, we were actually relieved to get back.   Twice the clouds came down, to swathe Bel Air in their delicate folds of moisture for twenty-four hours.   On the second occasion, the five of us walked in cloud half way to the Col de Fer.   By road, of course. The exercise acted like a cure.   I never remember feeling fitter in all my life.   And the music of the orchestra of waters we could not see was unforgettable.

Old Rowley's death was forgotten—or so it seemed.   Jonah had written to Falcon, but the latter's courteous acknowledgment had given no news.

It was, I shall always remember, upon the first day of July that we took the two cars and drove to Paradise.   This was one of the loveliest places we had found, and it lay perhaps thirty minutes from our front-door.

To reach it, we ran through Lally, turned to the right and on to the road to Pau : before we came to Nareth, we switched to the left, threading a thunderous gorge and taking the curling road which climbed by Cluny and Jules up to the Spanish frontier some twenty-five miles off.   Some of the handsomest country lay this way, and he who left the road could have it all to himself.   Once in a while, a tent would argue the presence of some enthusiast : sometimes a lonely angler fished some stream : but ninety per cent of the visitors stuck to the road, content to survey the prospects which we went up to and proved. But we were not visitors. Living among them, we had the freedom of the hills.

We slowed through the village of Cluny, hanging on our heel at the Customs, to give our assurance that we were not bound for Spain : then we swept on up the gorge, for a short two miles. And there we left the road for a ramp on the left.

Few would have marked this track, for the beeches grew thick about it, interlacing their boughs above it, as though to keep it hidden from curious eyes. Fewer still would have taken this track, for who could say that you could turn, when once you were down ? And it was not a place up which to drive a car backwards. . . . But turn you could, at the foot of the shadowed ramp ; or you could berth your car there and, getting out, take your choice of the pleasances there displayed. Each was five minutes' walk, and it always seemed strange to me that two so different havens should have lain side by side.

Turn to the left, and you came to a blowing meadow of fine, sweet grass. It was very small, very retired with oaks and chestnuts about it, to offer a grateful shade., It was a true mountain lawn ; but it might have been plucked from the English countryside. Lying there, supine, by merely moving his eyes, a man could command on all sides the peaks of the Pyrenees, could mark their bulwarks and tell their glorious towers, observe their hanging forests and glancing falls, could doze and dream of beauty—and wake to find the truth more lovely still.

Turn to the right, and you came to a little path which led some sixty feet down to the torrent's bed. To more than its bed—to a natural bathing-pool. Fringed by a strip of sand, this actually shelved to a depth of eleven feet. In fact, for a third of the year, the torrent passed it by, detailing a waterfall to feed it and keep its burden running and ever fresh. Because it lay full in the sun, except in its depths, it was never cold as the torrent, while the burly rocks about it grew hot and gave off heat.

Little wonder we gave such perfection the name of Paradise.

This particular morning we spent at the pool, and I have a photograph still which Carson took. Watched by Jill and Thérèse, Daphne and Berry are playing a game of backgammon upon the strand ; Jonah is waist-deep in the water ; and I am poised on a rock, about to dive.

At one we adjourned to the meadow, and there, despite Berry's misgivings, we ate our lunch.

It was then that we spoke of the virtue of Lally's water. . . . Berry emptied his glass and called to Carson for another bottle of beer.

" I do take it," he said. " I take it in my coffee and quite a lot of it goes to the preparation of my food. I probably swallow some when cleaning my teeth."

" Not that water," said my sister. " The other. The—the thermal spring. The stuff that invalids drink. It's warm and sulphurous."

" All right. You take it," said her husband. " I've more respect for my stomach. I'm not going to insult it with a beverage reminiscent of rotten eggs."

" Roger says it's not bad," said Daphne, " and terribly good for the chest. He says, if you drink it, you never have a cold the next winter. And here it is, at our door."

" Have you entered the establishment ? " said Berry. " And seen the vomitories ? "

My sister repressed a shoulder—which meant that she had.

" You don't have to use them," she said. " They just give you your dose, and then you go out and sip it."

" If I'm going to be sick," said Berry, " I'd rather——"

" Be quiet," said Daphne. " Nobody's going to be sick. And they're not vomi—vomidaries. They're for gargling."

" The one day I was there," said Berry, " there was a very large woman——"

Shrieks of protest cut short the memory.

" I know," said Daphne. " It's filthy. It oughtn't to be allowed. But that doesn't alter the fact that the water is beneficial. I think it's absurd not to take it."

" My sweet," said her husband, " for all I care, you can drink a gallon a day. I decline to be interested in an evil-smelling liquor which wells from the bowels of the earth. When you spoke of ' the Lally water,' I thought you meant that exquisite crystal fount which serves the taps of Lally, the surplus of which runs in the gutters of Lally by day and night, while we, who live five hundred yards off, must have it dragged to our door in a donkey-cart. Now if we had that on tap—well, I shouldn't drink it all the time, but if we ran out of beer, you never know."

It was about half past two that Jill and Jonah and I strolled out of the meadow towards the forest-clad heights which were opposed to those upon which the road had been cut.

Our way led past a toy barn : that this belonged to the meadow was very clear, for it was built against it, just under the lea of a rise.

Where there is grass in the mountains, there is always a barn, substantially built, as a rule, with dry stone walls and a carefully slated roof. In the upper part, under the slates, the hay is stacked, while the lower part, unfloored, is used as a byre.

Jonah spoke over his shoulder.

" If I believed in camping, I think I should make an endeavour to buy this place. The barn and the meadow, I mean. Half an hour's walk from Cluny . . . good shelter against rough weather, which you could elaborate . . . a bathing-pool at hand . . . and utter privacy."

I nodded.

" You could spend five months of the year here. No doubt about that."

" Why don't we do it ? " said Jill.

" Because, my sweet, I am too old for camping—unless I must. If I've got to do it, I will : but I like to get home to dinner, and a well-found bathroom suits me down to the socks. The lusts of the flesh get a grip, when you're over a certain age. As you are ageless, you can't appreciate that."

" Comfort first," said Jonah, and left it there.

We climbed for twenty-five minutes between the trees : then we bore to the right, to gain a broad ledge or plateau, commanding the gorge we had left. We were now high above the road on the opposite side—we could see a car crawling upon it, making its way towards Spain. Far below us lay the meadow, where

Daphne was sitting by Berry, still fast asleep. Thérèse was talking to her, but Carson was not to be seen.

"Higher," said Jill, relentlessly.

Nearly an hour went by before we passed out of the forest on to a second plateau which fairly deserved that name. A thousand square yards of downland commanded a prospect which made a man hold his breath. To the north, we could look down the valley, no longer a gorge, and could trace its glorious run to the gap through which we had driven, which led to the lowland plains. Cluny was round a bend, and just out of our sight. To the west, rose peak upon peak, in that superb disorder with which no order on earth can ever compare. To the south, where three gorges met, a miniature Jules lay land-locked, beside a glittering serpent of blue and white ; and, beyond her, the Pic du Midi, queen of the range, lifted her lovely head to the westering sun.

"I think," said Jonah, "we can't be far from a path of which I've heard. It runs from Lally to Jules, right over the tops of the hills. If I'm right——"

"Hush," said his sister, setting her head on one side. "I may be wrong, but I think I heard someone calling."

The three of us listened intently.

After a long moment, a very faint "*À moi*" was borne to our ears.

"Over there," said Jill, pointing south-east . . .

We hastened over the plateau, moving that way.

After five minutes, we stopped to listen again.

And heard nothing.

"Call again," I shouted, cupping my lips.

"*À moi*," came the answer, from well away to our right.

The plateau rose sharply to the east, but to the south it ran level, until it came again to the trees. Here the ground ran up in a very steep ramp, and, as I scrambled ahead, I saw that I was approaching the top of some ridge. And then I perceived that it was not a ridge at all, but the edge of some cliff, for the trees stopped short at the top, and there was the Pic du Midi, fairly ablaze in the sunshine, clear to be seen.

As I threw myself forward, the cry for help came very clear. "*À moi, à moi !*"

And then I knew that the cry was coming from over and down the cliff.

I called to Jill to keep back and to Jonah to have a care.

Then I lay down on the ground and drew myself up to the brink.

I have not a good head for heights, and when I saw what I saw, the palms of my hands grew wet and my senses reeled.

I was lying on the edge of a cornice. Beneath me was a sheer drop of well over a thousand feet.

On a ledge beneath the cornice, some twelve feet down, was standing a youth. The ledge was three inches wide. He was holding himself to the cliff by the brittle, protruding roots of one of the firs which was growing close to the brink. The ledge was too close to the cornice for him to hold himself straight : the projecting portion of cliff was thrusting his head and shoulders away from the wall. Seemingly miles below him, Jules looked smaller than ever ; and the glittering serpent beside it, a thread, for some reason, of gold.

The upturned eyes met mine, and the tongue spoke French.

" My rope has broken. That was three hours ago. But I think that, if you will help, there will still be enough. The tree on your right."

I looked at the tree on my right.

About its trunk was a fragment of climbing rope.

Before I had this unfastened, Jonah was lying down and looking over the brink.

I measured the fragment of rope.

" Say thirteen feet," I said : " and his shoulders are seven feet down. We should be able to do it, provided it holds."

Together, we examined the fragment, which was old, but seemed to be sound.

My cousin made a slip-knot and drew the loop wide. Then we lay down again, and he lowered it over the edge.

It was not very hard to drop the loop round the boy's neck. The rope now lay upon his shoulders.

" Get it under your arms," said Jonah. " First one arm and then the other. When you have done that, I'm going to draw the rope tight."

" But——"

"Do as I say, you young fool."

Red in the face, the other did as he said. The manœuvre presented no danger, for one hand was quite enough to hold him to the face of the cliff.

Then, very gently, my cousin drew the rope tight.

Our end now reached the edge with sixteen inches to spare. While Jonah took hold of this, I tied a knot as close to the end as I dared.

"And now what?" said Jonah.

"I think we must risk it," I said, wiping my palms on the ground for the fourth or fifth time. "I don't like this blasted cornice, and I'm not too sure of this rope. But I don't see what else we can do. True, I can hold him here, while you go for the rope in the car. And Carson. But that means a delay of two hours, and he says he's been there three. If he faints before you get back, as he very well may . . ."

"I agree," said Jonah. "And now you lay hold on life, while I take off my shirt."

As I took hold of the rope, I heard a movement beside me.

"I must see, Boy."

Jill.

"Get back, for God's sake," I cried.

"My weight won't make that difference. And if you're both going down, I'd like to go, too."

"Jill, I implore you. For my sake . . ."

My small cousin kissed my ear—and wriggled back from the edge. A moment later I felt her firm hands on my ankles, holding most tight.

Jonah had folded his shirt and made it into a pad. This he inserted between the rope and the edge.

Then he looked down to the boy.

"We're going to pull you up," he said. "But the rope is so short that we're very close to the edge. Much too close for my liking. That can't be helped. So when I give the word, you must try and take some of your weight by climbing yourself."

"If I could have climbed up, I should not have called for help."

My cousin looked at me, and wrung the sweat from his eyes. Then he returned to the youth.

"If you answer me back again, we shall leave you to die. Your life is worth nothing at all, compared with ours : yet we're risking our lives to save it. And now stand by. When you hear me say ' Go,' you will forget this rope and will try to climb up the face."

I took a turn round my wrist, which left some eight inches of rope between my hand and the edge.

Then slowly I drew myself forward, until I could kneel. Jill must have moved with me, for her hands were still fast on my ankles when I was upon my knees.

Jonah got to his feet.

"Go back, Jill," he said gently. "Ten paces back, my darling. We'll be all right."

And, with his words, the thing happened.

A sudden pull on the rope, for which I was quite unready, jerked me violently forward. When I flung out my left hand to save me, this met with nothing at all. For half my body was actually over the edge.

And there was the boy, with his face three inches from mine.

Ignoring Jonah's instructions, without any warning at all, the crazy fool had attempted to climb the rope.

But for Jill's hold upon my ankles, I must have gone down. As it was, I was quite helpless. My left arm was beating the air, and my right was holding a rope upon which was hanging a weight of somewhere about one hundred and forty pounds.

My cousin, Jonathan Mansel, did the only possible thing.

In a flash, he was lying beside me. Then he stretched out his hand and seized the boy by his hair, which was happily long.

Then he spoke to his sister, Jill.

"Try to pull Boy back," he said quietly.

Jonah was taking much of the weight on the rope : this enabled me to get my left hand on the edge, and, when this encountered the root of a neighbouring fir, I was able to help my small cousin to drag myself back.

After what seemed an age, only my head and shoulders were over the brink.

The boy had a hand on the edge . . .

"All together," cried Jonah.

The boy was up and in safety—I felt his foot on my back.

As the rope was jerked out of my hand, Jonah fell backwards and sideways across my legs. As I sought to thrust myself back, a good foot of the cornice gave way.

When the block of soil went down, I thought I was done. Indeed, I went down with it, so far as my trunk was concerned, for all my weight had been planted upon that piece of soil. But, mercifully, Jill had my ankles, and Jonah himself was lying across my legs.

I heard him cry out in French . . .

And after what seemed a long time, two hands, which were stronger than Jill's took hold of one of my legs. Then Jonah seized the other, and the boy and he, between them, dragged me away from the brink.

* * * * *

A nice picture we made, sitting on the edge of the plateau, just clear of the trees.

Jonah, stripped to the waist, was streaming with sweat ; his chest and his stomach were smeared with blood and dirt : my shirt was torn and stained, the fingers of my left hand were bleeding, and the rope had ripped open the skin of my other wrist. Jill, in shirt and shorts, sitting back on her heels, was kneeling between us two, one arm about Jonah's shoulders and one about mine. A bleeding bruise was spreading above one exquisite knee.

" Close call, that," said Jonah, wiping his face.

" You're telling me," said I. And then, " I'm through with these blasted brinks."

" What we want," said Jill, " is a brook."

" We passed one somewhere," said I, " about a week ago."

" D'you feel like that, too ? Never mind. I'm so glad you're alive, Boy darling."

" You must thank yourself, sweetheart. If you hadn't had hold of my ankles, I must have gone."

" And that's God's truth," said Jonah.

Jill got to her feet.

" Come," she said. " We ought to be getting back."

As we stood up, a figure approached from our left. Strangely enough, we had quite forgotten the youth.

" I have to thank you," he said. " I was very badly placed."

" That's all right," said I. " But don't do it again."

" Don't do what ? " said the boy.

" Any of it," snapped Jonah. " Don't climb alone : don't use a rotten rope : and, above all, don't disobey orders when people are risking their lives on your behalf. Where d'you come from ? Lally ? "

" Yes," said the other. " My father is there just now."

" If you like to follow us down, we can give you a lift. Your parents will be anxious if you are too late."

With that, we set off.

We stopped at the spring we had marked, to wash the dirt from our scratches and bathe my wrist ; and there we were joined by Carson, who always became uneasy, if Jonah was gone too long.

" Ah, Carson," said Jonah. " We could have done with you a little while back. But that's for later. Take this young gentleman with you and go on ahead. Take him and Thérèse in the Andret and drive back to Lally at once. Drop him at Lally, and then take Thérèse to the chemist's to get a bandage and stuff for Captain Pleydell's wrist. And then go back to the villa. We'll take the Rolls and be there as soon as you. Tell Major Pleydell what you're doing and say that we're just behind and that no one is hurt."

" Very good, sir. But what of yourself ? You're short of a shirt."

" See that my coat's in the Rolls. That'll see me home."

" Very good, sir."

Jonah addressed the youth.

" If you go with him," he said, " he will drive you back to Lally without delay. Goodbye."

" I am much obliged," said the boy. He hesitated. " I am sorry about your shirt, and I must thank you again. I was very badly placed." He put a hand to his head. " Do not think that I blame you," he added, " but it is very painful to pull the hair."

By the time we reached the meadow, the Andret was gone. But Carson's shirt was hanging on the door of the Rolls.

* * * * *

At eight o'clock that evening, Jonah put a letter into my hand.

"From Falcon," he said.

June 29th.

DEAR CAPTAIN MANSEL,

Secret

Sir Steuart Rowley.

I should have written to you before, but I have been hoping to be able to tell you that we had got our man. As you will see from the papers, the Coroner's jury yesterday returned a verdict against some person or persons unknown. In fact, we know who did it, but he has disappeared.

As you thought likely, the murder was done by a servant whom the Judge had dismissed : and, as you thought that he might, Mr. Shapely showed some reluctance to point to the man. But in fact I had him in view, before Mr. Shapely returned.

The facts are these.

Albert Edward Tass was employed as chauffeur at Dewlap when Lady Rowley died. He was an excellent chauffeur—but he had only one eye. This affliction had always worried Sir Steuart—I think, rather naturally. A chauffeur should have two eyes. But Lady Rowley had pleaded that he should stay. Everyone, including Tass, was aware that, but for Lady Rowley, Tass would have gone. Three months after Lady Rowley's death, Tass was driving Sir Steuart when he nearly knocked down a child. The child was on his blind side—the left. That evening the Judge sent for Tass. In the presence of Mr. Shapely and his sister, he told him that he must drive no more. He did not dismiss him. He offered to keep him on, at the same wages, to look after the cars and to do odd jobs. But Tass would have none of that. Either he drove, or he went. In fact, he lost his temper, and there was an unfortunate scene. He told the Judge to his face that ' he wouldn't have dared to sack him, if his mistress had been alive.' Then the Judge did dismiss him—quite rightly, of course. He could hardly keep a man who had spoken like that. Whereupon Mr. Shapely engaged him, there and then, to be his chauffeur and valet from that time on.

Once he got going, Mr. Shapely was perfectly frank.

D

" *I'd no right to do it,*" *he said ;* " *and I'm sorry now.   I did it to rile Old Rowley.   Tass was nothing to me.*"

I asked why he disliked Sir Steuart so much.

"*First,*" *he said,* " *I hated to see him sitting in my father's seat.   Secondly, he persuaded my mother to keep my allowance down to twelve hundred a year.   He thought a man should work for his living—or some of it.   I didn't agree—in view of the fact that my mother had rather more than thirty thousand a year. Thirdly, by her Will, my mother left him the whole of her income for life—and Dewlap and everything.   I had my twelve hundred —no more.   That meant that he had the whip-hand.   I don't think he spent the money.   I don't believe he touched it, except to keep Dewlap up.   But I was the son and heir, and he had accepted my birthright . . .*"

He laughed there.   Then he went on.

" *That's the sort of motive you like, isn't it ?   Just as well for me that I was in the South of France.*"

Entirely between you and me, I think it is.

To return to Tass.

Mr. Shapely and Tass left Dewlap the morning after the scene. Six weeks later, master and man went abroad, with a caravan. And in May of this year they came to the Pyrenees.   By this time Mr. Shapely was beginning to realize that he had cut off his nose to spite his face.   Tass was becoming a nuisance.   He did not enjoy caravanning or 'foreign parts.'   To use Mr. Shapely's words, " *he wouldn't have lasted a month, if he hadn't had a dud eye.   But I knew that that might prevent his getting another job. For that reason I stuck him—as long as I could.   More than once I went to a hotel, just because I couldn't stand him about.*" *Finally, in the mountains—not far from where you are now— Mr. Shapely paid him off and told him to go.   He gave him his fare to England, and Tass packed his suit-case and went.*

That was on Sunday June 7th, about nine-thirty a.m.

That night he must have travelled to Paris, for we know that he landed at Dover the following afternoon.   (His passport-number was taken at Calais and Dover that day.   And a man with an eye-shade is easy.   He was noticed again and again.   And we traced a five-hundred-franc note that he changed on the boat. This was given to Mr. Shapely by Lloyd's Bank, Pau, five days

*before he fired Tass.)   Tass did not proceed to London, but left
the harbour on foot.   From Dover to Dewlap is just about two
hours' walk.   The murder was committed that night, not before
half past ten and not after a quarter to twelve.   I think there can
be no doubt that the murderer opened the garage and took ' the
family car.'   Any way, that car was taken and presently found
at Hampstead at eight a.m. the next day.   From Dewlap to
London by night would take a good driver considerably less than
four hours.   Tass left Victoria Station by the early boat-train that
day : he passed by Folkestone and Boulogne—passport-number
checked at each port—and went on to Paris at once.   And there he
disappeared.*

I have left to the last one very important point.

*' The family car ' was so called because it was at the disposal
of Mr. Shapely, Miss Joan Shapely and her sister, now married
and in America.   Each had a key of the garage and of the switch.
When Mr. Shapely left England, he forgot all about these keys.
He noticed them some time later and dropped them into a pocket
of his dressing-case.   According to him, he never gave them a
thought until the conversation he had with you at Pau.   That
conversation, of course, suggested Tass as the possible murderer.
And then he thought of the keys.   When he left you, he went at
once to look at his dressing-case.   And when he did so, he found
that the keys were gone.*

To sum up :—

(a) Against Sir Steuart, Tass had a violent grudge,

*(b) Tass was six miles from Dewlap four hours before the
murder took place,*

*(c) Tass was familiar with Dewlap as with Sir Steuart's
ways,*

(d) Tass had access to the keys of the garage and car,

(e) Those keys have disappeared,

*(f) Tass left England immediately after the murder, after a stay
in England of less than eighteen hours,*

(g) Tass has vanished.

*It looks pretty clear to me.   But the French don't seem able to
find him.   It shouldn't be hard, should it ?   An Englishman,
short of one eye ?*

Are you staying on at Lally ?

I'm going on leave before long and I have a feeling I might come down that way.

Yours very sincerely,

RICHARD FALCON.

As I handed the letter back—

" O fortunate Jonah ! " I said. " How many would give their eyes for a letter like that ? "

My cousin smiled and put the letter away.

" I am very lucky," he said. " But I've helped the Yard once or twice, and they never forget a friend."

" They probably value your opinion."

" I don't know about that. In any event I don't think they want it here. Friend Tass is for the high jump, if ever they run him to earth."

" I'll say he is. Those keys . . . Still, why's Falcon coming here ? "

" I imagine, to have a look round. After all, Tass knows this country—or some of it. He may have made a friend in some garage—some little garage right off the beaten track. The French won't ask any questions, provided he's good at his job. And what price the local police ? And don't forget that even Paris is not particularly interested. This is an English murder. ' What's Hecuba to him ? ' "

" Yes, that sticks out," said I. " Any way to hear Falcon talk will be great fun. Didn't he send Oxen down ? "

" He did," said Jonah. " And Baal. He's a very good man."

* * * * *

Dinner had been served and eaten, and we were distributed about our gargantuan suite. As those who had borne the burden and heat of the day, Jonah and I were enjoying the mighty sofa. (Each of us had his feet up, with room to spare.) His coffee and brandy beside him, Berry was enshrined in one of the sumptuous chairs : the other comfortably accepted Daphne and Jill.

Thérèse slipped into the room.

" Madame will receive Monsieur de Moulin, the lawyer ? He is the father of that insufferable youth. But he is of the old school. He desires to thank in person the *Messieurs* who saved his son."

" Of course," said Daphne, rising.

We all got up, as Monsieur de Moulin came in.

He was a man of fifty or thereabouts, stout, cleanshaven, well-groomed, with a very pleasant expression and keen, gray eyes.

He bowed, first to Daphne and Jill, and then to us.

" Mesdames, Messieurs," he said, " may I know whom to thank or saving, at the risk of their own, the life of my only child ? "

Berry came forward and took the lawyer's hand.

" Let me introduce my cousins, Captains Mansel and Pleydell, the second of whom is also my brother-in-law. Between them, they did the job."

Monsieur de Moulin took our hands, one in each of his own.

" There are occasions," he said, " when words are inadequate. Life is a precious thing. After all, it is all we have. And you two risked that thing to save a stranger from death. You will please believe that I am—very grateful . . . You see, I know the spot. When I was younger, I used to climb myself. Do not think that that graceless youth would have told me everything. He is an egoist. But I am not a lawyer for nothing. I dragged the truth from him, as one draws a nail from the wood. When he contradicted himself, I tripped him and threw him flat on his back. Question upon merciless question, till I had the truth in my hands. I know how he flouted your instructions, the assassin, and nearly brought both of you down to a terrible end. He has made the admission with tears. And I had to come instantly— first to try to thank you, and then to apologize."

" Monsieur," said Jonah, " pray think no more of the matter. Your son is young and will learn. And it gave us both great pleasure to do what we did." Thérèse appeared with coffee and brandy. " You'll join us, of course."

The lawyer bowed and sat down.

" First the son and then the father," he said. " But there you are. You belong to a generous race. And now may I have your account ? "

We gave it him faithfully, while he sat on the sofa between us and said no word.

When we had done—

" God is good," he said quietly. " It was the nearest thing.

I have told you I know the place. It is one of the very worst in the Pyrenees. One of the guides was killed there nine years ago, since when no one has touched it. My son, of course, was forbidden to climb without a guide. I fear he found such instructions a reflection upon his skill. . . . Need I say more ? I think not. Except that he will not climb for another two years. To-morrow he leaves for Lyons, to stay with an aunt." He touched my arm. " I fear the rope cut your wrist when you took the sudden strain."

" That's right," I said : " but it's nothing."

" Such a wound can be very painful. And that little brat is complaining about his hair."

" To do him strict justice," I said, " he stood his ordeal very well. Not many boys of his age could have hung on that cliff for three hours."

De Moulin frowned.

" Not more than two, I think. He left at ten this morning and would have reached the cornice at two. And you relieved him at four. Still, two is quite long enough. For himself, I have hopes of his ' service.' The Army, I think, will do him a world of good. And now if you please, we will talk about something else." He raised his glass. " Mesdames, Messieurs, your very, very good health. I trust you are happy here."

" We are, indeed," said my sister : " it is such a lovely spot."

" Ah, Madame, there is only one Lally. My home is at Pau, you know : but I have a small villa here, to which I often resort. But you have the better part, for you are upon The Evergreen Mountain, and so better placed."

For a quarter of an hour, we talked. We told him how we came to be there, and that honest man gave us a sympathy which very few people had shown.

When he rose to take his leave—

" Well," he said, " I am very happy to think that you have found peace in these hills. This is, of course, a poor lodging, though I see that you have done something to make it habitable." He caressed an arm of the sofa. " You will have to be very careful whom you receive, for once they sit down in this room they will never get up. But I wish the house was better. If it was, you could stay here longer."

" How long can we stay ? " said Daphne.

" Till mid-October, Madame, if the autumn is fine.   You see, you will get the sun here, when Lally is in the shade.   All through the winter, Evergreen gets the sun.   And people who live at Lally walk up this road in mid-winter, to warm their bones."

" I can well believe it," said Berry.   " You could live here all the year round in a house which was properly built."

" You could, indeed," said the lawyer.   " And now let me give you counsel.   Why don't you build a small villa half way between here and Besse ?   The peasants would be very ready to sell you some land."

" To tell you the truth," said I, " we've been playing with the idea.   But, you see, there's no water.   Even for this little house, we have to get water from Lally twice in the day."

De Moulin stood very still.

Then—

" Would you like to build there—higher up, along this road ? "

" Yes," said my sister, " we should.   But we cannot consider building, because—well, a cottage with water is better than a palace without."

" Indubitably, Madame," said the lawyer.   He fingered his chin.   " It is strange you should raise this point.   Every year for the last six years, Besse has asked for the Lally water—and Lally has always refused.   It is not that we have not to spare— I am on the Town Council, you know—but pipes cost money to lay and Besse is very small and has two very good springs.   At a meeting of the Council on Friday, the request will come up again. . . ."

Jill was trembling with excitement, and Daphne had a hand to her mouth.

Nobody said anything.

De Moulin was frowning upon his finger-tips.

Then he looked at Daphne and smiled.

" Madame, I can promise nothing.   I have but one vote. But they sometimes take my advice, and—and, but for your brother and cousin, I should be bereft to-night."

*   *   *   *   *

Our state of mind was now curious.

Until that first morning, when I had remarked ' the site,' we had had no idea whatever of building a house : and such is human nature that, had ' the site ' been practicable, I doubt if we should have given it very much thought. As it was, we had played with the idea, because we knew very well that it was only a game. We had never taken it seriously. . . . And yet, as time went by and the neighbourhood tightened its spell, the game had come to mean a good deal to us. In fact, it had come to mean this—that, if ever, in days to come, we thought of building, we should dismiss that thought—because no site could compare with the one between Lally and Besse. And now, in a flash, the situation had changed. In two days' time the game might be no longer a game. . . .

The next morning, Thursday, after breakfast, we had things out.

" Let's get this clear," said Berry. " If the Council gives Besse the main water, do we really desire to build ? "

" Yes," said Jill.

" I think so," said Daphne. " Quite a small place, of course. If it's not going to cost too much."

Berry looked at me.

" I'd like to," said I, " simply because I'd like us to have a home. I decline to live in a town, and after White Ladies— well, no home in the English country would be of much use to me."

" I'm with you there," said everyone.

There was a little silence.

Then—

" I could bear a home here," said Daphne.

" So could I," said Jonah. " That is because the contrast would be so very marked."

Berry fingered his chin.

" I frequently wonder," he said, " where you would be without me. I don't deny the site is attractive. Ludwig, the mad king of Bavaria, would have thrown a fit about it. But we are neither mad nor monarchs : and this is a practical age. The fact that the main water may be available to such a site is a phenomenon. But that is not going to make it practicable.

Houses have to be built—and damned well built, if I'm going
to live in them. Of bricks or stone or whatever they build them
of. And this site is not on the level. Show it to a contractor,
and he will become either insolent or unwell. And who shall
blame him? From his point of view, the site is like a bad
dream. And what of electricity? I know you can make your
own, but that pastime is over-rated—unless you can have a
turbine; and there's no head of water for that. So the lack
of water is not the only snag. For all that, I hate being beaten.
I like this place. And I'd like to wake up in the morning—in a
bedroom worth sleeping in and right on the top of the world.
And so I say this. If de Moulin can wangle the water, let's buy
the fields—if we can. They shouldn't cost very much; and, if
we get stuck, we can always sell them again. And when we
have bought the fields, then we can collect ourselves and consider
the fences to come."

"We'll fly them all," said Jill.

"He's right," said Jonah. "There may be other snags. But
I refuse to see them."

"So do I," said my sister. "I want my ivory tower."

Jill had hold of my arm.

"Oh, Boy, it'll be all right, won't it? Our dream'll come
true?"

"God knows," said I. "But, if we can get the water, we're
over the biggest fence."

So much for Thursday morning.

The Council was to meet on Friday at four o'clock.

To say these two days were trying means nothing at all. In
a way, this was natural enough; for upon the result of that
meeting, our future would largely depend. At the moment we
had no plans: we had no home and we knew not where we should
go or what we should do. But if the Council were to give the
main water to Besse—well, I think we all knew in our hearts
that upon the site we had chosen would rise our new home. Be
that as it may, we could think of nothing else; and the more
we thought of the matter, the more glaring became the
advantages, not only of building a home, but of building it upon
Evergreen, midway between Lally and Besse.

Berry was as bad as anyone.

"It isn't as if, if we build there, we shall be out of touch. I've just been working it out. We can lunch at the Savoy on Thursday and breakfast here—on our terrace, on Friday at nine o'clock."

"Never!" cried Daphne.

"We can. Afternoon 'plane to Paris, and then the night train to Pau. That gets in before eight—and there you are. Then again . . ."

And so on.

We strolled towards Besse and surveyed the site from below : we strolled on through Besse, gained the upper road and surveyed the site from above : armed with field-glasses, we drove through Lally and on to the road to Pau—to survey the site from the opposite side of the valley, two miles away.

After lunch on Friday—

"This is absurd," said Jonah. "Who's coming with me to Pau for the afternoon?"

Daphne and Jill refused to leave the house, but Berry and I found Jonah's suggestion good. We made odd purchases there and presently entered a garage in search of some cotton waste. Whilst the people were getting this, I was looking round, and there, in a row of cars, was Shapely's caravan.

I pointed her out to Jonah, and together we looked her over from stem to stern.

"Close quarters for two," said my cousin. "Except for that, she's a very convenient job."

This was no more than the truth, for most caravans must be trailed, or else are too unwieldy to use upon lesser roads. But this was compact—about half as big again as a full-sized limousine.

"Come on, you two," called Berry. "It's nearly a quarter to five, and we may as well be in at the death."

Forty-five minutes later, the Rolls stole up to Bel Air. . . .

Daphne looked up from a *chaise longue* beneath the limes.

"No news yet," she said. " Jill's up at a bedroom-window, watching the road."

Not until six o'clock did a servant deliver a note.

This was addressed to Daphne.

We crowded about her to read the momentous words.

Madame,

I have the great pleasure to inform you that, at the meeting of the Town Council this afternoon, it was decided by four votes to three to give the Lally water to Besse. The pipe-line will pass up the road and any owner of property on the mountain called Evergreen will naturally be conceded the right to a branch. The work will be put in hand this autumn.

I need hardly say that, if I can be of any service in approaching the present owners of any fields which may attract you, I am entirely at your disposal.

With profound respect, Madame,
Most cordially yours,
JEAN DE MOULIN.

CHAPTER IV

IN WHICH THREE FIELDS BECOME OURS, AND DAPHNE AND JILL PRODUCE A WORK OF ART

ON Sunday, at a quarter past twelve, we showed de Moulin the meadows we hoped to buy.

We chose that hour, because from twelve till two the peasants are within doors, and we saw no sense in publishing what we proposed to do. Indeed, we were perfectly sure that the lawyer himself was accustomed to lunch at midday, so he and Madame de Moulin were going to share our meal. While Daphne entertained the lady, the rest of us walked with her husband up to the site.

" Those three fields," I said, pointing. " The one on the road, the one directly above it, and, again, the one above that."

" But that is simple," said de Moulin, " for the *ruisseau* (rill) edges all three." He took out a little note-book and made a rough sketch. " I shall check them to-morrow upon the cadastral plan. And then I will send for the owners." He pointed to the field by the road. " That is the most valuable, for it is not only more flat, but it lies on the road. I think it belongs to old Coulie ; but we shall see."

I looked at the elegant meadow that lay to the right—the one that the grotto graced, with the trough at its foot.

" It would be nice to have that."

The lawyer shook his head.

" Later, Monsieur, later. On no account now. In fact, if you take my advice, you will purchase but two, to begin with, instead of three. You see, the thing is like this. I shall, of course, say that you mean to build a house. Now any one of these fields would very well contain such a house as a peasant would build. That you should need two for one house will make him open his eyes. But that any man could need three, he simply will not believe. ' Hullo,' he will say, ' there is something behind all this. These strangers are speculators.' And up will go his price, in the hope of sharing the profits which you are certain to make. They are simple serpents, the peasants : don't forget that."

" Yes, I see that," said Jonah, " but let me put it this way. The third field may not be essential—and by the third, I mean the field at the top. But we must build well back from the road, and I am inclined to think that, when we cut into the mountain, as we shall have to do, we shall either reach that field or else undermine its edge. And then, if we do not own it, we shall be sunk : for we shall have to have it—at any price."

De Moulin nodded.

" I see your point," he said. " And in building one never knows. Very well, then. These three fields. But you must not buy more for the present—unless you are millionaires."

" Which brings us," said Berry, " directly to the question of price. We must, of course, accept that, now that the water is coming, any property here is worth twice as much as it was."

De Moulin smiled.

" Monsieur," he said, " dismiss such a notion at once. The peasants will not give it a thought. They use so little water, compared with you. Besse only desired Lally's water that she might be able to boast. For all that, I must tell you at once that you will be forced to pay much more than these meadows are worth. Take this first meadow, for instance. If a peasant was to buy this, he would pay at the very most some thirty-five pounds. It is roughly ninety yards long by some forty deep ;

but land so far from a town is of very little value and, when it is sloping, as this is, it is of less value still. But you will be asked three hundred."

"Good lord," said everyone.

"And will pay one hundred and fifty—about five times its value, yet half what its owner asks." The lawyer spread out his hands. "I shall do my best for you. You may count upon that. Of course, if you are prepared to wait for six or eight months——"

"We aren't," said Jill.

"Precisely, Miladi. If you could wait for so long, the owners would come to heel. But if you cannot wait, you will have to pay."

"Say, roughly, four hundred for the three."

"Thereabouts," said the lawyer. "Mark you, I may be wrong : but if you will leave it to me, I will bear that figure in mind. In a little while now, you will come to know the peasants : and then, when you want more land, you will deal direct. But now you are strangers . . . That makes a big difference, you know. But you will come to like them, and they will come to like you. And they will be proud to know that you are to be their neighbours."

"Well, we leave it to you," said Berry. "We won't fix any figure, until we hear what you say. But let me make this clear. We are well content to pay more than a peasant would pay. Much more. It's only fair. But we're not content to be robbed. The money apart, they'd only despise us if we were."

"Permit me," said de Moulin, "to commend that point of view. If you take that line with the peasants, you will get on very well. They will both like and respect you. And that is everything."

"You think," said Jill, "that they will be willing to sell ? "

"Miladi," said the lawyer, "have no concern as to that. It is only a question of price. When we can agree about that, the fields will be yours."

* * * * *

The lawyer was right.

By the following Wednesday night, three ' agreements to sell and to purchase ' had all been signed.

For the meadow by the road, we had agreed to pay one hundred and sixty pounds : for the one above that, one hundred and forty pounds : and for the one above that, one hundred and twenty-five. With the government tax and the fees, the three would cost us, roughly, five hundred pounds.

So the site became ours.

*   *   *   *   *

The second crop of hay had been recently cut. A third was to come. In return for this third crop of hay, the vendors had agreed to give us immediate possession ; for two or three weeks would elapse before the three deeds were signed.

The following morning, therefore, we all walked up to the site, clambered into the lowest meadow and started to climb.

When Berry had fallen twice, he sat up and spoke to the point.

" The first thing to build," he declared, " is a decent flight of steps. A gradual, curving ascent, with several rests. No good building a house if you can't get near the swine."

" We'll have to be careful," said Daphne : " we don't want to spoil the grass."

" Spoil the grass ! " said her husband. " You wait till they start to build."

" Oh, they'll make a mess, of course. But steps are permanent."

" All right. Don't you have them," said Berry. " One thing we shall be spared, and that is visitors. Those that survive will warn all the others off. And for those that don't—well, the graveyard is nice and close. We'd better keep a bier in the garage."

" Don't be absurd," said his wife. " If we build the house I want, it will take more than a mountain lawn to keep people away. They'll simply fall over themselves to see inside."

" They'll fall over themselves all right," said Berry, grimly. Here Daphne fell down herself. " There you are. Supposing you'd been dolled up, with your Jaeger step-in on and your co-respondent boots. You'd feel like going on up and sliming round some woman who hadn't got broken knees."

His apology having been accepted, I pointed to the foot of the bluff, where our second meadow adjoined the elegant field.

" There's a shelf there," I said. " A sort of half-ledge, half-dip, where we can sit down."

With one consent, we all converged upon this haven. After all, it is exhausting to survey a slippery site whose gradient is one in two.

My recommendation proved better than I had dreamed. The shelf was nearly level, jutted out a little and lay precisely in line with where we proposed to build. We were, therefore, ideally placed to consider the site of the house, yet could do so in comparative comfort—that is to say, without standing on the side of the foot.

One by one we reached port.

As Berry lay down on his back in the shade of a walnut tree—

" One thing," said Daphne. " I won't have an architect."

" I'm with you there," said I. " Let's have our own house."

" No staircase, no architect," said Berry. " Let's think of the things we won't have. I know. Don't let's have a tennis-court."

" Be quiet," said everyone.

" Daphne and Jill," said Jonah, " can get out the plans : Boy and I can look after the actual building ; and Berry can do liaison."

" What do you mean—liaison ? " said Berry.

" Well, the girls can sit here and watch, and we shall be up at the house. And you can move between us, conveying ideas and instructions and, occasionally, a tankard of beer."

" And there you're wrong," said Berry. " I shall design the house, and I shall lie here on a couch and see my orders obeyed."

" Concrete," said Jonah. " Proportion of sand to cement ? "

Berry waved him away.

" Such bestial detail," he said, " is beneath my mind. I shall confine myself to the sweep of the roof, to the hue of my bath-room, to the spread of the terrace upon which I propose to bask. And what about drains ? Do we have a septic tank ? Or just install a shoot and hope for the best ? "

After arguing for two hours, we came to a rough conclusion regarding the size of the house and where it should stand ; and Carson, who was in waiting, produced a number of pegs and drove them into the ground.

" And now," said Jonah, " we can't do much more here, till
we get a contractor up. But we can get out a plan. This will
have to be to scale." He looked at Daphne and Jill. " When
we've done the plan, could you do a model—in paste-board ?
I mean, if you could, it would save a lot of time. You see, we
send for a builder and show him the model first. Then we show
him the site. Then——"

" —we hold him down," said Berry, " until the fit has passed.
We'd better have a cork ready to shove up his nose."

When order had been restored—

" Then we tell him," said Jonah, " that we want that house
on this site. ' Can you do it or not ? ' we say. ' And, if you can,
what will it cost ? ' "

This very simple idea was well received, and we made our way
back to Bel Air in excellent cue. And directly after lunch, Carson
went off to Lally, in search of some cartridge-paper made up
into blocks. Knowing his patrons, he took care to bring back
five blocks—and half a dozen pencils and box-wood rules . . .

I pass over the next few days.

Enough that they were distinguished by many visits to the
site, by brain-splitting excursions into the realm of lower mathe-
matics and elementary draughtsmanship, by some of the most
violent disputes to which I have ever subscribed and by a wealth
of destructive criticism which frequently declined from the level
of calculated offence to that of personal insult.

" But I tell you it is," screamed Berry. " Only a blue-based
baboon that was mentally deficient——"

" The trouble with you," said Daphne, " is that you can't
divide. Forty-seven by nine is five and two over."

" But you're adding in the wall," raved Berry. " The wall
that divides the two rooms."

" Well, you've got to have a wall," said my sister. " You
can't have a wall-less room."

" Oh, give me strength," yelled her husband. " How many
times have I told you that in all my calculations I add half a
wall to a room ? "

" What you mean," said Jonah, " is——"

" Look here," said Berry, savagely. " If anyone tells me what
I mean again, I'll shove his face through his head."

"All right, all right," said Jonah. "But you can't have a room with one wall."

Berry took a deep breath.

"This particular apartment," he said, "is an outside room. I don't count outside walls, as being part of the shell. Now bearing that postulate in mind——"

"Listen," said Jill. "I think I've got it this time. If we bring the morning-room down to twenty-five feet——"

"You mean the library," said Jonah. "The morning-room was twenty-five."

"Not with the fireplace. If——"

"One minute," said Daphne. "What did we say the width of the terrace was?"

"Seven ells," said her husband. "With or without an 'h.' To reduce that to roods you multiply by five and divide by eight and a half above the Plimsoll line. You then hand the result to any blue-based baboon who will immediately dispose of it in the traditional way."

With that, he rose to his feet, pitched his block out of the window and, ignoring the storm of protest, stalked from the room.

One minute later he was back.

He set his back to the door and threw a look round.

"Shape of the house," he said. "We're damned well stuck, aren't we? Well, what of the letter 'T'? Cross-piece facing due south: stem running back to the mountain. Principal rooms in the cross-piece: offices, servants' quarters all in the stem. The two completely separate. Simple to build, and plenty of light all round. Can anyone beat that idea?"

Nobody could. We all admitted as much. No architect would have approved it. But on the following morning the paste-board model itself began to take shape.

*   *   *   *   *

Henri and Jean Lafargue were two efficient men. So much one could see at a glance. We had been advised that they were the best of the builders who practised in the Basses Pyrénées.

Together, they regarded the model, which was really a work of art. It was, of course, to scale—three centimetres to a metre

—and it was very well finished within as without. The walls separating the rooms had been carefully done, and every doorway and window had been most carefully cut. Even the shutters existed, painted in blue. Moreover, the model itself could be taken apart. The roof could be lifted off, and then the first floor, so that it could be examined from stem to stern.

Henri turned to my sister.

" It does not surprise me, Madame, that you desire no architect. He would be superfluous."

" Well, if you don't mind not having one . . . "

The brothers laughed.

" Madame," said Jean, " we shall not regret his absence. We have suffered too much in the past at architects' hands." He returned to the model. " Twenty-eight metres long, you desire, by twenty deep. This will be a big villa, Madame."

(A metre is three feet three inches.)

" Not very big," said Daphne. " One thing you've probably noticed—we couldn't get in the stairs."

The brothers laughed again.

" Many an architect, Madame, has broken down over the stairs. But we will submit some suggestions. And, if you will permit me to say so, you have done a most beautiful job."

" If it makes things simpler . . ."

Henri took up the running.

" It does two things, Madame. First of all, it speaks for itself : secondly, it shows us that you, Madame, know your own mind. If, as I hope, you employ us, we shall, I know, find it a pleasure to do your will. And now may we see the site ? "

Jonah and I led the way. We surveyed the site from the road. Then we made our way to the ledge and surveyed it from there.

" You mentioned a terrace, Monsieur."

" That's right. We want a broad terrace, running the length of the house. Say, four metres fifty in width."

I saw Henri bite his lip.

" What we feel," said Jonah, " is this. If we are to build we don't want to waste any time. Now we cannot build in the winter, because of the frosts. But neither can we start building, until we have shifted a very great deal of soil. I mean, to build upon a mountain the house that we want, you must first make a ledge or platform—do you agree ? "

" Certainly, sir."

" Well, to make your platform, you cut soil out of the slope and, with the soil you displace, you raise the ground below you to the level at which you stand."

" Quite so."

" In this way, when you have dislodged five metres of soil, you will, in fact, have a platform eight metres deep—not ten, of course, because of the wastage : but I think you can fairly say eight. So far, so good. But three of those metres will be ' made ' ground : and on ' made ' ground you cannot build safely, until it has settled right down. If, then, we begin the excavation at once, the soil can settle through the winter and we can build in the spring."

The brothers looked grave.

Then—

" Monsieur," said Jean, " we should like to consider the matter. Please remember this. You have asked us to build, not a chalet, but a château—a large, substantial home." He paused. " To-day is Friday. Will you receive us on Monday at ten o'clock ? "

" That will do well," said Berry. " Always provided that you bring some concrete suggestions. I don't want to rush you un-fairly ; but autumn is coming on and we do not want to waste time. And if you cannot help us, we shall have to ask someone else."

The brothers bowed.

" Monsieur may count upon us. On Monday we will submit a definite plan."

When the two had gone their way—

" Are they scared ? " said Daphne.

" No," said I. " They're only overwhelmed. It's a bigger private house than they've ever built before ; and, from their point of view, the most damned awful site that they've ever seen. But they're out to get the contract. Just look at the advertise-ment. You'll be able to see the house for seven miles."

This was literally true. Once built, it would be a landmark.

" They're most deeply impressed," said Berry.

" And what are they saying at this moment—in the safe seclusion of their car ? "

" That all English are mad," said everyone.

" But we aren't, really," said Jill.   " If it comes off, it'll be the most perfect thing."

" I entirely agree," said Berry.   " If it comes off."

*   *   *   *   *

The brothers were back on Monday at ten o'clock.

Jean had a roll of tracings under his arm.

When the two had paid their respects, Henri addressed himself to Jonah.

" Monsieur insisted on Friday that before the house could be built, a platform must first be prepared upon which to build. Very good. Monsieur is right. But we do not like ' made ' ground, and to delve for twenty metres into the mountainside is quite unthinkable. Besides, who wants a house let into a mountainside ?   Indeed, if we delve for five metres, that will be quite enough. But your house, with its terrace, is twenty-five metres deep. Very well, then, we build a wall. We build a wall which is thirty metres long, directly across the slope and exactly twelve metres *below* where you wish your house to stand. That wall is immensely strong and exactly twelve metres high. Now when that wall has been built, there will be a V-shaped gulf between it and the mountainside. That gulf we shall cover with a platform—a platform of ferro-concrete. And upon that platform, Monsieur, we build the house. The terrace and two thirds of the house will stand upon the platform ; the remaining third will rest on the mountain itself."

We all cried out at the excellence of the idea.

" What is more, we can start at once. With luck, our wall should be up before the hard frosts come in. The platform, no. But we can get all ready against the coming of spring ; and during the winter we quietly cut our five metres out of the mountainside."

" The wall will have wings," said Jonah.

" Quite so, Monsieur. Wings at each end which rise with the wall and run into the mountainside. And the platform itself will be supported by piers."   Jean began to unroll the tracings.

" The wall will be all of stone—from the quarry across the valley, two miles away. It is a kind of granite, and very suitable. Its foundations will be of ferro-concrete, and at every four metres it will be girded with steel."

" Wings and all," said Jonah.

" Precisely, Monsieur. So it will be, so to speak, welded into the mountainside. The base of the wall will be two metres thick : and it will taper gradually to half a metre thick at the top. Such a wall and its platform will cost you five hundred pounds."

There was a little silence.

Then—

" That's a lot of money," said Berry. " I mean, to pay that out, before you begin to build . . ."

Jean Lafargue spread out his hands.

" Monsieur, what will you ? That is the price of building on such a site. But I must be frank with Monsieur. Unless we may build such a platform, we cannot undertake to build such a house. And it will have advantages. The excavation, for one thing, will be very slight. And excavation costs money. The house will require no foundations and will be as dry as a bone. You will have a most spacious chamber beneath the house —such storerooms, work-rooms and cellars as never were seen."

" It's a grand idea," said Jonah. " We must think it over, of course : but I give you best. A mighty retaining wall. And the earth from the excavation goes to make terraced gardens on either side."

" Monsieur should have been a builder," said Henri fervently.

" Terraced gardens be damned," said Berry. " What of the terrace itself ? Fifteen feet by ninety, full in the sun—and commanding as fine a view as I ever saw. Projected, as it were, into space. It'll be the eighth wonder of the world. And less than twenty hours from the grill-room of the Savoy."

We studied the tracings forthwith. . . .

It was very clear that the brothers desired the contract. They and their draughtsmen must have worked to all hours to produce plans so clear and so finished in such a short time.

Finally—

" Monsieur permits us to visit the site again ?"

" Of course."

We all went with them.

Less than two hours later, Carson had marked with pegs the outline of the foundations of the retaining wall.

*   *   *   *   *

Henri was to return the following afternoon. He had to recruit local labour and obtain official permission to quarry the stone we required. The local labour would be leavened by men from his staff at Pau. The latter would lodge at Lally during the week, and a lorry would take them home on Saturday afternoon. A foreman, whose name was Joseph, would be in charge, and one of the brothers would be there three times a week. The work would actually start in three days' time—at six in the morning of Thursday, to be precise. But Henri was to see us on Tuesday at five o'clock—to learn our decision regarding the entrance-drive.

Jonah put it clearly enough—on Monday afternoon.

"The first thing they've got to do is to make a drive into the meadows out of the road. Now the level of the first meadow is six feet above the road at its lowest point. To gain that six feet, or more, they must make a considerable ramp. More. Because the road is so narrow, the entrance itself must be wide : otherwise no big vehicle will be able to get in. Now we don't want to do more damage than we can help ; so the drive which is cut for the lorries which bring the building stuff must be the drive which will afterwards serve the house. We must therefore decide here and now where we want the entrance and how the drive is to run."

"Entrance by the *ruisseau*," said I.

"That's what I think," said my cousin. "The other end of the field would really be more convenient, for, if we enter by the *ruisseau*, everything coming from Lally will be faced with a hairpin turn : but the ground at the other end runs into a ridge and to cut a drive out of that would mean easily twice as much work."

"What about the middle ? " said Jill.

"That's out of the question," said I, "for the middle is where they will work. They must have a clear space there, in which to mix their mortar and shoot their sand and stones. The middle, in fact, will be the builder's yard. And there they will set up the crane they will have to have."

" Did you say a crane ? " said Daphne.

" Of course," said Jonah. " The platform will be forty feet up—forty feet from the foot of the wall. Say, roughly, seventy feet above the drive. Well, you can't climb seventy feet with a lot of rocks in your arms."

My sister put a hand to her head.

" I'm beginning to get frightened," she said. " What have we done ? "

" One minute," said Berry. " For reasons best known to yourselves, you seem to have decided that the entrance should be by the rill. You're probably wrong, but I don't dispute your decision, because I can't see that it matters the flick of a turkey's eyelid where we go in. But then you said we must settle how the drive is to run. Well, that's a very different cup of tea."

" I shouldn't have said that," said Jonah. " You see, there's only one way in which the drive can run. And that's parallel to the road, about twenty feet inside the meadow, which happily, just to begin with, is very nearly flat. You enter by the *ruisseau* or rill and then drive straight along across the foot of the site. And there's the garage waiting, right at the other end."

" Who cares about the garage ? " said Berry. " How will a car proceed from the road to the house ? "

" It won't," said I. " It will proceed from the road to the foot of the front-door steps.

" Don't quibble," said Berry.

" He isn't quibbling," said Jonah. " Just before it enters the garage, a car will pass the foot of the front-door steps. These will debouch upon the apron on which the cars are washed."

" But you said just now that the house would be seventy feet above the drive."

" About that," said Jonah.

Berry looked wildly round.

" One of us is insane," he said. " You can't have a hundred and forty front-door steps."

" Thereabouts," said Jonah. " To take a drive up to the house, we should have to buy two more meadows ; and then the drive would cost us five hundred pounds to build. Of course there'll be two flights of steps, one front and one back."

As soon as he could speak—

" I see," said Berry. " And suppose you get down to the drive, to find you've forgotten your teeth ? "

" You ring up Thérèse from the garage and tell her to throw them down."

Berry left his seat and took a short walk.

On his return—

" What about a lift ? " he demanded.

" Out of the question," said Jonah.

" The other day," said I, " you were all for a flight of steps."

" I said a flight," said Berry. " Not a tread-mill. D'you honestly mean to tell me there's no way out ? "

" None," said Jonah. " I thought you realized that. We shall soon get used to them. After all, what are a few steps, if they're going to lead to a terrace ' projected into the air ' ? "

My brother-in-law swallowed.

" We'd better," he said, " we'd better have some quarters by the garage. Nothing much. Just a bedroom and bathroom, you know—in case I feel faint. Oh, and what do we do if it's raining ? "

" Fairly squirt upstairs," said I, " and into the porch."

" Remove that man," said Berry, excitedly. " Charge him with obscene libel." He turned upon Daphne and Jill. " Yes, you can laugh, you sirens. Not a word about steps yesterday. Slush about hanging gardens and terraces in the air. So I signed that blasted contract. Fancy paying five hundred quid to have your guts dragged out every time you come in."

" Darling," said Daphne, " it sounds much worse than it is. Besides, Jonah thinks about a hundred. Not more than that. And you won't have to run up and down them all day long."

" Are you trying to be comforting ? " said her husband.

" Listen," said I. " It is, of course, inconvenient. You can't get away from that."

" No exaggeration, please," said Berry.

" But it is unavoidable, unless, as Jonah says, we like to buy two more fields and then pay out five hundred pounds, half to be spent on labour and half on retaining walls. Which is absurd. But don't forget that the garden will be on the house-level. The steps will only be used when we want to go out in the car."

" Only," said Berry. " Say twice a day. That's a hundred

and fifty thousand a year. Talk about blue-based baboons.
. . . We'd better call the house ' The Postman's Delight.' "

"Do you agree," said Jonah, " that the entrance should be
by the *ruisseau* ? "

"Oh, I suppose so," said Berry. " The bottom's fallen out
of my soul—but what of that ? "

"And the garage the other end ? "

"Provided that it has a retiring-room. I won't climb a hundred steps every time I want to powder my nose."

This remark was very properly ignored.

Jonah got to his feet.

"Come on then," he said. " Let's go and peg out the entrance,
so that there's no mistake."

Berry joined us before we had done.

"Must they start at cockcrow ? " he asked.

"At six," I said. " Not cockcrow."

"Same thing," said Berry. " Oh well . . . But I'm damned
if I'll shave."

"Do you mean to be present ? " said I.

"Of course. Am I or am I not the head of the family ? "

"You are."

"I should damned well think so," said Berry. " As such I
have my rights. You can keep your hundred steps—and put
them where they belong. But my prerogative remains. No
one shall take it from me. Be the hour dawn or dusk, I'm going
to turn the first sod."

CHAPTER V

IN WHICH BERRY TURNS THE FIRST SOD, AND JONAH TELLS
FALCON HIS GUESS

IN fact, no sod was turned ; but a stone was prized out of
the wall which kept the soil of the meadow from sliding
into the road. The ceremony was duly performed soon after
six o'clock on the twenty-third day of July. Joseph subscribed
to the rite with great solemnity. Indeed, by his suggestion,

we each pulled out one stone, while the workmen looked on. Then we stood away, and the little band fell to work.

We all took to Joseph at once, and Joseph took to us. He was a small merry-eyed man, wonderfully fit and strong and immensely capable. The men liked, but feared him. He was always first on the scene, and was always the last to leave. He knew his job inside out and could do any artisan's business rather better than the artisan himself. Certain pieces of work he would let nobody touch—they were for his hand alone. He was never idle. He never stood watching, but worked with his underlings. Yet he had an eye like a hawk, and a man who wasted time disappeared at the end of the week. The summer working-day was ten hours long : Joseph's was always eleven, and often longer than that. The man had *amour propre*. More. Never before had those for whom he was building displayed any interest in the work : but we took an intelligent interest in everything that was done. This carried Joseph into the seventh heaven, and he gave us the finest service that ever five people had.

By Saturday evening, two things had become most clear. The first was how wise we had been to decide that the entrance should be at the western end of the site : the second was that, though the ground there was lower than at the eastern end, the miniature cliff of soil, which, by cutting into the meadow, the men had laid bare, would have to be held. Indeed, this had had to be revetted to allow the work to go on—roughly revetted with timber, to hold the soil back. But this was not too safe, and the struts, of course, diminished the width of the entrance itself : and so, since, sooner or later, a wall would have to be built, the masons were coming on Monday to start the work.

And there you are.

Before we could build our house, we had to build a platform on which it could stand : before we could build the platform, we had to build a forty-foot wall to hold the platform in place : and before we could build that wall, we had to build a twelve-foot retaining wall, to make the entrance safe for the lorries to go to and fro.

That is the price of building upon a mountainside.

Those first nine days flew by.

Joseph had set a hand-rail which climbed to our ledge, and

that ledge was our battle-headquarters from that time on. There Daphne spent most of her day, and thither we repaired when we could no longer stand up. Jonah and I spent much of our time at the entrance, lending a hand with the mortar or shovelling soil : Carson helped Joseph to build an eyesore hut : and Berry and Jill spent hour after hour at the *ruisseau*, clearing the brambles that choked it and shoring up its banks where they had given way.

And then at last the foundations of the great wall were laid : six feet six inches across and ninety-seven feet long—a raft of ferro-concrete, to carry the wall itself. The work was done one Saturday. On the following Monday morning, the wall itself was begun.

There were now seven masons and thirty-two men in all. The brothers Henri and Jean were determined to waste no time. Two masons were still at work on the little retaining wall at the mouth of the drive. Three lorries were plying all day, bringing now sand, now cement and now the stone from the quarry two crow's miles off. Three men were working at the quarry, hewing and blasting and breaking from dawn to dusk. The water had been piped from the *ruisseau* to a spot by Joseph's hut : Joseph and Carson together had done this job. And a primitive crane had been reared, to hoist giant buckets to a scaffold along which trucks could be pushed to the foot of the great, big wall.

So for fourteen days . . .

Then a proper, steel crane arrived—with an extensible tower, and a man to drive its engine and manage its arm.

The wall was now twelve feet high and had tapered to five feet thick. Its wings, too, were taking shape . . .

In its western wing a doorway was being built—a Norman doorway worthy of the wall and its stone. This would admit to the chamber beneath the platform, and wood and coal and such stores could be brought in by this way. The doorway had been Joseph's idea.

And now it was Sunday evening, and all of us, except Jonah, were standing on the site of the drive, gazing up at the wall.

" How much higher ? " said my sister.

" It'll be rather more than three times its present height."

" Boy ! "

"Plus another three feet six for the parapet."

My sister covered her mouth.

"I feel quite frightened," she said. "Whatever will everyone say?"

"I can't imagine," I admitted. "I confess there are times when I feel uneasy myself."

"The quarry will give out," said Berry. "There can't be so much stone."

"Plenty of stone," said I. "Remember Chartres cathedral."

"They won't let us have that," said Berry. "Destroying ancient monuments."

"Fool," said his wife. "Will the quarry really give out?"

"I'll take you there to-morrow," said I, "and you shall see for yourself what, if I were to tell you now, you would not believe."

"I'll believe you, Boy. Go on."

"We seem to have used next to nothing." That was the truth. "Broken up and set in mortar, a cubic yard of stone goes an absurdly long way."

It was a gray-brown stone, very pleasing to look on and very hard. It was, of course, used rough—that is to say, undressed. The effect was admirable. (One 'girdle' was already in place. This was not to be seen, for it lay in the heart of the wall and was faced with stone. But it was there all right—girding the wall to the wings and the mountain beyond. 'Grapple them to thy soul with hoops of steel.')

We climbed to the masons' scaffold and turned to look at the view.

"And this is nothing," said Jill. "By the time it's three times as high . . ."

"We shall have to be roped," said Berry. "It won't be safe."

"With a decent parapet?"

"Well, a good, strong one. I'm not as young as I look."

"With flags on its top," said Jill. "All nice and warm. D'you think we could get some flags?"

"I know we can," said I. "They cut them twenty miles off!"

"Oh, Boy, it'll be like England."

"That's the idea, sweetheart."

This was most true. One and all, we wanted an English home.

"There now," said Daphne. "Tell me. I've always forgotten to ask. I really think my brain's going."

"I know it is," said Berry. "I'm always afraid you'll lick de Moulin good night."

"You filthy beast," said his wife. "But for heaven's sake tell me before I forget again. The house itself—the façade—will be twenty-eight metres long. Why then is the terrace thirty? I mean, the terrace will be the length of the wall."

"That," said I, "was Henri and Jean's idea. And a devilish good one, too. It will give us a way off the terrace on the western side of the house. A step or two down to the garden. So we can reach the terrace from either garden or house."

"Brilliant," said Daphne. "We'd never thought of that. What a mercy they did."

"That," said I, "is the awful part of building. Five times out of six, you think of a thing too late. But Jonah has vision, and Joseph's a tower of strength."

"I warn you," said Berry, "we shall make some frightful mistakes. Only after we've dug the cesspool——"

"We shan't if we look ahead."

"We've made one already," said Berry.

"What's that?" said everyone.

"This wall won't be high enough. What's forty feet? If it was to be ninety feet high, we could call our residence 'BABEL' and look the world in the face."

Here Jonah appeared.

"Falcon's at Pau," he said. "I've just been speaking to him. He's coming to stay at Lally for two or three days."

* * * * *

"You think he's down here?" said Jonah.

"In this region," said Falcon. "Except for one thing, I've little enough to go on. But at least he does know this district. They went to Portugal first: then they came up to France by sea: they entered the country at Bayonne and gradually made their way east: so they spent just over two months in the Basses Pyrénées. And that is the only part of the Continent that he does know—except some of Portugal. But I don't think he's there, and the French say he hasn't left France."

" ' Except for one thing,' " said Jonah.

Falcon smiled.

" My instinct. Officially, that doesn't count. But it has been right. I have a definite feeling that Tass is somewhere down here."

There was a little silence.

Then—

" You're going to look round ? " said my cousin.

" Yes. Shapely told me roughly the way they came, and I shall start from here and cover that ground. Unofficially, of course. Have you ever heard of a place called Luz Ortigue ? "

" I have, but I've never been there. You turn to the right after Cluny. There's no habitation there."

" That's where Tass was dismissed. He walked from there to Cluny to get a 'bus into Pau."

" If you'd like to see it, I'll take you there to-morrow. I'd like to see it myself."

" That's very kind of you. In my job seeing's believing. I'd give a great deal to run that fellow to earth."

" It was a barbarous crime."

" Yes. And very well timed. The man was in Paris before the Yard was informed."

" Purchase of the chloroform ? " said Jonah.

" The French say it can't be traced. That's likely enough. And it may very well have been purchased in Portugal."

" Finger-prints ? "

" Yes. I didn't say so in my letter. There are things one doesn't write. On a packet of French cigarettes, that had fallen between the front seats of the family car."

" Those of Tass ? "

" Yes. As soon as I had seen Shapely, I sent a man out on the chance, to look at the caravan. The tumblers stand in a rack. After Tass had left him, Shapely had to shift for himself. He'd only used the first three—washed them and used them again. The other three had last been handled by Tass. At least, they bore the same prints as the packet of cigarettes."

" Dead case," said I, and stood up.

" I think so," said Falcon.

" No other prints ? " said Jonah.

" Not one."

" Careless," said Jonah. " I don't mean dropping the packet, That's easy enough. But leaving your prints on a thing that you might so easily drop. And otherwise he was so careful."

" That's very true. But I fancy he made the prints when he purchased the packet in France."

" Probably. What did he look like ? "

" Nondescript," said Falcon. He took his note-case out. " There's his passport photograph—the only one we can raise. He would never be photographed, because of his eye. Neither dark nor fair. Well-covered. Height five feet ten. But you can't get away from the eye-shade. That stamps a man. I don't think the French are trying—and that's the truth."

" Looks more than likely," said Jonah, handing the photograph back. " But what a queer case."

Falcon looked at him very hard.

" What d'you mean by that, Captain Mansel ? "

" In the first place, vengeance cools. Well, it didn't cool here. It stayed hot—for, say, seven months. In the second place, the timing was perfect : the whole crime might have been rehearsed. Thirdly, the murderer leaves you in no doubt as to who committed the crime—eye-shade, passport and keys are simply presented to you. His one card is disappearance—the poorest card in the pack."

" I entirely agree," said Falcon. " It's worried me quite a lot. But everything points to him, and there's nobody else. I looked very hard at Shapely. He had a motive worth having for rubbing Sir Steuart out. But his alibi's copper-bottomed. His passport shows that he wasn't in England this year until June 14th. And the murder was done on the 8th. I can't believe he was dropped. And who took him away ? And Captain Pleydell saw him at Lally on June 9th."

" That's right," said Jonah, slowly. " Shapely couldn't have done it ; and Tass undoubtedly did. I do hope you get him, Falcon. It was a wicked show."

*　　*　　*　　*　　*

We all went to Luz Ortigue the following day.

As the Andret slid out of Cluny, I saw the Rolls ahead pull

into the side of the road.   Then one of its doors was opened and Falcon got out.

As we drew abreast—

" I'm being a nuisance," he said.   " At Mrs. Pleydell's suggestion.   She's very kind.   You see, I didn't know that there was a Custom House here.   Shapely said nothing about it.   And I saw them take our number.   That suggests records of some sort, and I've got a letter here."

I berthed the Andret forthwith and followed Jonah and Falcon back to the Custom House.

Falcon's letter worked wonders.   When the Custom Officers saw it, they were most deeply impressed.

" We are at your disposal, Monsieur.   Pray ask us what questions you please."

" I saw that you took the number of our car.   Do you keep a record of every car that goes by ? "

" But certainly, sir.   And of the passengers."

" What exactly is your procedure ? "

" As Monsieur may know, the frontier is eighteen miles off : but, since the frontier is bleak, this little village is used as the frontier-post.   It is the same in Spain, on the opposite side. Very well.   Between this post and the frontier are many beauty-spots, which tourists delight to visit, without going into Spain. And so we have three classes of passers-by—those who are making for Spain ;   those who are going for a picnic and mean to return the same day ;   and those who mean to camp in the mountains for several days.   The first, of course, we deal with in the regular way.   We accept the word of the second that they will return the same day—but we note the number of the car and the number of passengers :   and if they do not return, the guards go out. Of the third we demand their passports :   these are not stamped, but are kept here against their return."

" And the car and the passengers are noted ? "

" Most certainly, sir.   We have one book for each class."

" May I see your book for Class Three ?   I should like to see the entries for the beginning of June."

As the officer moved to a shelf—

" Yesterday morning," said Falcon, " I saw the caravan. There was nothing of interest there, but I thought it a nice-looking job.   On the small side, of course.   All right for a honeymoon couple—for whom, I assume, it was built."

Here the sergeant returned with a book.

" There are the entries, sir, for the first week of June."

There were only four, and the caravan was the third.

> *EXIT on June 4th, at 11.30 a.m., caravan, dark blue, no. OE567 G.B. (Triptyque) : passengers two—English owner and English chauffeur—passport D77894 Shapely and passport G19632 Tass.*
>
> *RE-ENTRY on June 7th, at 11.0 a.m., chauffeur only on foot —passport G19632 Tass returned : on June 10th, at 5.0 p.m., caravan no. OE567 G.B. and owner—passport D77894 Shapely returned.*

Falcon said nothing, but pointed to *June 10th.*

" And here," said the official, " is a note which the chauffeur bore."

A piece of note-paper passed.

The note was written in French.

> *To the Custom Officer on duty.*
>
> *Please give bearer, Albert Edward Tass, his passport and help him to take the 'bus to Pau.   He will not be coming back.*
>
> F. C. SHAPELY.

Falcon laid down the note.

" Were you on duty that morning ? "

" No, sir," said the official.   He raised his voice.   " Jacques ! "

Another man entered the office.

" I think you received this note."

The other examined the paper.

" Yes, that is right.   A poor man with one eye, I remember. He was bearing a heavy suit-case, and it was very hot.   He was hard to understand, but the note explained things for him.   He caught the 'bus for Nareth : and there, no doubt, he would take the 'bus to Pau."

" Would you know him again ? " said Falcon.

" Oh, yes.   He had but one eye."

Falcon laid four photographs down—of men who were wearing shades over one of their eyes.

" Can you pick him out ? "

The man bent over the four.

At last, he looked up.

" Monsieur is asking a lot."

" I know I am. Do your best."

" It is one of those two, for I know that he had no moustache. But I cannot say which."

One of the two he had picked was the portrait of Tass.

" Monsieur is seeking this man ? "

" I want him badly," said Falcon. " If you should see him, detain him : if you should hear of him, please telephone at once to the Chief of the Police at Pau."

" That is understood, Monsieur. It is a serious charge ? "

" Murder," said Falcon, simply—and left it there.

There was a wide-eyed silence.

" What happens at night ? " said Falcon.

" The post is closed, Monsieur. Classes Two and Three may return ; but no car may go out."

" And for persons on foot ? "

" It is closed also, Monsieur. The way is lighted and barred, and a guard is on duty all night. As you see, the way is most narrow, and the men have orders to shoot."

" Yes," said Falcon : " no one, I think, could get by. Well, thank you very much . . ."

The three of us took our leave.

As we returned to the cars—

" June 10th—not 9th," said I. " That alters the shape of the case."

" It may and it mayn't," said Falcon. " Shapely was unsure of his dates. And living and moving as he was, it's easy enough to forget the day of the month. Even the day of the week. And forgive me for pointing out that you were not caravanning and yet you said that you saw him on Tuesday June 9th."

" I know. But wait a minute. Let's get this straight. I'm not excusing myself, but I'll swear that Shapely said Tuesday when we were talking at Pau."

" Remember his words ? "

" Yes. ' I passed through Lally on Tuesday, *en route* for the Col de Fer.' I know he said that, for I thought ' Was it Tuesday

or Wednesday ? '   But we'd had such a busy week that I thought
' Oh, he's probably right,' and let it go."

I saw Falcon frown.

" He was less definite with me."

" It looks," said Jonah, " like an attempt to mislead. But
I can't believe that it was, for Shapely was well aware of the
entries which we have just read. And they are proof positive
that he wasn't in Lally on Tuesday and, incidentally, that he
couldn't have committed the crime."

" I entirely agree," said Falcon. " His alibi is cast-iron,
because at the time of the murder he was on the far side of this
post. But why didn't he tell me that ? "

My cousin shrugged his shoulders.

" *Qui s'excuse s'accuse*," he quoted.

Falcon laughed.

" You will look at Shapely, won't you ? "

" I think anyone would," said Jonah.

" And where does Tass come in ? "

" D'you really want my guess ? "

" I'd love to have it," said Falcon.

" It was murder by proxy," said Jonah.   " Tass did the job
all right, but Shapely set him on."

*   *   *   *   *

A short four miles from Cluny, we turned to the right.   For a
mile a rough road danced to the tune of a lusty water, with
forest on either hand and a ragged ribbon of blue to speak to
the sky.   Then forest and water fell back and the rough road
lost itself in a mighty sward.

Luz Ortigue is a glen.   On one hand the mountains rise from
an upland lawn : on the other the forests come down to a sturdy
torrent, so that its blue and white water is dappled with light
and shade.   The grass is sweet and close-cropped and is studded
with clumps of oaks.   In a word, I cannot imagine a fairer
camping-ground.   It is, of course, not so private as Paradise—
because it is more convenient, more ' indicated.'   There were
traces of more than one camp, and a tent had been pitched a
short furlong from where we stopped.   But it was a most lovely
spot and made, at a guess, a wonderful starting-point.   The

tent we saw was empty. Its owners had clearly gone off, to prove the depths of the valley or capture the topless hills.

" I wish I liked camping," said Falcon. " If I did, I should settle down here for the rest of my leave. But, to tell you the truth, I'm too soft."

" So are we all," said Berry. " Camping is all very well when you're not more than thirty years old. After that, its shortcomings emerge—from the quilt of rapture with which you have smothered them up. Certain rites should be followed in comfort."

" That will do," said his wife. " I know you mean washing-up, but not everyone would."

" I'd love to camp here," said Jill. " I'd love to explore that valley, before the sun was up and the dew had gone."

Falcon smiled.

" I'm sure you would. But you give the lie to Shakespeare—and very few can do that."

Jill looked at him very gravely.

" What do you mean ? "

" I may be wrong," said Falcon, " but I don't think you feel any older than you did at Shakespeare's age."

" What age was that ? "

" Sweet and twenty," said Falcon.

Jill looked round delightedly.

" Isn't that a nice thing to say ? But, if I was ever that, then it's perfectly true. I don't feel older at all. But, in their heart, I don't think anyone does. There's no reason why they should. I mean, you're just you—whether you're twenty-one or a hundred and six. Age is a law of Nature like everything else ; but all her laws are so wise that if you obey them truly, you can't go wrong." She threw back her lovely head and looked at the sky. " It was awful, you know, when Piers and my babies were killed. They went down in a 'plane together. But I knew that they were all right. Better off than if they had lived. So I had nothing to grieve for—except, of course, that I'd love to have seen them again." Two tears welled out of her eyes, but she dashed them away. " The point is—they were all right. And, if they'd lived, they might have been unhappy—you never know. After all, death's quite natural. And everything that's natural is right. I often think that the dead must be simply wild when people mourn. It's really like getting a peerage—being moved up. It's only that you can't see them, though they can see you. And love goes on, you know. Love's stronger than death."

There was a long silence.

Daphne was biting her lip, and Berry was unashamedly wiping his eyes. Falcon got up and walked off. Jonah was very carefully filling a pipe. And Jill was still looking at the heaven, as though there were something there that her eyes could see.

I rose and followed Falcon.

After two or three minutes of silence—

" Lady Padua," said Falcon, firmly, " does not belong to this earth."

" She never has," said I. " She's out of the golden world."

" And quite unsullied," said Falcon. " I've never seen such a thing."

" I think it's unique," said I. " She knows no wrong. It killed us to give up White Ladies : but, though she doesn't know it, she saw us through. She is entirely selfless, and so—well, she gets things straight. Of course, her life is sheltered. We do our best."

" By God, I don't blame you," said Falcon. " ' And whosoever shall offend one of these little ones . . .' "

" And, with it all, she's wise."

" You don't have to tell me that. The thing is, she's natural. She is the most natural being I've ever seen. And you have seen her grow up."

" She's never grown up," said I. " She's just as she always was."

" Marriage ? "

" Made not the slightest difference. She took the state in her stride. My cousin, Jill, is a throw-back. As I said just now, she's out of the golden world."

Falcon looked round.

" She belongs to these parts," he said.

" I think she does. She can hear the tongues in the trees and read the books in the brooks."

" Ah, but go on," said Falcon.

" You're right," I said. " That is her secret. And how
many can ? What happens to her is right. Her faith passes
all understanding. And that is why she is—Jill."

*   *   *   *   *

Two days had gone by, and Falcon was about to be gone.
One day he had spent at the site, talking with Joseph, working
on the *ruisseau* with Jill and watching the great wall rise as if
it belonged to him. Unless he was playing up, he was silly
about the place. I remember that Daphne asked him if he
thought we were mad. " Mrs. Pleydell," he said, " you are
sane—in a frantic world. I'm proud to have seen the foundations
of something worth while."

And now he was about to be gone.

He would not go without viewing the site once more ; so
Jonah and I had gone with him : and we three were sitting
together upon the ledge.

" I hope," said Jonah, " you'll let us know how you get on."

" Of course I shall."

" And if we can ever do anything, let me know."

" I shall indeed," said Falcon. He hesitated. " Captain
Mansel, I've given your ' guess ' a great deal of thought."

" I'm not sure it was worth it."

" I know it was. But it makes it still more important that
Tass should be found. More. If your ' guess ' is a good one,
Shapely's in touch with Tass."

Jonah raised his eyebrows.

" He probably knows where he is. I wouldn't put it higher
than that."

" For the moment, no : but sooner or later . . ."

" Yes," said Jonah, nodding, " I think you're right. Tass
will have to be succoured from time to time. But that's going
to be difficult, Falcon—I mean, to have Shapely watched,
perhaps for month after month."

Falcon shook his head.

" Not in this case, Captain Mansel. I have the Home Office
behind me as never before."

" Then I think it's a question of time. I believe if you stick
to Shapely, Shapely will lead you to Tass."

CHAPTER VI

IN WHICH HADRIAN'S WALL IS FINISHED, AND A VILLAGE IS ENTERTAINED

FALCON left Lally on Thursday, the twentieth day of August, exactly four weeks since Berry had ' turned the first sod.' On that day was finished the little retaining wall at the mouth of the entrance-drive. In fact, it was not ' little ' : but the great wall itself diminished all other masonry. Falcon had compared it to Hadrian's Wall ; and for us it went by that name from that time on.

To return to the ' little ' wall. This was full twelve feet high by thirty feet long : it was very slightly ' battered,' that is to say, sloping back, and it had been built in a curve to conform to the spacious sweep of the mouth of the entrance-drive. It did not touch the soil which it had been built to retain : between the two, there was a void of six inches which had been packed with stones. At regular intervals pipes of terracotta protruded for an inch from its face. These had been laid, of course, as the wall was being built, to let pass any water that otherwise might have collected between the soil and the wall.

Now that this work was done, two more masons were free to work upon Hadrian's Wall. Until this was ten feet high, the gulf between it and the mountain was likewise packed with stones : and, as with the little wall, pipes had been laid through its depth, to drain any water away. I have spoken before of the doorway, gradually taking shape in the western wing. Its threshold was ten feet up from the foot of the wall : if, then, you entered by this, you stepped directly on to the wedge of packed stones. This surface we proposed to concrete without delay, for so there would be a magnificent storeroom and workshop, ready to hand. Its dimensions would be those of the terrace, which would, when the platform was built, lie directly above.

On the following Monday, the plans of the house arrived, and the brother contractors with them.

" Mesdames, Messieurs," said Henri, " we do not propose, by

your leave, to discuss these plans to-day. We propose, instead, to leave them with you to digest. And then, after two or three days, we two will return. By that time you will know them almost as well as we do, so that we shall, so to speak, stand upon level ground."

" Or a platform," said Jean, mischievously.

" You will find," said Henri, smiling, " that they very closely resemble the beautiful pasteboard model which Madame and Miladi have made. Admittedly, we have made some suggestions : but if these are not to your taste, you have only to say the word. We are not architects. We are here to do as you wish, for you are to live in the house and you know what you want.

" And now I come to a matter of great importance.

" It would be a great mistake to decide in any haste upon the plans of such a residence. And there is no reason for haste ; for the house cannot be begun until the platform is built, and the platform cannot be built until next spring. But wait ! I am not quite sure that we must wait till the spring."

" You mean . . ." began Jill, excitedly.

" Miladi, we promise nothing. It would not be right. The hard frosts may come in early. But we have made such good progress that we are inclined to think—and Joseph, whose opinion we value, agrees with us—that with a little good fortune, the thing might be done. It will mean a great effort—a spurt, to beat the frosts. But, if we can do it—well, we shall gain three months : and that will mean that about this time next year, you will be installed."

A chorus of acclamation greeted his words.

As it died down—

" And now, Mesdames, Messieurs, I come to my point. The construction of the platform does not depend entirely upon the whim of the frosts. It also depends upon you. I will tell you why. The platform will not be of earth—or even of brick. It will be of ferro-concrete—cement and steel. And once the concrete has set, it must not be touched. Any holes in it, therefore—holes through which pipes will pass—must be left in the structure, *before* the concrete is laid. That is vital : for, once it is laid, Mesdames, it can never be pierced. Well, now, pipes must pass—the plumber, the builder's foe, will not be

denied. Drain-pipes, waste pipes, pipes for central heating. . . .
And so I ask for your help. Not for one moment do we ask you
to pass the plans, as a whole. But we do ask two things. First,
that you should make sure where your bathrooms and lavatories
shall be built : and secondly, that you will engage what plumber
you please and tell him to visit me as soon as ever he can. He
will have your instructions and I shall give him a duplicate set
of these plans ; and, when he has worked things out, he will mark
on the plan of the platform where he desires his holes."

" How long can you give us ? " said Jonah.

" Let me put it like this, Monsieur. Provided that the weather
is kind, we should like to run in the concrete four weeks from
to-day. But please remember this. We make this suggestion
in your interest, and not in ours. If you feel that it cannot be
done, then the platform must wait. But if you can do it,
Monsieur, and if the weather is kind—well, then, you will be in
your house by this time next year."

*   *   *   *   *

To say that we fought for those tracings is very nearly true.
Berry tore one, by snatching, before the brothers were fairly
out of the house.

" The stairs," shrieked Daphne. " Where have they put the
stairs ? "

" I can't see them," said Berry. " They must be outside."

" There they are ! " cried Jill. " Oh, isn't that clever, Boy ? "

It was very clever indeed—to our simple minds.

Thanks to Berry's brain-wave, the design of the house was
exactly the shape of a T, with the cross of the T facing south
and the stem of the T running back to the mountainside. In
the front or upper part of the cross of the T lay all the principal
rooms, both upstairs and down : behind these rooms lay two
galleries, one above the other, running the length of the cross.

Where the cross of the T met the stem, the brothers had hung
a semicircular stair : the galleries were untouched, for the
stairway was sunk in the stem—a broad, agreeable stairway
which curled, with the wall on its right, from the ground-floor
up to the first. Not only was this a most convenient place, but
it broke in an elegant way the line of the galleries. And when

we perceived that, directly behind these stairs, on the opposite side of the wall, the brothers had hung the back-staircase, we gave the two of them best.

But not all their suggestions were so helpful.

Appalled, as we had feared they would be, by the simplicity of our design, a turret rose on the left and a bay bellied out on the right, and a 'rustique' balcony ran the whole length of the house. Still, it was simple enough to strike out suggestions like that, and all things that really mattered they had embodied or improved.

The outside walls would be solid and twenty inches thick. All inside walls would be solid and ten inches thick. The outside walls would be built of quarried stone : the inside walls would be built of blocks of concrete, turned out of a mould. Between the ground-floor and the first and between the first-floor and the attic, rafts of ferro-concrete were to be laid ; and, except, of course, for the frames of the windows and doors, no wood would be used in the construction until the attic was reached. The roof would be hung with tiles which came from the north of France and were guaranteed against changes of temperature. The terrace and its parapet were to be laid with flags. The floors were to be of parquet. The downstairs gallery and the stairs were to be of marble, and the stairs would be graced by a wrought-iron balustrade. The fireplaces would be of brick, with recesses on either side, to contain the logs. All woodwork throughout the house was to be of seasoned oak. The shutters upon the ground-floor were to be of steel : those on the first-floor of oak. The plumbing, the wiring and the tiling of the interior were to be our affair.

" And very nice, too," said Berry. " I've always wanted to live with a marble stair."

" But what on earth," said Daphne, " is all this going to cost ? "

" They take care not to say," said Jonah. " Nothing appears about price."

" We shall be ruined," said Daphne. " Marble and parquet and tiles from the north of France."

" I will have my marble," said Berry. " No one shall take it away. I shall probably be painted upon it. Besides, if we're building our home, we may as well make it nice."

"I agree," said I. "We mustn't dishonour the site."

"I'm with you," said Jill.

"Listen," said Jonah. "All these details can wait. All that we have to decide without any delay is whether the bathrooms and lavatories are where we wish them to be ; where else we want running water ; where we want to have radiators ; and the site of the furnace-room."

"Is that all ? " said Berry.

Jonah shrugged his shoulders.

"You heard what he said. If we want that platform this year, we must do our part. Once the concrete's run in, no holes can be made. Damn it all, it's going to be ten inches thick."

My sister put a hand to her head.

"We seem to be building a fortress."

"Why not ? " said Berry. "An Englishman's home is his castle—or so they say."

I put in my oar.

"I support the brothers there, and Jonah will, too. A house such as we have designed will be an enormous weight. In the ordinary way, the weight of a house doesn't matter—nobody gives it a thought. But that is because most houses are built on the earth. But two-thirds of the weight of our house will not be borne by the earth. Hence Hadrian's Wall and a platform ten inches thick."

"Well, we've plenty of time," said Jill, " to settle the things Jonah says. The brothers said a month."

"My darling," said Jonah, "we have not plenty of time. We have not one moment to waste. We've got to find a plumber who's willing to do the work. We've got to show him the plans and exactly what plumbing we want. He will then do his sums and render his estimates. And when we've accepted these, then—and not before—will he be in a position to mark on the plan of the platform the holes which he will require. And from what I know of plumbers, if he is in that position four weeks— not a month—from to-day, we shall have achieved a record. In fact we have less than four weeks ; for Joseph will want to know where these holes are to go at least four days before the concrete's run in."

An interview with Joseph the next morning shewed forth the

truth of these words, and we spent the rest of that day deciding exactly the plumbing which we should require.

By the plans, the furnace-room would stand just clear of the platform upon the soil : and the servants' quarters, scullery and pantry would also be built upon earth : those, then, could wait. But the bathrooms and lavatories serving the principal rooms would all be above the concrete which must not be pierced. These appeared almost exactly where we had suggested they should stand, but it was clearly important that we should inform the plumber whereabouts, for instance, in a bathroom the various fittings should go.

" Drains will be drains," said Berry. " You can't get away from that. Once the platform is made, it will be no good lamenting that of course the bath should have lain where its lesser brother must stand."

" But it's frightfully difficult," said Daphne. " I don't know the width of a bath."

" Roughly a metre," said Jonah. " That's three feet three. And two metres long. If you work on those dimensions, we can get a catalogue to-morrow and check them from that. The bathroom doors and windows will really dictate where the various requisites go."

" ' Requisites,' " said Berry. " What a very beautiful word. Which reminds me that the condition of the western hinge of the requisite upon the ground floor of this residence is causing anxiety."

" Carson's fixed it," said Jonah. " And now this plumber business. I think we should see de Moulin and ask him to give us a line on the plumbers of Pau. And to-morrow we must go in and see for ourselves."

" How the hell does one choose a plumber ? "

" By references," said Jonah. " There's no other way. You go to a man and ask him what work he's done. Then you go to the people he's worked for and ask them if his work works."

" I see," said Berry. " Well, I think I'll leave that to you. I don't want to spend my day discussing water-waste-preventers with women I've never seen. Besides, we shall be arrested. ' Pardon, Madame, but am I right in thinking that the amenities of your beautiful home were recently crowned by the installation of a closet of unusual convenience ? ' I know this is France, but——"

" If it works," said Jonah, " they'll show you with all their might. If it doesn't, they'll say so—at length. I repeat— there's no other way. We must have a damned good plumber ; otherwise we shall be sunk."

De Moulin named three plumbers and prophesied evil of all. This was borne out by the households we visited. At the end of the second day we entered a very small shop which was not on de Moulin's list. After a little delay, a man was fetched from the workshops which lay behind.

When we said what our business was, the other smiled.

" You are, then, the Messieurs who are building a château by Lally ? "

" That's quite right," said Jonah. " How did you know ? "

" There is a saying, Monsieur, that a city which is set on a hill cannot be hid. Besides, my nephew is your foreman."

" What, Joseph ? " said I.

" That is right. A conscientious lad."

" Would you like to do the plumbing ? It'll be a pretty big job."

The other bowed.

" It would be a fine order for me, sir, but I must tell you this. I am in a small way at present. I should have to ask you to pay me sums on account. The makers of baths, for instance, will give me but little credit : but you would not lose by that, for we should get a discount for cash. And if you would like a reference, Monsieur de Tourey of Lescar would speak for me. I put in his central heating at the end of last year. He is very enthusiastic. You see I was apprenticed in Switzerland, where the plumbing is very good."

We arranged to take up the reference and let the man know the next day.

And the day after that he came to inspect the site . . .

" Joseph," said I, " why didn't you mention your uncle ? I think he's the man for us."

" Monsieur," was the reply, " one should not commend one's relations, however good they may be. But I am very glad you have found him. His work will be very well done ; and, for me, it is always pleasant to labour with someone one knows."

That day the plans were passed and Felix Arripe, plumber, was appointed to practise his mystery in our behalf.

We felt that the choice was wise. His showroom was not garnished with coloured porcelain baths ; but on his shelves were the catalogues of all the principal firms. He had but three workmen ; but then he worked himself. About wholesale and retail prices he was almost distressingly frank. His reference was first-class. Finally, we were quite sure that, had he been Joseph's twin, Joseph would not have commended a man whom he did not trust.

By the first of September, Hadrian's Wall and its wings were twenty-seven feet high.

Within the space which the wall and its wings enclosed, ten pillars or piers had been founded, to carry the beams upon which the platform would rest. Pillars, piers, beams and platform would all be of ferro-concrete, and all would be welded together into one whole.

The doorway in the western wing not only was now finished but admitted to a fine level floor, some ninety feet long by fifteen ; and the brothers had already arranged for a cable to be run from the valley which would bring electricity up ; so that when they started work upon the platform, the men who were working below should have plenty of light. But that work could not be begun, till Hadrian's Wall had reached its appointed height.

Ferro-concrete is this—rods or grilles of steel, sunk in a very strong mixture of pebbles, sand and cement. The steel must be laid in position : and when it is as it should be, the mixture is poured and rammed all round the steel. The mixture must, therefore, be liquid—not, of course, like water, but rather like very thick gruel. But gruel will not stick to a thing, unless it is held. So, beneath or around the steel, there must be a layer or coffer ; and this is of wood. Once the concrete has set, the wood can be taken away : but it must be there to hold up the steel and the concrete, until the latter has set. Such work is called shuttering—and costs very nearly as much as the ferro-concrete itself. Since the area of the platform would be some six thousand square feet, six thousand square feet of shuttering had to be done : and every pier and beam must be coffered, or boxed about.

Already the lorries were bringing up piles of rough planks and pit-props. . . .

The site was becoming an eyesore—a scar on the countryside.

The weather was still very fair and the days were immensely hot. We had had next to no rain, and only once had a storm interfered with the work. The *ruisseau* was running low, but still gave water enough for the masons' needs. So far we had had no frost.

Everyone now was working with all his might.

On Monday, September the seventh, the steel began to arrive. The rods were of all sizes—some as thick as a pencil and some as thick as my wrist.

" Ah," said Jonah. " And now we can do something better than lend a hand."

He hastened in search of Joseph, and after a moment or so, the two went into the hut.

When they emerged, Jonah beckoned . . .

" Joseph is going to teach us to make a grille. He's going to make one as a pattern. And when he has made it, then we shall make the rest. That will mean he has four more men to put on the other work."

" Four ? " said Berry.

" Four," said Jonah. " You'll soon get into the knack."

" It is hard on the hands," said Joseph, and picked up a pair of cutters, as long as my arm.

We followed him up to the doorway, set in the western wing. Behind us, two workmen were bearing a sheaf of rods.

As we all passed on to the concrete—

" Observe, Messieurs," said Joseph, " the very great value of a work-room right on a building site. It is, indeed, without price."

In a flash he had drawn his rule, had measured a length on the concrete and marked it off : very soon he had chalked a rectangle, roughly six feet by three. Then he picked up a rod, measured a length of two metres, took the cutters from Carson and cut the piece off. Ten such lengths he cut : then he laid them upon the rectangle which he had chalked. Then he cut twenty lengths of one metre and laid these across the lengths already in place. More or less evenly spaced, they made a rough grille.

" Messieurs will observe," said Joseph, " that the ends of the rods protrude from the rectangle which I have drawn."

He picked up a coil of soft wire, snipped two inches from this and tied together a couple of rods where they crossed. This he did again and again, until, when he lifted the grille, the rods did not move. Then he turned the grille about and bent the protruding ends over, two at a time. But he only bent over the ends of the one-metre rods.

" The others I leave," he explained, " for they will hook on to the bars which wait to receive them, which will hold the grilles in their place." He rose to his feet. " Well, Messieurs, there is the pattern. Of these, we shall need thirty-six ; but the others will not be so big. It is but dull work, but it must be carefully done. And, as I have said, you will find it hard on the hands."

" That's quite all right," said Jonah. " A pair of pliers, perhaps, just to bend the ends of the rods."

" I send them at once," said Joseph, and left us alone.

" Now let's get this straight," said Berry, possessing himself of the rule. " I'll do the measuring off, Carson can do the cutting, Boy will lay them in place and you'll tie them up."

" Give me the rule," said Jonah. " Two to a grille."

With that, he drew a fresh rectangle, six feet away from the first.

As he stood up—

" You'll work with me—I know you. And Carson will work with Boy."

Berry swallowed.

" As you please," he said. " All the same——"

" I shall do the cutting and laying, and you will do the ties."

" I shall lacerate my fingers," said Berry.

" Just to begin with," said Jonah, mercilessly.

I picked up Joseph's grille, to lay it aside. To my surprise, I found that it weighed a great deal. And Joseph had turned it about, as though it were a page of a book.

And there you are.

Joseph had made his grille in ten minutes of time. And he had been working alone. Carson and I took eighteen minutes exactly ; and the others—thanks to Berry—took twenty-four. I felt most deeply ashamed . . .

Still, we did improve.

Before the day was out, Carson and I held the record with eight minutes dead; and Jonah and Berry had done it in under ten.

Joseph had left us alone—except that from time to time more rods were brought up. But at four o'clock he appeared, to see what we had done.

When he saw the piles of grilles, he pulled off the little beret he always wore.

"Messieurs," he said, "I make you my compliments. If I had four workmen like you, what could I not achieve? What is more, I need not check them. I know they are true to the pattern in every way."

"It's our house," said Berry, licking the blood from his fingers and wiping the sweat from his face.

Joseph smiled.

"And if it was not, Monsieur, they would be just the same. I know. It is *amour propre*. If one were to do bad work, one would not be able to sleep."

Between us, we made all the grilles, while the men who should have made them did other work.

The steel cores of the pillars were boxed in the next two days, and, before the week was out, they had been embedded in concrete for almost the whole of their height. In every case a foot of steel was left bare; this would run into the beam which the pillar would help to support, so that pillar and beam would be locked together with concrete—so locked that even an earthquake could never tear them apart.

On Thursday the wings were finished; the cores of the beams were laid on that and the following day; and, as they were laid, they were coffered. By Saturday afternoon this work had been completed, and all the coffers were propped. And on Saturday evening Hadrian's Wall was done—six weeks to the day since we saw its foundations laid.

It was, I think, a great triumph to have raised such a wall in six weeks; but a much more signal achievement remained to be won. In a word, in the following week, the steel-work of the platform had to be laid—and tied to that of the beams as well as to that of the girdle which was to lie on the top of the

wings and the wall; and the platform had to be shuttered—
that is to say, a staging had to be built beneath where the platform would lie, to hold up steel and concrete, until the latter had
set. All this must be done in one week. And then, if the weather
permitted, the concrete could be run in.

Till now I have said nothing of the interest our venture aroused
not only in Lally and Besse but the neighbouring countryside.
Any building upon Evergreen was bound to excite remark;
rumour apart, such a thing could be seen for miles. Husbandmen
could see it from the meadows and shepherds could gaze upon it
from many a mountain lawn; from a third of the rooms in Lally,
observation upon its progress could well be kept: and every car
that used the main road on the farther side of the valley could
keep the construction in view for more than a mile. Any building on such a site was bound to arrest the eye; as for Hadrian's
Wall . . .

I tremble to think of the number of working hours which
were lost in contemplation of that great work of men's hands.
Husbandmen neglected their labour; flocks and herds cared for
themselves; people sat still at windows, propping binoculars;
the road between Lally and Besse became a promenade; and
once I counted six cars drawn up by the side of the way, directly
across the valley, two crow's miles off. At first we declined to
believe that people journeyed from Pau to see what we had done,
but Thérèse declared it was so, and at last I proved it myself.

On the Sunday morning which followed the actual completion
of the wall, Berry and I walked leisurely up to the site. Daphne
and Jill and Jonah had gone to Church. As we passed the
elegant meadow, we saw four people ahead in the midst of the
way—two men and two women, all French, engaged in argument.
Their gestures left no doubt that they were discussing the wall.

As we made to pass by—

"*Pardon, Messieurs,*" said a voice.

The elder of the two men was speaking.

"It is possible that you can assist us. You see, we have
come from Pau, to see this important construction of which we
have heard. Even now, we dispute the matter."

"How can I help you?" I said.

"Monsieur, we were informed that a château was being built.

Very well. The walls are there : before long the roof will go on. But where are the windows that such a château should have ? "

"That's not the house," I said. "That wall will support a platform upon which the house will be built."

The other man put in his oar.

"I cannot accept that," he said. He pointed to the construction. "Those are plainly the walls of the château, and there on the left is the doorway in which the front door will be hung. Some steps, no doubt, will approach it : and a porch of glass will protect it against the rain."

One of the women leaned forward.

"My husband," she said, "is expert. His cousin is a building-contractor with whom we are on excellent terms."

Berry picked up his cue.

"A building-contractor ? " he cried. He took off his hat. "I salute a colleague. I have a step-aunt who is a bricklayer's mate." He laid a hand upon my shoulder. "I present my wife's brother—also, alas, my cousin. He has spent many years in prison, but is reformed. He will very shortly take orders."

The eyes of his audience were starting out of their heads.

"And now for the problem," said Berry. "Did I understand you to say that a flight of steps will protect the porch from the rain ? "

With a visible effort, ' the expert ' marshalled his wits.

"The—the château has no windows," he stammered. "We perceive a doorway worthy of such a house : but we have been finding it strange that there should be no windows through which the occupants might consider this very beautiful view."

Berry roared with laughter and clapped him upon the back.

"My old friend and colleague," he chirruped, "you are behind the times. An architect from Paris has designed this residence. Those who live there will do so by artificial light. It is the rage, you know. In all the best quarters of Paris the windows are being filled in."

The Frenchman swallowed.

"But that," he said, "is formidable. To build a house in the sunshine and live in the dark."

"Everyone to his taste," said Berry. "And how did you leave my uncle ? "

The other put a hand to his head.

"Monsieur, I think, mistakes me for somebody else. I have not the honour——"

"You are Monsieur Le Dung," said Berry. "We met in Montmartre one morning at two o'clock. My uncle was regrettably drunk; and you and Fifi were——"

"Never," shouted the other. "I am not Monsieur Le Dung."

"That was the name," said Berry, "which Fifi used. Ah, Fifi!" He blew a kiss into the air. "Never mind. The next time you see my uncle——"

"I tell you," screamed the other, "that you have made a mistake. I do not know this Fifi. As for your uncle . . ."

Berry was looking back, whistling, as though for some dog. Then he returned to our companions.

"Never keep a bear," he said gravely. "A dog, yes. But a bear is disobedient."

"A bear?" cried one of the women.

"I used to have two," said Berry; "but one took a fancy to babies and so I gave it away. I'm not too sure about this one. They get very jealous, you know. If they see you talking to someone . . ." He turned to me. "See if he's coming, will you? I want to get on."

I walked back towards Lally, calling "Butcher!"

By the time I looked round, Berry had the road to himself. He led the way to our ledge and threw himself down.

"We shall get into trouble," I said, "if you go on like this."

"Impertinent fools," said Berry, "must be discomfited. When four adult beings, the youngest of whom will never see forty again, after well marking these bulwarks, decide that they are those of a windowless house, and are then offensive to people who put them wise—well, such persons must be corrected."

"Madame Le Dung will correct her husband all right. Her face, when you mentioned Fifi, argued suspicion confirmed."

"The point is," said Berry, "they won't come back this way. When they heard you call Butcher, they fairly legged it for Besse. You know, that wall is a corker. If it was not well done, it would let the landscape down. As it is, it's right in the picture. . . . Walls are so old. They're nearly as old as the hills. Balbus and Romulus built them. We'll have to take care with the house : but, whatever we build above it, that wall will always be the feature of the estate."

" We should," I said, " have put a canister within it containing our names and particulars, some coins of the realm of England and a copy of *The Times*."

" So we should," said Berry. " Never mind. We'll put one in a wall of the house. A proper document on parchment, which you shall draw up. Oh, and what do we do to-morrow ? "

" Help to run the concrete into the beams."

Berry fingered his chin.

" That doesn't sound too bad. Entirely between you and me, I've lost interest in grilles. They'll be improved by burial. The thought that I'm treading their graves will warm my heart. By the time I'm through, I shall probably feel the same about the beams. ' Run in.' I suspect the transitive use of such intransitive verbs. It sounds as if we were going to suffer some liquid to pass. My instinct tells me that that is too good to be true."

" We may have to work it a bit."

" Quite so. Again the transitive use of an intransitive verb." He examined his hands. " I suppose they can graft on new finger-tips. And I can wear some false nails."

" To-morrow," I said, " will impose a strain on the palms— the juncture of the palms with the fingers."

" Blisters ? " said Berry.

" It's just possible. Crowbars are unsympathetic."

" Hell's guts," said Berry. " They wouldn't allow this at Dartmoor. They dress for dinner there now. And now let's examine the latest work of men's hands. I remember a crumb of mortar I meant to remove."

Eight hours later we learned that our stock had soared in the little village of Besse. Thérèse was our informant.

" But Monsieur is terrible. How the village of Besse has laughed. All were emerging from Mass, when four strangers arrived at a run. They were greatly deranged. They said there was a bear in the way, and, when they were asked whereabouts, they said that it was approaching ' the windowless house.' Then all the world discerned the footprints of Monsieur. The strangers were interrogated, and, sure enough, Monsieur le Major Pleydell was found to be the owner of the bear. And of a second bear which had devoured infants in arms. Imagine how Besse has roared. And all the windows in Paris which are being bricked up! But who would believe that four grown-up individuals could be such imbeciles? And Monsieur le Capitaine, the felon, who is soon to become a priest! But when they came to Monsieur Le Dung, then Besse has broken quite down. Monsieur le Maire had to be helped to the café, and tears were running on Monsieur le Curé's cheeks. And the strangers are furious, because they have not been believed. And they would not walk back down this road, but sent for a car from Lally to take them back. Ah, Monsieur has made a number of friends to-day; for the bourgeois despises the peasant, but now the country has had the laugh of the town."

"And the moral?" said Berry. "Don't say that Besse missed the moral."

"The moral, Monsieur? Ah, no. But that is too much. Monsieur cannot deceive Thérèse."

"There's an excellent moral," said Berry, "a present of which I make to Monsieur le Curé free of charge. He must use it in his sermon next Sunday. If those four strangers had gone to Mass, as they should, they would not have fallen foul of a disobedient bear."

"And Monsieur?" said Thérèse. "Monsieur was not at Mass."

"Monsieur was receiving instruction from his cousin, the priest to be."

Thérèse gave a shriek of laughter and disappeared.

CHAPTER VII

IN WHICH FORTUNE FAVOURS THE BOLD, AND TWO STRANGERS
APPROACH OUR GATES

THE next morning brought a letter from Falcon.

September 12th.

DEAR CAPTAIN MANSEL,
                Sir Steuart Rowley.
I promised to let you know what progress I made.

I left Lally, as you know, on August 20th. From there I drove to Oloron, where I spent two nights. Then, for a week, I rambled about the country, visiting villages and towns, till I came to the sea. There I turned north and made my way to Bayonne. At Bayonne I turned east and made my way back to Salies. There I spent two nights. I reached Orthez the following day. That was September 3rd. I stayed at La Belle Hôtesse, *which no doubt you know—to find that I had missed Shapely by thirty-six hours.*

I won't detail the action I took, but will tell you what I found out.

Shapely reached Pau from Paris by the early-morning express on Thursday September 1st. He drew from the cloak-room some baggage which he had left there in June and drove direct to the garage at which he had left his van. He gave orders for the van to be serviced and ready by half past ten. At that hour he returned, paid his bill and left, driving the van. That evening, at half past six, he came to La Belle Hôtesse, *where he spent the night. The next day, September 2nd, he drove to Bordeaux. There he made arrangements to ship the van and caught the night train to Paris, arriving at Croydon at four o'clock the next day.*

I saw him on September 7th.

I pointed out that Orthez was twenty-five miles from Pau— a distance which even a van can cover in less than eight hours. I asked which way he had taken and how he had spent that time.

His answer was this. That, whilst he was touring with Tass, he had made a photographic record of the way by which they had gone. That record had been incomplete, because he had run out of films. Having occasion to fetch his van, he had taken the opportunity of making good that gap. He showed me the pictures he had taken of the country by Navarenx.

I do not believe his explanation. I think that he went to meet Tass. He was plainly shaken by my questions and feared I knew more than I did.

The region south of Orthez is being carefully combed.

Yours very sincerely,

RICHARD FALCON.

" My God," I said. " What shocking bad luck ! Falcon was sitting at Salies, while Shapely was ten miles off."

" Wicked," said Jonah. " But observe, if you please, that Falcon doesn't complain. He's used to hard knocks."

" I hope he's used to hard nuts. Shapely will take some cracking. Fancy having those photographs ready."

" Yes," said Jonah. " He's up against something there."

" There remain," I said, " two things which are too hard for me. First, why did Shapely lie—say that he passed through Lally the day before he did ? "

" You believe that it was a lie, and not a mistake ? "

" Yes," I said. " For this reason. If you are right, and Shapely directed the crime, the vital dates would have been engraved on his mind."

" So they would," said Jonah. " That's one to you."

" Secondly, why didn't he tell Falcon that his passport was with the Customs on the day that the crime was done ? I know you say that he probably shrank from producing so perfect an alibi. But I don't feel that that's the answer."

Jonah raised his eyebrows.

" I can give you no other," he said. " But, whatever answer you get, it won't alter the facts of the case. That Shapely directed the murder, I do believe : that would explain the timing —and other things : but he took the greatest care to secure himself. By staying beyond that post at the critical time, he made himself as safe as he would have been if he'd been locked up in some jail. To all intents and purposes, he *was* under lock and key."

" That's very true," said I. " How easy it is to fail to see the wood for the trees."

With that, we went up to the site : but all that day I was thinking of Falcon's letter and how Fate seemed to favour the men who had conspired to put Old Rowley to death. Of Shapely's guilt in the matter, I now had no doubt. Shapely had a strong motive—a very strong motive—for sending his step-father down. Tass had gone straight from Shapely—straight as an arrow from Shapely, to do the deed. Shapely's alibi bore the stamp of design. And Tass was not to be found ; but Shapely had visited the district where Falcon believed him to be—and had paled when Falcon had asked him how he had spent his time. Here was no proof ; but add together these facts, and they made, to my mind, a strong case—not a case, of course, for a jury ; but many a felon has never come to be tried.

I shall always maintain that such an outlook was fair. I admit that we had liked Old Rowley, had never liked Shapely, had never set eyes upon Tass. But Shapely's cast-iron alibi got me under the ribs. That it was accidental, I simply could not believe. And if it was not accidental—well, what of a man who does wilful murder by proxy, and takes the greatest care to secure himself ?

* * * * *

Everyone worked all out for the whole of that week ; but what laid stripes upon us was that on Thursday night the temperature fell.

We had finished the beams on Tuesday, and they had been carefully covered against a possible frost. So they were safe. But now, though all was ready by Saturday night, though all had fought against time to lay and tie and shutter six thousand square feet—and won the fight, such labour might be in vain. We could take no risks with the platform on which the house was to stand.

There was nothing to do but go on—and hope for the best. I stood on Friday with Joseph and watched the sun go down.

" And never a cloud," he muttered. " Who ever saw such weather ? And autumn coming in fast." He shook his head. " There will be a sharp frost to-night."

" Tell me," I said. " If it's like this on Sunday evening . . ."

" Then to run in the concrete on Monday would be a criminal act. You see, Monsieur, it is like this. In the first place, once we begin, we have got to go on. Such a platform cannot be laid piecemeal. By working with all our might, we can do the job in two days. And in two days, do it we must. In the second place, if we run that concrete in and then we have a hard frost before the concrete has set, the platform will never be safe. In such a case, therefore, we should be faced with the task of taking the whole of it down and starting afresh. All the material would be wasted, and as for the labour—well, demolishing ferro-concrete is not amusing work. In this case, such a task is unthinkable. Six thousand square feet ! Tied into these beams and these walls ! " He threw up his hands. " I am bound to tell Monsieur the truth. Unless the weather changes, we must not attempt the work."

" Can we telephone to you on Sunday ? "

Joseph smiled.

" I shall be here, Monsieur. I shall not leave Lally this week-end. And early on Monday morning, I shall decide ' yes ' or ' no.' At the moment I am not hopeful. I am ready to take a risk. To start at all at this season is taking a risk. But to take that risk is worth while, for, if we succeed, we can work right through the winter, except for two or three weeks. Not at this pace, of course : but choosing our time. And walls can be covered while they are being built. And if a frost catches us napping—well, it is not a very great business to pull down six feet of wall and build it again. But the platform— no."

" Exactly how long do we need without a sharp frost ? "

" For this platform, Monsieur ? Five days. Two to run in the concrete, and three for the concrete to set." He shrugged his shoulders. " Four would do, but I would rather have five. Well, we have done our best. On Monday all will be ready. If the weather holds out against us, it cannot be helped."

" The weather is very capricious. It may be like this on Monday, and ten days later there may be no frost at all."

" That, Monsieur, is perfectly true. But every day that passes increases the risk which we are prepared to take. We are very high up here—two thousand six hundred feet. And once October is in, to hope for five days running without a sharp frost would be to tempt Providence." He shook his head. " No, Monsieur. I am in charge. And so long as I am in charge, if we cannot lay the platform next week, we must wait for the spring."

*　　*　　*　　*　　*

It was just before one o'clock on Saturday afternoon that I noticed a change in the wind.

Because the work was so urgent, the break for dinner had been cut from two hours to one, and the men were on their way back from Lally and Besse. Jonah and I had broken our fast at the site.

I hastened to Joseph, standing beside his hut.

" The wind's changed, Joseph."

His chin was up in a flash.

Then—

" I cannot feel it," he said. " But Monsieur was higher up." He raised his voice. " Ulysse."

One of the men replied.

" Monsieur Joseph."

" Monsieur le Capitaine says there is a change in the wind."

" That is so, Monsieur Joseph. Myself, I remarked it as I was coming from Besse. If it lasts, the drought will be broken within twelve hours."

Joseph turned to me.

" Monsieur brings me good tidings," he said. " Ulysse is knowledgeable. He has been bred as a shepherd, and his advice is better than that of a weather-glass."

I think it was. It was certainly four hours ahead of our barometer. This began to fall about five o'clock. And a golden sun went down in a bevy of cloud. . . .

When I woke on Sunday morning, the opposite side of the valley was not to be seen.

I walked up to the site before breakfast.

Hadrian's Wall was looming out of the mist, and a sound of hammering came from the heights above.

I made my way to the waste of steel above wood.

Joseph was there, with the rain running down his face, checking the shuttering and putting finishing touches to the holes for which the plumber had asked.

When he saw me, he pulled off his beret.

" Good morning, Monsieur. That we are the favourites of Fortune, there can be no doubt. This is the weather I have prayed for. While it lasts, there will be no frosts—there was none last night—and, for what we have to do, it is the finest weather that we could have. Give me a week of this, and your house will stand as though it were built upon rock. The sun is not good for concrete, until it has set : we should have had to water with watering-cans, and, with the *ruisseau* so low, we should have had to bring the water from Besse. Oh, we are very lucky. But I wish that to-day was to-morrow, and that is the truth."

" Have you seen Ulysse ? " said I.

" My weather-glass, Monsieur ? Yes. I walked up to Besse this morning and turned him out. He says that this will certainly last for three days—and possibly more : but he adds that, when it clears, there will be a very sharp frost."

" Oh, hell," said I. " If it only lasts three days . . ."

" We must pray," said Joseph. " We must work, and Mesdames must pray very hard. And in case their prayers are not heard, I am having tarpaulins sent up. And braziers. I do not like the idea. I shall not be satisfied. But, with weather like this, I am bound to take a chance. It is too promising."

*   *   *   *   *

I may have worked harder than I did in the next two days, but, if I have, I cannot remember when. Each evening, at six o'clock, I could hardly stand up. Jonah and Carson worked, I think, rather harder—and seemed not at all fatigued. On Tuesday morning Berry's back gave out—this to his genuine distress, but to no one's surprise. The day before he had worked for eleven hours, for quite six of which he had been soaked to the skin. This was, of course, asking for trouble. Muscular rheumatism has been his familiar for years.

Sand and stones and cement . . . sand and cement . . . sand and stones and cement . . .

This was mixed on the ' drive ' and shovelled into buckets which could have contained a boar. The buckets were hauled to the scaffold, some seventy feet above : there their contents were emptied into the travelling trucks. These ran on a little railway, along the foot-bridge scaffold and up to Hadrian's Wall. There the lines branched and ran to right and to left, up to the end of the platform, now being made. (These lines were continually shifted, according to where, upon the platform, the concrete, so mixed, was required.) When they reached the point at which the masons were working, the trucks were tipped and their burden fell on to a raft : and from the raft it was shovelled on to the waiting steel. Once there, it had to be 'worked.' And when it had been well 'worked,' so that every rod was embedded and there were no 'pockets' left, then it had to be carefully levelled just to the top of the steel. Then the grilles were laid and tied : and then a finer mixture was spread upon them. And when these, too, were embedded and out of sight, then the whole was levelled to precisely the height of the wall.

The men worked magnificently. After all, it was not their home. But everyone knew of the gamble and what was at stake. It became a point of honour that the rafts should never be empty, that the trucks should not wait upon the buckets nor the buckets upon the trucks.

All day long the lorries were bringing sand and cement. All day long men were shovelling and hauling, their bodies streaming with a mixture of rain and sweat. All day long men were 'working' the concrete, stirring, slicing with trowels till it shuddered like any quicksand and found its level itself. All day long the masons were finishing the surface, checking it with square edge and level and leaving it true and flawless, as only a craftsman can.

One or other of the brothers was there the whole of the time, while Joseph directed the battle and fought himself. His energy was inspiring. If ever a hitch occurred, he was there and was bearing a hand before anyone else : when a section of railway jammed, he had it free before I could send for a pick : one moment he would be on the scaffold, urging the mixers below, and the next he would be at the farther end of the platform, checking a level with a mason or tying a grille into place. And once, when a truck jumped the rails and men were straining like madmen to keep it from spilling its load, he seized a raft and carried it single-handed and set it down by the truck in the nick of time. I mention this, because it was not only a great feat of strength but, to me, a great example of presence of mind. He saw that the men were failing, that even his added strength could not hold the truck up, that Mahomet must be brought to the mountain—and that at once. And so he did it somehow. Not one man in a thousand would have ' got there.' But Joseph did.

At half past six on Tuesday, the platform was done—and the cloud was still thick about us, filling the valley with vapour, drenching the world with rain too fine to be seen, and blotting out things material at fifty yards. In fact this weather prevailed until Saturday afternoon ; but by Thursday night it was clear that the game had been won. No frost, however severe, could now damage the work of our hands : the concrete had set—and that, under perfect conditions—conditions seldom encountered upon the plains.

On Friday, by our desire, the men were told that the morrow would be a day off, though all would be paid : by this, rather natural gesture, Joseph was deeply impressed and, because, I think, of what he had said, every man came to thank us, high and low : but he would not avail himself of it and spent the day, as usual, upon the site.

He was, of course, jubilant. So, indeed, were we all : for a very great effort had been made—men had done their utmost, and Nature had rewarded their efforts as they deserved.

As though to ram this home, on Saturday evening a glorious sun set red. That night the sky was clear, and, as Ulysse had predicted, there was a very sharp frost. When we awoke the next morning, the mountain-tops were covered thick with snow. And the forests had changed their habit. Autumn was in.

We all went to Church on Sunday—out of pure gratitude.

And then we walked up to the site and took our stand on the platform which we had helped to build.

It was an impressive experience.

For the very first time we could capture the days to come and could tell what it would feel like to live and move upon the terrace of what was to be our home. We could see exactly the prospects which we should command and could hear exactly the sounds which would reach our ears. We could judge when the sun would meet us and when he would take his leave ; and we could consider the lay-out of the gardens we meant to make.

" Oblige me," said Berry, " by keeping twelve feet from that brink. I know it's quite all right and that all last week men did contortions upon it and waltzed all over the scaffold and never fell down. But to me, standing here, the illusion of depth is frightful. I shan't feel safe till they get that parapet up."

For this point of view there was a lot to be said. The waste of concrete jutted into the air. In fact, it concealed at most a forty-feet drop : but, standing back from its edge, we could not see the valley, but only its opposite side, rising out of the depths, and a man who had been taken there blindfold and then permitted to see might well have supposed that he stood upon the brink of some canyon which might be bottomless.

My sister lifted her voice.

" I don't want to be silly, but——"

" I know," said Berry, " but don't you take it to heart. It's an accident of birth. And we'll always protect you, darling. Forget the word ' asylum.' People may stare sometimes, but——"

" Come and look at the view," said Daphne, advancing towards the edge.

" No," screamed Berry. " I forbid you. It makes me go all bugbears—I mean, goosegogs. U-u-ugh ! "

" Am I wise ? " said Daphne, who has a good head for heights.

" You're Pallas Athene," howled Berry. " If I'd been Paris, you should have had the apple. My sweet, I implore you . . ."

" That's much better," said Daphne, turning. She was less than one foot from the edge. " And now I'll begin again. I don't want to be silly, but I simply cannot believe that this is where we're to live. It—it's so fantastic."

" It's like a dream," said Jill. " Think of waking up in the morning and seeing this—this bird's eye view."

Berry looked up from the business of drying the palms of his hands.

" Think of coming home in the evening and seeing two hundred steps between you and a drink."

" Good for muscular rheumatism," said Jonah. " If you'd

had steps to climb for the last twenty years, you would not in your old age——"

" No doubt," said Berry ; " no doubt. And if I'd been making grilles ever since I was ten, what stumps I had left would now be tipped with horn. And what's biting The Blue Boy ? "

" I've been thinking," said I.

" Stop that noise," said Berry, addressing The Columbine. " The sage is in travail. And may we, poor scum, be permitted to foul the luscious meads of philosophy on which you stroll ? "

" You," I said shortly, " would foul a neglected grease-trap. All the same, this is a matter to which you must be admitted. I mean, it's of some importance—even to you."

" Oh, Boy," said Jill, " don't say you've discovered some snag."

" Call it a snare, my beauty. But I think I must point it out."

" Oh, I can't bear it," said Daphne.

" Don't worry," said I. " It's going to be quite all right. About three weeks ago, the one and only Joseph asked me in so many words why we had chosen this site. I said that we'd looked all round and we liked it best. He said that no doubt we were right, but that, the evening before, he had walked up to Besse, and that he had been struck by that meadow."

I pointed to the one on the other side of the *ruisseau*—a really beautiful field and easily twice the size of any one of our three.

" He said that, had we built there, the ground rose so much more gently that Hadrian's Wall need not have been half its height and that, since the road is very much higher just there, we could have made a drive that ran right up to the house. I said that we'd marked all that, but that any house built there would be looking straight on to the graveyard, and that it was for that reason that we had turned it down."

This was quite true. The graveyard stood on a spur on the southern side of the road which ran from Lally to Besse—the only spur that there was in all that mile. It was very beautifully placed, and I think the dead must lie happy in such a spot. But graveyards in France have not the beauty their fellows in England have ; and, in any event, it would have lain full in the foreground, and that was a shade too much. But, because the road curled higher up, from the platform itself we could only see the edge of its wall.

"Well, Joseph is very polite and he said that he quite understood. But to me it was clear that he didn't. He could see no objection at all to looking over a graveyard ; and he found our distaste peculiar—no doubt about that. Now his point of view is the point of view of the French. Till then, it hadn't entered my head : but now I'm perfectly sure that, had we been French, and not English, we should have built in that field.

"Well, there you are. This house will attract much attention. What we have done so far seems to be the talk of the *Basses Pyrénées*. Is it too much to suppose that any day somebody else may think that to build up here is not such a bad idea ? And may stroll up here to look for a possible site ? And may be struck, as Joseph himself was struck, with the eminent desirability of that very handsome meadow next door ? "

"Oh, Boy ! "

"Exactly," said I. "It's very instructive to stand where we're standing now." I pointed to the elegant meadow, down on our left. "We need have no fear of that. No one could ever build there. It's much too wet. But what of the other side ? We never intended our home to be one of a row. And how should we like some Frenchman's conception of beauty slapped down in that field ? For one thing alone, it would blast our view to the west."

"It would ruin everything," cried Daphne.

"The bare idea," said Berry, "has given me a pain in the stomach. I mean, that's quite true. I very much doubt if I can eat any lunch."

"Lunch be damned," said Jonah. "Boy's perfectly right. If we can buy that field, we must buy it at any price. A residence there, however beautiful, would simply tear everything up. And, as Boy hinted just now—well, we all know what the French architect can do when he really tries."

"Conceive," said Berry, "a neo-Moorish trifle in ruby pink, kitchen-yard running down to the *ruisseau*—convenient for garbage and washing and clear of the sanitation which would enter slightly below. I wonder where they'll put the conservatory."

With one voice, we insisted that he should hold his peace.

" I'm thankful you saw it," said Daphne, " but it is a bit of a blow."

" It'll be all right," I said. " But we mustn't waste any time."

" But what do we do ? De Moulin ? "

" He's back in Pau. Besides, he advised us next time to deal direct."

" But we don't know the owner," said Jill.

" We'll soon find out," said I. " I'll talk to Joseph to-morrow He's no damned fool. But neither are the peasants. We'll have to pay through the nose."

" That can't be helped," said Jonah. " If they like to ask the earth—well, we've got to have that field."

*   *   *   *   *

It was a question of protection. When you build a house in the country, you hope for a country-house. High upon the list of amenities stands privacy. And, with never a tree between, a dwelling sixty paces away will kill that privacy dead. In our case, too, we had selected our site for the very lovely prospects commanded on every side. And a house built right in the foreground would blot out those to the west.

The meadow, which now we called Naboth, at no place touched the road. Between it and the road, lay a long rectangular field— very steep and narrow, not fit to be built upon. This had been proved by its owner, for the ruin of a half-built cottage stood in its midst : whoever had started the construction had given it up in disgust, for the steepness of the ground was against him and a landslide of earth and stones was its only occupant. And above this poor neighbour stretched Naboth—broad, deep, well walled and good to look upon.

And there, of course, lay the danger. Forget the graveyard and it was an attractive site. As house-agents say, ' it offered.' And if someone accepted its offer—well, we were sunk.

*   *   *   *   *

On the following morning, Monday, men were set to cut into the mountainside. This, of course, directly behind the platform for we needed twenty feet more than the platform gave. Th soil which we cut away was to go to make the garden : this was to consist of terraces—two or more on either side of the house. But terraces must be retained. And so, with Joseph's assistance, we settled the lines they should take. And, when we had settled their lay-out, the masons began at once to build the retaining walls. This labour was simple enough. We only required a long wall, some six feet high, with a wing at either end to block the gap which would yawn between the wall, when built, and the mountainside. Into the enclosure thus made, the soil would be tipped, and when the soil was flush with the top of the wall and its wings, we should have a long, flat terrace, some five yards wide. As soon as this terrace was done, the masons would start upon another directly above. We expected to have enough soil to make, perhaps, four terraces, two upon either side of the house itself. Between these and Hadrian's Wall, a space of four yards would be left. Here would rise the steps which led to the house : and those same flights of steps would serve the terraces.

To return to the excavation.

Once this was well under way, the building of the house would begin. But not before that, for the trucks must have room to leave the excavation and reach the enclosures where they would tip their soil. Then the front of the house could be started— that is to say, the whole of the cross of the T. The stem of the T must wait until the delving was done.

In the evening, when the last man had gone, I spoke to Joseph of Naboth and told him how we felt.

He heard me out gravely. Then he turned and looked at the field.

"Mesdames and Messieurs are wise. That meadow is dangerous. For you to have buildings there would be a catastrophe. And it might very easily happen, unless you make it your own. But Monsieur must move with great care—unless Monsieur wishes to pay the eyes from his head. I will help, of course. But I must not go directly, for I am not of the country and shall be suspected at once. There are one or two workmen, however, that I can trust. I will approach one of them, and he shall find out for Monsieur what Monsieur desires to know."

"I want to know the name of the owner and where he lives. And whether, of course, he will sell."

Joseph smiled.

"Monsieur can omit that question. It is only a matter of price. I think I had better say that Mesdames and Messieurs are thinking of making a drive. You see, it must not be dreamed that you desire the meadow to deny it to anyone else. In that case the price would soar. The owner would get ideas. He might even search for another purchaser ; and seek to play him against you, to raise your price. And so I shall say that you have a drive in mind—a drive to come up through that meadow and gain the house." He looked at me sharply. "But that, sir, is only a ruse. I beg that Monsieur will never adopt such a plan."

"Not on your life," said I. Joseph expired with relief. "Oh, no. We'll never do that. Once we were up in the field, it would be easy enough. But to gain that field from the road . . . A railway cutting, Joseph."

"Monsieur has said it."

"And I think we shall have built quite enough retaining walls."

Joseph made a wry face.

"With the terraces, six to date. But there is another to come." He turned and pointed at the mountain. "This excavation, sir, is going to make us think. We have made a start—yes. In one spot even to-night we are nearly two metres in. But, after that, we have four metres to go. It does not sound much, Monsieur. And it does not look very much. But here the eye breaks down. One cannot measure into a mountain-side. And the ground is against us just here. You will have your four terraces, Monsieur. In fact, it is my belief that you will have six."

"Six ? "

Joseph nodded abruptly.

"Monsieur will see. And Monsieur must think of this—that the walls of our excavation cannot rise sheer. They must be sloped and planted, so that the soil will not fall. This, of course, above the retaining wall : and that, I think, will have to be fifteen feet high."

"My God," said I. "Are we going to dig a quarry ? "

"Monsieur has used the word which I had in mind. But

never mind. It shall be done. It is but a question of patience. Only, it is a good thing that we have no more than six metres to excavate. If it were ten—well, Monsieur would have to erect a second Hadrian's Wall."

I walked home thoughtfully.

Another retaining wall—this time, some fifteen feet high : a semi-circular wall, for the sides must be retained, as well as the back. And a good, stout wall, to hold the mountain itself from sliding on to the house. . . .

And that is, of course, what happens when people seek to build houses where houses were not meant to be built. Cottages may perch on or cling to a mountainside : but a residence must be built into the mountain itself. And there you come up against Nature. It looks so simple. But to cut twenty feet from a mountain whose rise is, say, three in four and to slope your excavation to four in five—well, a mathematician would have done the sum in his head ; but we were not mathematicians and so had not realized that there was a sum to be done.

I could not do the sum now : but, if I could, I would not. For no one who did not know would allow that my answer was right. All I can say is this—that if anyone feels that he must have an amphitheatre, let him send for bricks and mortar and have the thing built : but never let him scoop one out of a mountainside. But, you will say, that is idle, for there is the backing all ready and, before he begins to scoop, his work is half done. I know. That is what we thought . . . Of course we had no choice. The mountain was there, and the mountain had to be removed. But I never would have believed there was so much soil.

* * * * *

At mid-day on Wednesday Joseph made his report.

"I spoke to Levillon, Monsieur—the son-in-law of Ulysse. The meadow is owned by a forester, Pernot by name. He lives at Lally, in the Street of the Waterfall. Levillon saw him last night and told him what we had agreed. But Pernot cut him short. He is sorry to disoblige Monsieur, but he does not intend to sell."

"Good lord," said I.

Joseph shook his head.

" I find it astonishing, Monsieur. As Monsieur knows, I never expected that. And Levillon, too, is astounded. It is not, for instance, a question of sentiment, for the field is not family land. Pernot only purchased it four years ago. But the man was most definite."

I fingered my chin.

" This is very awkward," I said. " I mean, if we could be sure that he will stick to his guns—well, that's all right. If the man doesn't want to sell, that is his affair. But if somebody else comes along and tempts him with a big price . . ."

" I know," said Joseph. " And that is what worries me. Not all are so scrupulous as Monsieur. If somebody wants that meadow and they take the good Pernot to a *café* and thrust the notes under his nose . . . And Monsieur will wake up one morning and find that the field is sold—sold for less, perhaps, than Monsieur was willing to pay."

" And yet," said I, " what can we do ? We can't . . ."

The sentence was never finished.

Two strangers were standing in Naboth, men of the town. Their car, which was chauffeur-driven, was waiting below in the road. With a sweep of his arm, one was indicating the prospects . . . Then they turned to survey the meadow. After a little conversation, one of them took his stand, and the other began to pace forward—precisely as we had done before we had purchased our site.

CHAPTER VIII

IN WHICH BERRY SITS DOWN WITH A BEAR, AND IT IS A VERY NEAR THING

I CANNOT describe the consternation which my news was to cause at Bel Air.

Jonah was at Pau for the day, but Berry, Daphne and Jill were seated upon the small terrace, discussing photographs of bathrooms and arguing about tiled floors.

As I concluded my tale—

" D'you mean they're there now ? " cried Daphne.

" Well, they were when I left," said I. " I tell you, they were pacing the field. From the length of the façade, as they paced it, I'm not at all sure they're not out to build a hotel."

Jill clapped her hands to her face.

" A hotel ? Up there ? Beside us ? Oh, Boy, that would be the end—before we'd begun."

" I know," I said. " It wouldn't be worth going on."

" Don't stand there talking," said Berry. " What do we do ? "

" We must try and get hold of Pernot—before they do."

" But Pernot says he won't sell."

" If he really means that, we're safe. But if those two wallahs mean business . . ."

" We must bump them off," said Berry. " Invite them on to the platform an'—an' help them down."

" Don't be a fool," said Daphne. " Besides, they're only the first. You can't murder everyone who wants to purchase that field."

" I could," said Berry. " Easily. Still, I see your point. If we did it too often, we might get wrong with the Mayor."

" We must try and see Pernot," I said. " He might give us the first refusal, and that would mean we were safe."

With my words, came the sound of a car, descending the road from Besse.

In silence we watched it go by.

Its occupants were very plainly in excellent cue, for they were lolling and laughing, as men who have stolen some march.

" My God," I breathed. " Don't say they've got Pernot's address ? "

" Where does he live ? " said Daphne.

" Bang opposite us," said I. " They'll have to go by his house."

" And he will be there. He's bound to come home for dinner. They always do."

" If I know them, they'll have their lunch first. We're safe until half past one."

And there we heard a step upon the terrace . . .

Joseph.

Béret in hand, he bowed to Daphne and Jill.

" Mesdames will excuse me," he said, " for coming upon them like this. But it is about that meadow. They are seeking to buy it—those two that have just gone by. They overtook me on the road, as I was walking to Lally, before I had reached the short cut which I always take. And they stopped the car and asked me to whom the meadow belonged. And—God forgive me—I told them that it was owned by a cousin of mine . . . the Mayor of Louvie-Juzon, half way between here and Pau. He does own a meadow up here, but that is far above, on the upper road. And to-day he will be at Oloron—that I know. But I did not tell them that. So we have, I hope, twenty-four hours. But Monsieur must get hold of Pernot as quickly as ever he can."

" Well done, indeed, Joseph," said I.

" Monsieur may talk like that when the meadow is his. I said that I hoped that we had twenty-four hours. But we may have less. Monsieur the Captain and I were not the only two who saw them pacing that field. And tongues are now wagging in Lally . . ." Joseph drew himself up. " I go to my dinner now—and to find out where Pernot may be. I will come again on my way back, at ten minutes to two." He bowed to Daphne and Jill. " *Bon appétit*, Mesdames, Messieurs."

" *Bon appétit*, Joseph, and thank you so very much."

And then he was gone, padding down the miniature drive . . .

At a quarter to two he reported that Pernot's wife was at Nareth and that Pernot himself was cutting wood in the mountains and might spend the night in a cabin up on the hills.

" Tell me," said I. " Those strangers were business men. They will go to Louvie-Juzon to see your cousin at once. We know that he will not be there. But will he be there to-night ? "

" Oh, yes, sir. About six o'clock."

" Well, if they await his return—as I think I should do—because they are business men, they will soon find out their mistake."

" I confess that is likely," said Joseph.

" Then what will they do ? "

" I think that to-morrow morning they will visit the Land Registry at Pau. They will show the clerks the meadow upon the Cadastral Plan. And the clerk will tell them at once who the owner is. And in two hours they will be here with Pernot's name and address." Here Joseph lugged out his watch. " Monsieur will excuse me, but I must be on my way."

" We'll come with you," said I ; " and talk as we go."

As we walked up the road towards Besse—

" This is damned serious," said Berry. " Where exactly is Pernot at work ? "

Joseph shrugged his shoulders.

" Levillon would probably know, but, as luck will have it, I gave him the afternoon off, to go to Bielle. But we will try Ulysse."

Five minutes later, Ulysse was standing before us, cap in hand.

" My son-in-law," he said, " is a fool. Pernot will sell. But Monsieur must talk with him. To-morrow, if not to-day, he will be at his house."

" Where is he now, Ulysse ? "

" Directly opposite, Monsieur." He pointed to the forest-clad mountain, facing the site. " There are two plateaus up there, though they do not appear. And he is at work in a dip to the left of the first. He is cutting wood for my cousin, who has a plot there."

" Why, we—we might run into him," said Berry. " We had meant to walk up to the plateau this afternoon."

Ulysse turned to glance at the sun.

" If Monsieur means to do that, he should start at once. To reach the first plateau from Lally, we reckon an hour and a half ; and the moment the sun goes down, it is very dark in those woods."

" Come on," said Berry, turning. " So you think he will sell, Ulysse ? "

The old fellow smiled.

" If Monsieur talks with him—yes."

Twenty minutes later, Jill set us down in Lally, at the foot of what guide-books call ' The Vista Promenade.'

*　　*　　*　　*　　*

The Vista Promenade.

This is, of course, a misnomer. In the first place, there are no vistas, for the forest stands thick about you from first to last. In the second place, a promenade suggests an effortless stroll. It does not suggest a steep zig-zag quite three miles long, the surface of which is copiously studded with rocks and strewn with roots of trees and is frequently not to be seen for the falls of soil from above.

With one eye, so to speak, on the clock, we climbed as fast as we could, and, cool as it was in the forest, were very soon streaming with sweat.

"We'll never do it," said Berry. "And if we do, we'll never get down alive. We can't do this stuff in the dark."

"I've a torch in my pocket," I said.

At the end of the first half-hour I decreed a five-minute rest. Berry leaned against the wall of the zig-zag and closed his eyes.

"We should," I said, "be about a third of the way. D'you think you can make the plateau?"

"I've got to," said Berry. "You can't go on alone. It's as good a place as I've seen for breaking a leg."

"We can turn back," I said. "And hope very hard that Pernot comes home to-night."

"That won't do. If he doesn't come back to-night and those skunks get on to him to-morrow . . . Oh, no. It's too big a risk. If that meadow is built in, we're sunk. So we've got to go on." He drew in his breath. "*Sic itur ad astra*. We seemed to be doomed to a series of fights against time. Look at that blasted platform. We tore ourselves to pieces, to get it done. And now this desirable field. No leisurely discussions in a café. Not on your life. A spurt up the flanks of Hell against the clock. And no alternative. Never mind. I'll say it's worth it, to own that field."

In that spirit, we made our way on.

The higher we went, the rougher became the path.

By the time we had climbed for an hour, I was by no means sure of the wisdom of going on. By what Ulysse had said, we ought to reach the first plateau by four o'clock. But, after that, we must find the dip to the left: and at four o'clock the sun would be going down behind the range of mountains which stood to the west.

And what tale could we tell to Pernot, if we ever located the man ? If we said we had come to see him, the fellow would smell a rat. Unless there was a great deal at stake, no two men in their senses would make such a journey so fast. Yet I did not feel up to finesse. I was not exhausted, but I should have been glad to sit down and collect my wits. And though Berry would not show it, I knew that he was distressed. Yet, to turn back now seemed dreadful. I know few things more repugnant than to take your hand from the plough . . .

So, after a rest of five minutes, we held on our way.

At two minutes to four, the trees fell back about us, and almost at once the path ran on to the plateau for which we were bound.

Berry made his way to a tree-stump and sat himself down.

" Not too bad," he panted, and wrung the sweat from his face. " Am I to understand that people do this for pleasure ? "

" They go up to the second plateau and over the top and down."

" *Chacun à son goût,*" said Berry. " You might tell me if you see a bear coming. Not that I can attempt to elude him— my legs won't work. But I can discourse to the brute. They say that bears are sympathetic—I don't know whether it's true."

" I seem to have heard that the best thing is to ignore them."

" Oh, be your age," said Berry. " You can't ignore a bear in a spot like this. I know they don't eat flesh if they can get roots : but supposing we meet one that's slimming or short of Vitamin B." He looked round uneasily. " You know, I'm not mad about these precincts. They're simply made for a bear-garden."

In the failing light, the place was unattractive. So far as I saw, the trees prevented all view, and the turf was scrubby and was strewn about with boulders and the aged remnants of trees.

' A dip to the left.'

I pricked my ears, to listen for the stroke of an axe. But the silence was absolute. If Pernot was hereabouts, he had finished work for the day. And there I did not blame him. Dusk was about to come in. Which meant that, if we were to find him, we had no time to lose.

" Ready ? " said I.

"One minute more," said Berry. "It's the first time I've rested in a bear-garden, and as, if I can help it, I shall never do so again. . . . Look at that lump of timber. It looks just like a bear in this ' dim, religious light.' It's probably a statue of the brute that founded this place."

I must confess that it did resemble a bear. No doubt, had the light been stronger . . .

Here the ' statue ' rose to its feet and ambled away.

Together we watched its departure in the most pregnant silence that I have ever known.

As it disappeared in the shadows—

"Thank you very much," said Berry. "And now I can't help feeling we might be getting back. They can build a fish-market in Naboth for all I care. As for looking about for dips——"

A footstep beside us made us jump out of our skins.

Then a pleasant voice spoke in French.

"Just as well, Messieurs, that he was too sleepy to care. He has had his rest in the sun and has gone for a drink. But Messieurs are late. They were not proposing to go higher ? "

"Er—another time," said Berry. "You can go on ? "

"Yes, indeed," said the other, whom I was quite sure was Pernot, because of the axe he bore. "The second plateau is half an hour's walk from here. And then you go over and down the other side. The young de Moulin will tell you." He threw up his head and laughed. "But I think I address the messieurs who saved that young wretch's life."

"He did that," said Berry, laying a hand on my arm.

Pernot put out his right hand.

"I am glad to meet you," he said. "It was a valiant deed. And your life was worth more than his."

As I set my hand in his—

"But how do you know us ? " said I. "And what is your name ? "

"My name is Pernot, Monsieur."

"Pernot ! " cried Berry. "Are you the Pernot that owns the field next to ours ? "

"That is right, Monsieur. We are neighbours. *Ma foi*, but you are building a wonderful home."

" It would be much more wonderful if you would sell us your field."

Pernot lowered his axe and lifted his eyes to the sky.

" Ah, that. Yes, Levillon told me. And I said no. There are complications, Monsieur. And then you know, that field is a beautiful field. Compared with some I could mention, it is a paradise."

" True," said I. " It is a very nice field. But we are prepared to pay a very nice price. What are these complications, of which you speak ? "

" Always there are complications, or so I find."

" Well, I can't see them," said Berry. " But you are the best judge of that. All the same, we should like to have it. I don't wish to press you, Pernot ; but—well, I know that you bought it." Pernot started. " It isn't as if it was your family's land."

Pernot looked round. Then—

" Monsieur knows that I bought it ? "

" Well, so I've been told."

" It is true," cried Pernot. " I did. I paid the good money over—four years ago. By the laws of God it is mine."

" By the laws of God ? " said I. " And what of the laws of men ? "

Pernot smote with his axe upon the ground.

" I have no title," he said. " The sale was not registered. I thought to save the money the registration would cost. And now, when that rogue of a Busquet——"

" Wait a moment," said Berry. " Whom did you buy it from ? "

" I am telling Monsieur. I bought it of Émile Busquet, the son-in-law of old Puyou, who died last year. He lives in Paris, Monsieur, and he is not a nice man. When it comes to his knowledge that Monsieur desires this field, he will hand back the money I paid him and sell it to Monsieur himself."

" Do you hold his receipt ? " I said.

" I have it at home, Monsieur. Everything is in order— except for the registration I did not do." He hesitated. " I have been frank with Monsieur."

" I'm thankful you have," said Berry. " We'll go to Monsieur de Moulin and see what he can do to help us over the jump."

Pernot shook his head.

"He will advise Monsieur to deal with Busquet direct."

"I don't think he will," said Berry. "And if he does, I shall not take his advice. I have a weakness myself for the laws of God."

Pernot started forward.

"Monsieur means——"

"That I will buy from no one but you. Can you come and see de Moulin to-morrow and show him what papers you have? We'll drive you down, if you can."

Pernot took off his béret and put out his hand.

"I have always heard you could trust the English," he said.

"I should hope so," said Berry, shaking hands. "And now what about the price?"

"Monsieur will not find me unreasonable."

"I am sure of that. But before we see my lawyer, we must have agreed the price."

Pernot swung his axe to and fro.

"I am fond of that field," he said. "It is very deep and handsome—the best upon Evergreen."

"I don't know about that," said Berry. "But I quite admit that it is a very nice field."

"It is flat, too. Should Monsieur make his drive there, his work is already done."

"Scarcely," said Berry, "but we won't argue the point. What figure do you suggest?"

"I had thought of four hundred pounds."

"Well, I hadn't," said Berry, shortly. "Four hundred is far too much. We'll give you three."

"Ah, three is too little, Monsieur. Three hundred and eighty, perhaps."

"We'll give you three hundred and fifty—and that's a damned good price."

Pernot shrugged his shoulders.

"What will you?" he said. "Very well. Three hundred and fifty pounds."

We all shook hands upon that.

"You'll come back with us to Lally?"

"Yes, indeed, Monsieur," said Pernot. "I had meant to

stay here in the cabin : but if, to-morrow, Monsieur is to drive me to Pau . . . Besides, it will be dark in the forest. But I know the path we must take as the palm of my hand."

It was very nearly dark on the plateau—and very cold. I could only just see the line of the way we had come. And, though I used my torch when we came to the trees, it was abundantly clear that Pernot's assistance would prove invaluable.

There was no moon, and the darkness within the forests was that of the pit itself. That, if Pernot had not been with us, we should have got down somehow, I have no doubt : but that most unpleasant descent would have taken us hours to make, for, before we had covered a furlong, I tripped and fell, and though I tried to save it, I dropped the torch. But Pernot led us down in less than two hours.

It was natural to enter a café in the Street of the Waterfall. There, over some excellent brandy, a rough Agreement was signed ; and when Pernot insisted on paying for one more round, I knew that the price we were paying was higher than he had hoped. But we did not grudge it him. We did not even grudge it him the next day, when Busquet's receipt was produced. This showed he was making a profit of nearly seven hundred per cent.

*   *   *   *   *

De Moulin looked down his nose.

Then he glared at Pernot, sitting on the edge of a chair and wiping the sweat from his face.

" What fools you peasants are ! You seek to save a few *sous* and so throw a fortune away."

The unfortunate Pernot writhed.

" But no, Monsieur. Monsieur will save it."

" I do not know that I can. The sale can be registered—yes : provided you pay the fine. But there must be a proper Deed— which this Busquet must sign. And if he will not sign, then it cannot be registered."

" But he cannot refuse," cried Pernot. " I have his receipt."

" Oh, yes he can," said de Moulin. " At present the title is his. All that he has to do is to pay you back the forty-five pounds which you paid. And then he can sell to Monsieur . . . for three hundred and fifty, instead."

Pernot yelped with dismay.

" But Monsieur has said that he will buy only from me."

" Monsieur is very handsome in all that he does. But what of these strangers who have been seen in your field ? When they go to see this Busquet——"

" No, no," screamed Pernot.

" Calm yourself," said de Moulin. He turned to Berry and me. " I will tell you what I shall do. First, I prepare an Agreement which you and this fellow will sign. He will promise to register his title and then to sell you the meadow for three hundred and fifty pounds. That will only take half an hour. Then I prepare a Deed for the previous sale. This will go to Paris to-night by messenger. I shall send it to a colleague of mine. He will see this Busquet at once—and will do his best to obtain his signature. He may have to make him a present. That cannot be helped. For, if those strangers are who I think they are, if once they get hold of Busquet, the game is up."

" And who," said Berry, " who do you think they are ? "

" There are two men here who are seeking sites for hotels. It is an immense combination, with money to burn." He returned to Pernot. " You hear. I shall do my best—not at all for you, because you do not deserve it ; but for these gentlemen, who have sore need of the meadow you wish to sell."

" Thank you, Monsieur," said Pernot, humbly.

" I promise nothing. But I shall do my best. And now I prepare the papers. Yours, my friends, will be ready in half an hour. But I shall not be ready for Pernot till four o'clock. But he can return by 'bus."

As we took our leave—

" How soon will you know ? " I said.

" I shall tell my colleague to wire me. He is a man of parts, and I think he will do the trick. That is, of course, if the others have not arrived first in the field. But they will not do that unless they have smelt a rat. In which case they may telephone to Paris. . . . In any event, it will be a matter of hours. These business men do not wait. In half an hour, then . . ."

Half an hour later the protocol had been signed.

As Berry laid down his pen—

" And if they get to Busquet first, we may as well tear this up ? "

De Moulin spread out his hands.

" You put it bluntly, my friend ; but I cannot say no.   But you have done your best and I shall do mine.   And there is, you know, a proverb that Fortune delights to help those who help themselves.   You will ring me up here to-morrow at a quarter to six ? "

*   *   *   *   *

We seemed to be doomed to suffer these very trying delays, when everything hung in the balance, but the balance would not move for twenty-four hours ·or more.

We had had a great deal of good fortune.   I had had the luck to observe the strangers surveying the field.   We had had the luck to find Pernot the evening before—the man was on his way to his cabin, when he heard our approach, and came clean out of his way to see who it was on the plateau so late in the day.   Had we been five minutes later, we should not have met that night.   Best of all, de Moulin was a man of action. . . .

Still, we were far from easy.   The strangers were business men.

" Tell me again," said Jill, " about the bear."

" Oh, I wish you wouldn't," said Berry.   " I've had some shocks in my time, but this was the worst."

Daphne looked up.

" You can never relate it, for no one would ever believe you."

" Pernot saw it," said Berry.   " You can't get away from that.   No doubt, when he saw it, he knew that it was a bear. But I didn't.   I'm not familiar with the brutes.   When I take a—a stroll commended by every blasted pamphlet the *Basses Pyrénées* puts out, I don't expect that walk to be frequented by evil beasts.   ' Glorious views,' they say.   And that's a lie.   But they don't say ' Close-ups of bears.'   I tell you, the mammal was less than twenty yards off.   And it looked like a baulk of wood. Damn it all, I might have sat down on the swine.   Easily.   I thought it was a freak of nature.   Gray-brown, it was—like a piece of weathered timber.   And I called Boy's attention to it. If I hadn't been so done, I'd have gone up and had a good look. And then, without a word, the darling got up . . .   To say that

I

my intestines turned over means nothing at all. When I put a hand on my stomach, it wasn't there."

" I wish I'd seen it," said Jill.

" There was nothing to see," said Berry. " I tell you, my bowels were gone."

" You are disgusting. I wish I'd seen the bear."

" There's morbidness," said Berry. " There's——"

" It didn't do anything to you."

" It took five years from my life."

" It went away. It didn't come towards you."

" I refuse," said Berry, " to invest that bear with any qualities. No decent bear would practise deception like that."

" Which is absurd," said Jill. " It didn't mean to look like a tree."

" Of course it did," said Berry. " It actually stuck out a leg, to resemble a branch."

" Yes, but you thought it looked like a bear. And if it looked like a bear, then it wasn't being deceitful."

" I must decline," said Berry, " to continue this argument. I know a bear when I see one, and I was most grossly deceived. At the time the deception was practised, I happened to be without the use of my legs. Had I not been so embarrassed I should almost certainly have inspected what I took—and was meant to take—to be a phenomenon. Probably with untoward results—from my point of view."

" Well, I'm glad you didn't sit down on it."

" So," said Berry, " am I. More than glad. Almost rapturous. And now d'you think we could talk about something else ? Bears are all right—in their place. In a very deep pit, for instance—with b-bars all round. But, as a divan . . . D'you think I could have a small brandy ? I don't feel too good. I expect it's talking too much."

A flash of black silk, and Thérèse had her back to the door.

" Pardon, Mesdames, Messieurs, but I have only just heard. God in heaven, and Monsieur has sat down with a bear. With but five metres between them. Lally is full of the tale. And the bear has seen fit to retire. And Monsieur has called out ' *Bon appétit*,' as it withdraws."

" I believe you did," said I, laughing.

" And the bear said ' Trust Baldwin,' " said Berry, " and gave the Fascist salute."

" But it is true, then, that Monsieur has sat where he was, but the bear ran away ? "

Berry shrugged his shoulders.

" He need not have gone. There was plenty of room for us both."

Thérèse raised bright eyes to heaven.

" And Monsieur Boy ? He has subscribed to this madness ? "

" I was present," said I. " But there was no madness about it. Everyone behaved very well."

" Monsieur suggests it was nice feeling that caused the bear to withdraw ? "

" Possibly," said Berry. " Bears are sensitive things."

" No doubt that is why they devour the innocent lamb ? "

" So do you," said Berry. " But you like it roast, with mint sauce."

" I resign myself," said Thérèse. " I cannot argue with Monsieur. But it is not right that Monsieur should consort with the dangerous beasts. Monsieur is very brave, but on the next occasion I beg that it will be Monsieur who leaves the field."

" I'll think it over," said Berry. " Two glasses of brandy, Thérèse."

" *Parfaitement*, Monsieur."

She withdrew, to return with the spirit almost at once. As she poured it out—

" It is the old man, Ulysse, who has won the laugh of the day."

" And what did he say ? " said I.

" He said that, for him, the bear had waylaid Monsieur, because he was wanting news of Monsieur Le Dung."

But I knew that Pernot was not laughing—in the Street of the Waterfall . . .

Nor did we laugh the next morning, when Joseph's cousin arrived. In fact he drove up, to see Joseph, learn the truth of the matter and tell what he knew.

His report was ominous.

The two men had waited to see him till six o'clock. They had then returned to Pau : but at ten o'clock the next morning their car drove up to his house.

The interview was not cordial. Two minutes had sufficed to

convince them that they had been fooled, and they had left on the instant for the Land Registry at Pau.

" I heard the direction given—the *Rue de Liège*. And were they angry, Monsieur ? For me, a dangerous mood. They did not storm, but they looked most cold and black. And when I spoke of mistakes, one of them spat at me, ' I have seen these mistakes before.' And then they were gone."

" This was yesterday morning," said Jonah.

" Yesterday morning, Monsieur, at ten o'clock."

Jonah looked from Joseph to me.

" It's even money," he said. " No odds at all. The one who gets first to Busquet gets the field. Of course, if they telephone . . ."

I turned and looked at Naboth.

If a hotel was to rise there, we might as well throw in our hand. The view apart, such a neighbour would blast our home. The terrace, on which I was standing, would be commanded by windows—row upon row of windows—perhaps only sixty yards off. As for the noise and the traffic . . .

And then, at a quarter past five, a car drove up with a note.

Friday, October 2nd.

MY DEAR SIRS,

Do not trouble to telephone. All is well. Consider yourselves the owners of Pernot's field.

The Deed, which Busquet has signed, will leave Paris to-night, and to-morrow myself I shall register the sale and pay the fine.

Now it is over, I may say it was touch and go.

But when I heard—let us say that I have my spies—when I heard that our friends had been to the Land Registry, I spoke with my agent in Paris and told him, as they say, to be on the tips of his toes.

He has just spoken to me. He was with Busquet this morning at nine o'clock. And he offered him twenty pounds, if he signed the Deed there and then. So Busquet signed.

And as he left the flats, another taxi drew up . . . Any way, we have won. The meadow is yours.

Cordially yours,

JEAN DE MOULIN.

Well, there you are.

But it was a very near thing.

CHAPTER IX

IN WHICH JONAH COLLECTS A SUIT-CASE, AND CARATIB IS REDUCED

ON the following Monday morning a council was held at Bel Air.

"The thing," said Berry, "is this. This never-very-desirable habitation is rapidly degenerating into the best imitation of a makeshift mausoleum that I have ever seen. The temperature of my bedroom this morning was that of the tomb, and the pains of Hell gat hold upon me when I attempted to leave what, for the sake of charity, I will describe as my bed. To be five minutes' walk from the site is convenience itself : but I must point out that to be ten minutes' walk from the graveyard will, if I stay here much longer, be of almost equal convenience—to those of you who are not prevented by pneumonia from attending my funeral. More. I am given to understand that, before this week is out, the contractor in charge proposes to begin the work of laying down the aqueduct or conduit, soon to convey the main water from Lally to Besse. And if I know anything of contractors or aqueducts, the condition of this thoroughfare, which now, except in certain spots, accepts but one line of traffic, will very soon present considerable difficulties to any but the malignant and evil-smelling ruminant, so painfully reminiscent of one's nearer relatives. In all these circumstances, I venture to suggest that an early return to Pau is, as the French say, indicated. We can come up every day, if we're so inclined. We can indulge the spirit, yet spare the flesh. Any objection from those I love ? "

"Say that bit about the ruminant again," said Daphne.

"I don't believe I can recapture it," said her husband. "It was one of those pearls that just slide out of my mouth. They're mentioned in the Bible, you know. You're cautioned against it, of course : but I hope very much that you won't identify yourself with——"

My sister appealed to me.

"Are these studied insults ? " she said.

"Yes," I said, "they are. Ossa is being piled upon Pelion.

But I shouldn't pursue the subject. If you do, you will be compared unfavourably with a blue-based baboon."

" I was coming to them," said Berry. " I often wish they could hear our conversation. I mean, they don't have much fun. And they'd laugh themselves sick."

" Why," said Daphne, shakily, " would they laugh themselves sick ? "

" You must work that out," said Berry. " Search your heart some time, when you're entirely alone. And the answer may be vouchsafed. You never know. Any way, I want some more shoes. Who's going to London to get them ? There they are. Packed up in an excellent case. Thérèse did it under my eyes. And have them I must, if I am to winter at Pau."

The red herring did its work.

" I must have some stuff," said Daphne. " I never expected to be here for more than two months. I can tell you the trunks I want. They're numbered ' 9 ' and ' 13.' "

" Don't tell me," said Berry. " I'm damned if I'm going to get them. We shall be in England for Christmas, but I won't go back before then."

" Well, someone must go," said Daphne.

" I shall be with them in spirit," said Berry, piously. " But that's for later. Your duty is pressing—to find a rest in Pau for the sole of my foot. And it must have at least two bathrooms—I won't go on like this."

Daphne looked at Jonah.

" Can we have Carson ? " she said. " If yes, then Jill and I can go down for the day."

" Of course," said Jonah. " This morning ? "

My sister shrugged her shoulders.

" We may as well. It is getting cold up here. If we could find a nice flat . . . I mean, we'll be out so much, that we shan't want a lot of room."

" Truly constant hot water," said Berry, " would suit me down to the socks."

" You won't get that," said Jonah, " until we're installed. The French are much better than they were ; but they can't shake off the idea that a fire must be lighted if somebody wishes to bathe."

" Well, do your best," said Berry.   " And now I must get to work. I'm doing the dimensions of the soap-niche—the one in my bathroom, I mean. I've talked to Joseph about it. He's going to leave a hole in the wall."

That evening we had a flat, to which we proposed to remove in three days' time. And Jonah and I had tossed up as to who should travel to Town. And I had lost.

*   *   *   *   *

Meanwhile the excavation was progressing. We knew it must be, because the third terrace was rapidly taking shape. But for that, we should not have known, for, as they drove into the mountain, falls of soil from above kept the labourers where they were. It was a dreadful business. What was worse, it was now quite clear that even six terraces would not absorb the soil which we should displace. This was disquieting. The soil had to be disposed of : and if it was to be conveyed to the summit of Hadrian's Wall, there transferred to buckets and then let down to the lorries waiting below, to be by them removed to some desert place, all this would entail much labour and great expense and would entirely prevent us from beginning to build the house.

And then Jonah had an idea.

All the charm of the *ruisseau* lay in its upper half—that is to say, the reach above Hadrian's Wall. Below that, it ran in a gully, steep and gaping and ugly, of no account. Jonah's plan was simple. It was to pipe the *ruisseau* from where the gully began, and then to fill in the gully with the superfluous soil.

At this idea Joseph jumped. To pipe the *ruisseau* was easy —say two days' work, and a railway to the head of the gully would take but an hour to lay. After which, it was a question of tipping, and nothing more, for the soil would find its own level without any fuss.

" There is only one thing," he said.   " We must set a good, strong grille at the head of the pipe, for if that should ever be blocked, and the *ruisseau* in spate—" he raised his eyes to heaven "—well, Messieurs will have a new *ruisseau* before they can think. And God alone knows what course that new *ruisseau* will choose to adopt. Water is all very well, so long as it runs in its bed. But, once it is out, it can be a dangerous thing. I have seen it at work—and twelve feet of a road washed away, while men were asleep."

Before the end of that week, the house was begun.

There were, of course, no foundations, for the walls rose straight from the platform, now fit to bear their weight : and, when we arrived one morning, there before us was the outline of all the principal rooms. The outer walls were of stone, like Hadrian's Wall, but the inner were built of blocks. These had been moulded in the chamber which had been already built—that is to say, the chamber beneath the platform, where there was no fear of frost. There were the doors and the windows, the gallery and the rooms : but the first thing that struck us all was how very small everything was. We said as much to Joseph.

" But, Monsieur, the rooms are immense. Never have I been engaged upon such a private house. Consider the gallery only."

" Oh, it's quite big enough, of course. But it looks about half the size that we thought it would."

Joseph smiled.

" Wait till it is garnished, Monsieur," was all he said.

(Here, of course, he was perfectly right. For some strange reason, a rough interior looks absurdly small. But as soon as the floor has been laid and the ceiling and walls have been plastered, it looks absurdly big. Only when it is furnished, does that apartment assume its proper size.)

That Saturday marked the end of a busy week. We had left Bel Air for Pau : the business of laying the pipes which would conduct the main water from Lally to Besse had been begun : the foundations of a fourth terrace were being laid : the pipes, to contain the *ruisseau*, were lying by the side of the drive : the excavation was proceeding, and the house we had set out to build was actually taking shape.

Now that Jonah had solved the problem of soil disposal, we determined to have five terraces, rather than six—three to the east of the house, and two to the west. The lowest of the three to the east ran straight to the ledge from which for so long we had watched the building of Hadrian's Wall : and, had we owned the elegant meadow, above which the grotto hung, we could have built a miniature terrace, to run from the ledge to the grotto, about the foot of the bluff. I did not mention this fact, but bore it in mind. To be perfectly frank, I lusted after that meadow, with which, of course, went the grotto and the jolly, old trough below. Its head was daintily wooded, its bosom, because of the spring, was always emerald green, and I knew that with time and patience it could be turned into a bower.

* * * * *

We were fortunate in the flat which my sister and Jill had found. Daphne is wise. She had not gone to the agents, but to the porter of the Hôtel Splendide. We had known him for years, and he was a present help in such matters as this. If he did not know himself, he always knew whom to ask. Within the hour, my sister had three addresses—two flats and one villa, not upon the house agents' books.

The second of the two flats offered us very much more than we had a right to expect. It was new, it was comfortably furnished and had never been occupied. It had, in fact, been taken by a firm of furniture-makers, working at the village of Asen, twenty miles off. This, with the wild idea of displaying their goods, rather as London firms make up an attractive flat in the heart of their stores. But it was not in the heart of a London store : it was on the first floor of a private building in Pau : and when six months had gone by and the flat had brought in rather less than an order a month, the firm had made up its mind that the only thing to be done was to get its money back. So the flat was ' to let,' as it stood. We should have to find plate and linen and things like that, but heating and constant hot water went with the house. And there were no less than three bathrooms.

What was almost more to the point, the furniture was very good. It was not what we should have chosen, but every piece was well made. And we should need furniture. Some we had withdrawn from White Ladies before handing over our home, but not nearly enough to furnish another house. Here, then, was an excellent chance of actually seeing what the firm at Asen could do. And whether their wood was seasoned—would stand up to central-heating, a most important point. Indeed, it began to look as if their idea of a showroom was not to prove wholly vain.

Two or more of us drove to the site on five days out of six.

There was now no work we could do, for we were no longer fighting to beat the clock. But questions were always arising which we could settle better than anyone else, and a close liaison with Joseph was quite invaluable. I say this advisedly. So deep was the interest which we had displayed in our home—in every tiny detail of its construction, that Joseph had come to consult us on every step that he took. The expert knowledge was his : but he put this at our disposal before he gave an order or lifted a hand. And of this we were more than glad. For we knew what we wanted, and this was to be our home.

All was going well. Only the excavation hung over the venture, as a cloud : a cloud a great deal bigger than any man's hand. By the middle of the month of October, it had become a great scar on the mountainside. We were nearly six metres in : but we had to gain two more—one for the wall, to retain the excavation, and one for a passage between that wall and the house. Say, seven metres and a half. There were thirty men on it now, working eight hours a day . . . I used to dream about it. (Here I should say that, could we have procured such a thing, no ' bulldozer ' could have been brought to the site of the work—except, perhaps, at the cost of spoiling the blowing meadows beyond repair.)

Still, the front of the house was rising—the cross of the capital T. Every night they carefully covered the work that had just been done. And the weather was kind : we had no very sharp frosts.

*   *   *   *   *

On one very rainy day, Jill and I alone had been up to the site. For myself, I had been glad to get back—to a drink and a bath ; and I was dressing for dinner, when Jonah entered my room and shut the door.

" I've just written to Falcon," he said, " and before I send the letter, I'd like you to see what I say. You'll think I'm very secretive : but the truth is that what I did was a one-man job."

As I took the letter, I smiled.

" ' Superintendent Mansel,' " I said.

" That's just what I'm afraid of," said Jonah. " That's why I didn't take you. We have been seen with Falcon, and word gets round.   It simply must not be thought that we are in touch with the Yard."

SECRET.

October 17th.

DEAR FALCON,

Sir Steuart Rowley.

In your letter of September 12th, you said something which did not immediately attract my attention ; but a fortnight ago, for some strange reason or other, your words came back to my mind.

You said that, on his arrival at Pau on September 1st, Shapely ' drew from the cloak-room some baggage which he had left .there in June.'

It then occurred to me—rather belatedly, I confess—that it was strange that Shapely should have left any baggage at the cloak-room at Pau in June.   He was then travelling to London—he talked with my cousin and me a few hours before he left and seemed uncertain whether he would return.   Why then leave baggage at Pau ?

I decided, if I could do so, to clear this point up.

So Carson travelled by train from Nareth to Pau and put a suit-case in the cloak-room, receiving a ticket with a number in the ordinary way.   He then gave me the ticket, and ten days later I took the suit-case out.   As I had expected, I had to pay two or three francs—a fine of so much a day for leaving the suit-case there in safe custody.   This gave me an opportunity not only of observing the system followed but of making friends with the clerk.

The system at Pau is this.   When a piece of luggage is left, two tickets are torn from a book.   Each ticket bears the same number.   One is given to the owner and one is affixed to the piece of luggage left.   Then that number is entered in a book.   The book has three columns—one for the date on which the luggage was lodged, one for the number, and one for the date on which the luggage was withdrawn.

While the clerk was busy, I turned the leaves of the book.   I looked at the entries under June 13th, for that, I knew, was the day on which Shapely left Pau for London.   There were in all eight entries, but every one had been cleared before the end of the month. *This proves that the baggage which Shapely drew was not ' some baggage which he had left there in June.'*

That told me what to look for, and I found it almost at once. The baggage which Shapely drew on September 1st had been deposited on June 10th.

Well, there we are.

It wasn't Shapely who deposited it, because he was at Luz Ortigue, as we have reason to know. It was Tass who deposited it, having come straight from Paris. The entry was the first of the day, which suggests that he arrived by the early train. It was, no doubt, Tass's suit-case, which he desired to be rid of and was later afraid to collect. So he sent the ticket to Shapely. And Shapely collected the suit-case and handed it over to Tass somewhere not far from Orthez on September 1st.

There is no question of identification, for the present clerk took over only three weeks ago, when his predecessor suddenly died.

If I may venture to say so, I think I should keep this evidence up your sleeve. The book is there and will be there, when you want it, to prove what I say.

> *Yours,*
> *JONATHAN MANSEL.*

As I handed the letter back—

" Full marks to you," I said. " Get Tass, and you get Shapely, for here is a link between them which nothing on earth can break."

" It involves him," said Jonah. " Accessory after the fact. No more than that, of course."

We left the matter there.

Five days later Falcon's answer arrived.

SECRET.

October 20th.

DEAR CAPTAIN MANSEL,
> *Sir Steuart Rowley.*

I was about to write to you when your letter of October 17th arrived.

What a detective you would have made ! Honestly, I never gave the baggage a thought. I should have, of course. It's my job. Yet I passed it by, but you stopped. When I showed your

letter to the Chief, he nearly pulled my leg off. And he made me
promise to ‘ report to you forthwith.’

And so I do, though I have a poor tale to tell.

Incidentally, I am taking your advice and keeping your
valuable evidence up my sleeve. Tass comes first—that is, if he’s
ever placed.

Just listen to this.

In my last letter I told you that the district which Shapely
visited on September 1st was being carefully combed.

In the letter in which we made this request of the French, we
also asked that, on the next occasion on which Shapely visited
France, he should be carefully shadowed either by their people
or ours.

We have now received a reply.

This says :—

(a) that the district in question was very carefully searched
without result.

(b) that, as there is no charge against Shapely, the authorities
cannot consent to shadow him or allow our people to do so in
France.

(c) that since we ‘ permitted Tass to escape from England,’ we
had better await his return which will doubtless take place before
long.

Well, there we are.

> *Yours very sincerely,*
> *RICHARD FALCON.*

I looked from the letter to Jonah, filling his pipe.

“ And now what ? ” said I.

“ Finish,” said Jonah. “ There’s nothing more to be done.
Tass may lie low for years—if he has any sense, he will. If he
or Shapely are careless, they might give the Yard a chance. But
as long as they are both careful, the incident will stay closed.”

“ What a blasted scandal ! ”

“ It is. But what can we do ? Old Rowley’s blood cries out :
but they laid their plans too well.”

“ But the French can’t have combed that district.”

My cousin shrugged his shoulders.

“ I don’t suppose they have. You see, they’re not interested.

It isn't their show. And they're quite within their rights in declining to shadow Shapely. On the face of things, he's a perfectly innocent tourist.''

" Succouring a man who's wanted for murder ? ''

" So we say.''

There was a little silence.

Then—

" One thing beats me," I said. " Well, it doesn't exactly beat me, but it doesn't seem to fit in. Shapely told Falcon that Tass did not like ' foreign parts.' Well, that rings true. An English chauffeur doesn't. He doesn't like the food and he misses his beer and his ' scotch.' Yet Tass is faced with more or less indefinite exile. And he must have considered that, if the crime was arranged.''

Jonah tapped his teeth with his pipe.

" That's a good point," he said. " And it hadn't occurred to me. And I don't see the answer." He smiled. " But then I never do—to the questions you ask. You wouldn't last long at the Yard. You'd break their hearts.''

Jonah showed me his answer to Falcon, before he sent it off.

It was very short ; but at least it left the door open, and that was all I desired.

October 22nd.

DEAR FALCON,

I am very sorry for you. But irons cool quickly in this country, and this particular iron was never more than warm.

I can, of course, promise nothing ; but we have eyes and ears, and if Shapely should leave England, you might care to let me know. If you telegraph, call him ' Aunt Mary.'

Yours,

JONATHAN MANSEL.

* * * * *

" But I don't understand," said Daphne. " We asked you for estimates for tiling walls and floors, and we asked you to show us samples of the tiles you proposed to use. You asked for a copy of the plans, and that you had. We did not ask for these sketches.''

Monsieur Antoine Caratib bowed from the waist.

"So many have said that," he said, "and they have lived as will Madame, to bless my name. Regard this exquisite confection of black and green. That is the bathroom which I have produced from my brain for Mademoiselle. Believe me, I worked through the night." He produced another sketch. "And this for Madame herself—all brown and gray. Subdued, of course. But I know. It is the personality——"

"Look here," said Berry. "You may be very discerning, but that's neither here nor there. We did not ask for discernment. We asked for estimates—and samples. Can you produce them, or not?"

"Monsieur will be patient. He will not find work like this in the Basses Pyrénées."

"I'm not looking for it," said Berry. "Madame's judgment is quite good enough for me. She and Miladi, between them designed the house. If they could do that, they are presumably capable of choosing the hues in which the bathrooms should be hung."

The other spluttered with excitement.

"That is just where Monsieur is wrong. What is a house? A shell. A shell of bricks and mortar—to house a shrine. And I have devised three shrines—three . . ." He broke off to gaze upon Jill. "Did I hear Monsieur say 'Miladi'? I was not aware."

Berry flung himself down on the sofa, and Jonah picked up the torch.

"Monsieur Caratib, these sketches do not interest us. In any event they are useless. In this one, for instance, the bath is in the wrong place. The plumbing requires——"

"Plumbing?" cried Caratib. "You talk to me of plumbing. The plumber crawls before me. Show me your plumber, and I will spit in his face."

"Stop talking like that," said Jonah, "and listen to me. You had the plans—to assist your calculations. Have you brought us an estimate?"

"But, of course."

"Then be good enough to produce it."

Caratib re-opened his dispatch-case. As he rummaged among its contents—

" I should like to reconsider the bathroom I had designed for Mademoiselle. I did not know that she was noble. I did one in scarlet and gold for the Duchesse de Dome. I could not repeat that, of course, for a model must stand alone. Ah, here is what I was seeking. Three bathrooms, according to plan. There was a fourth, I believe ; but I have omitted that. I do not tile bathrooms for servants. In fact, they do not have bathrooms in the houses to which I go."

" Perhaps they don't have servants in the houses to which you go."

The fellow recoiled.

" Monsieur insults me."

" That," said Jonah coldly, " would be impossible." He put out his hand. " Give me your estimate—as a matter of form."

The paper passed.

Estimate for designing and carrying out three bathrooms in a villa to be built at Lally.

Two hundred and fourteen pounds.

One third of the above sum to be paid on the acceptance of the estimate and the balance on the completion of the work.

Jonah handed the estimate round.

Then he addressed Caratib.

" Your estimate is refused. Take your sketches and go."

" Refused ? " cried the other.

" Refused."

" But I do not understand what you mean."

Berry rose to his feet, made his way to the fireplace and touched the bell—twice.

Then he turned to Caratib.

" You understand perfectly well. We do not accept your estimate. That is not only because it is fraudulent. It is because to-day you have shown us that you are not the sort of person with whom we care to deal. For one thing only, we like and respect the plumber whom we have engaged. And strange as you may find it, we like and respect our servants, one of whom —" he glanced at Carson " —is waiting to show you out."

Caratib folded his arms and set his back to the wall.

Daphne rose to her feet and followed Jill out of the room.

As the door closed behind them—

" Take up your things," said Berry, " and go your way. If you don't, you will be assisted."

" Yes, that is easy," said Caratib. " You commission my works of art and then seek to withdraw."

Solemnly Berry regarded him.

" You know," he said " you'd be improved by death. You're a filthy, incompetent snob of the vilest type. You live by cheap bluff, and why you've survived so long I cannot conceive. And now get out."

" I will go," said Caratib. " But first you will pay me for making my estimate. Those very beautiful drawings took up a week of my time." He produced a bill, already receipted and stamped. " That is a nominal charge, but let that go."

Estimate, as agreed, ten guineas.

" What a fool you are," said Berry, " to try this stuff upon me. If you wish to pursue the matter, you'd better see Monsieur de Moulin. He'll put you where you belong."

" You refuse to pay ? "

" I give money to beggars," said Berry," but not to impertinent knaves." He glanced at me. " Has he got the plans in his dispatch-case ? "

Carson held the man, while I took them out.

Caratib was trembling with rage.

" You will pay for this," he snarled. " You forget that you are in France."

" I have yet to learn that France supports blackmailing swindlers. I happen to know what it costs to tile a bathroom. Go to the Courts, my friend, and show them this estimate."

" You have your plans. I demand that estimate back."

" Demand and be damned," said Berry. " Carson, remove this fellow. He gives me a pain."

Caratib seized his dispatch-case and bolted out of the room. . . .

Less than an hour later, Jill and I were seated in an old-fashioned ironmonger's shop.

" I think you're an agent," I said, " for Ulic tiles."

The ironmonger bowed.

" That is quite true, sir. They are the best in France."

" Can I see some samples and prices ? "

" Certainly, sir. I have a booklet here which I will give you at once. It is illustrated in colour. But that is never satisfactory : before an order is given, the tiles themselves should be seen. If Monsieur will mark in the booklet the tiles he would like to see, I will have the samples here within forty-eight hours. And if the samples do not suit, then Monsieur shall give me the colour and tiles shall be made."

" That's more like it," said I. " And the prices are in the booklet ? "

" Precisely, sir. They are the actual prices which Ulic lays down. My commission, of course, is included."

" Splendid," said I. " And now what about a tiler ? I suppose you don't happen to know one."

" I know a good tiler, sir. He bears an Italian name, but he is naturalized French. He is modest and conscientious and he does beautiful work. At the moment he is working at Lally."

" What could be better ? " said I. " May I have his name and address ? "

" With pleasure, sir. I believe I am right in saying that it is Monsieur who is building that wonderful château by Besse."

" A villa," said I. " It's a very beautiful site."

" If rumour is true, it will be a beautiful house. And may I say this—that if Monsieur requires many tiles, I shall, of course, make a reduction. I can afford and am allowed to do that."

" You're very good," said I : " but we shall be happy to pay the prices laid down in the book."

On the following day we made the tiler's acquaintance.

His name was Lavarini. He was tall and broad and fair and his eyes were of china blue. He stood before us, twisting his shabby beret in nervous hands.

" It would give me great pleasure, sir, to work at Monsieur's house. And Monsieur will not regret it. Always I do my best Monsieur Joseph will speak for me : he knows that I try."

" Can we see your work ? " said I. " Some work you have done."

He led us upstairs to a bathroom. He had done the floor and was now at work on the walls. It was the very best tiling that I have ever seen.

" And how do you charge ? " said I.

" By the hour or square metre, sir : whichever you please. If it is to be intricate, I would rather charge by the hour. This bathroom, to give an idea, will have taken me thirty-two hours. At half a crown an hour that is exactly four pounds."

I put out my hand.

" We can't ask fairer than that. Keep in touch with Joseph. We'll want you some time next spring."

" At your service, sir," said Lavarini. . . .

That evening we worked things out.

By employing Lavarini to hang the best tiles we could buy, the three best bathrooms would cost us some fifty-five pounds. Almost exactly one quarter of what Caratib had asked for inferior stuff—and, I have no doubt, for inferior workmanship. Good men do not work for masters like Caratib.

*　　*　　*　　*　　*

On the last Monday in October, I stood on the platform with Joseph and watched the men filing away.

" So Monsieur is going to England ? "

I glanced at my wrist.

" At this time to-morrow, Joseph, I shall have been in London for nearly an hour."

" But that is amazing, Monsieur. Monsieur is going to fly ? "

" Between Paris and London, Joseph. I shall travel to Paris by train."

Joseph drew out his watch.

" Very good. At this hour to-morrow I shall think of Monsieur in London—and Monsieur will think of me. I shall stand in this very spot, with my watch in my hand."

" That's a bargain, Joseph. And I shall be here again one week from to-day."

Joseph inclined his head.

" I shall look for Monsieur's return, and I hope very much that I shall have something to show."

I threw a glance round the site.

The house was slowly rising ; the five long terraces were finished ; where the gully had lain, a slanting barrow of earth had begun to form. In the road below, I could see the head of the trench which was slowly nosing its way from Lally to Besse, in which were to lie the pipes conducting the water which was to serve our home.

" Will the pressure be strong enough to carry the water up to the top of the house ? "

" I think so, Monsieur. The engineers say it will serve the ground floors at Besse, and they are about the same level as will be the roof of this house."

" If not, it means a cistern below : and that means a pump."

" An expensive nuisance, Monsieur. If we can avoid it, we must. I have a hose all ready for when the connections are made ; and the moment the water is flowing, I shall be able to tell."

" Where shall we bring the main water on to the property ? "

" Ah, I knew there was something. I am glad Monsieur raises that point. For me, I suggest down there, where the garage will stand. From there the pipe can slant up to where this platform ends and the mountain begins. A small branch can serve the garage, for washing the cars, and two other branches can serve the terraces. So we economise pipe. The terraces on the west will have to be served from the house."

" I think that's sound. Ask Captain Mansel, though. His judgment is very good." Here the horn of the Rolls was sounded. " And now I must be going. Miladi and Major Pleydell want to get home."

" *Bon voyage*, Monsieur."

" Thank you, Joseph. A week from to-day, then."

As I took my seat in the car—

" If you ask me," said Berry, " you've got this house on the brain."

" So have you," said Jill. " Who spent two hours this morning——"

" On a shrine," said Berry. " Not a house. A temple. But I got it right in the end. A mirror over a basin is no damned good. So I'm going to have two mirrors—one upon either side. Then you can get at the swine. But a basin shoves you away. But I wish I could think of something to floor that soap-niche with."

My suggestion that Bath brick would do was coldly received.

CHAPTER X

IN WHICH TWO IS NO COMPANY, AND JILL HAS CAUSE FOR ALARM

THERE is no dame like London, and I was more than glad to see her again. I had three full days with her—and a list as long as my arm of things to be done. On Friday evening I crossed the last thing out. That was a present for Joseph—a quarto volume on building, rich in photography. The photographs showed the details of every kind of construction from footings to chimney-pots, and, though, of course, the text was in English, with such a volume before him, a man like Joseph would have no need of words. The pictures spoke for themselves—to one who had eyes to see. And Joseph had.

All the luggage had been dispatched directly to Pau : I had been to Whitehall and had suggested someone to take 'Old Rowley's' place as one of White Ladies' trustees : Jill's wristwatch was in my pocket—a fairy trifle that I was afraid to touch, and a belt—so-called—for Daphne was hidden in one of my shirts.

And one other thing I had done—at great expense. Waterloo Bridge was gone : but I had purchased six of its balusters. These had been kept for me in a builder's yard. I had hoped they would stand at White Ladies : but now White Ladies was gone. And so I arranged for them to travel by sea to Bordeaux : and from there by train to Nareth—that they might end their days in an English garden deep in the Pyrenees. Good and faithful servants for one hundred and twenty years, they were to be pensioned off—and given a terrace to keep ; the clouds would wait upon them and wash them clean, they would sleek themselves in a sunshine that they had never known, and lizards would lie along their pedestals and mould themselves to their curves. 'End their days.' I should have said 'See out Time.' Age cannot wither the stuff of which Waterloo Bridge was built.

And then, on Saturday morning, the fog began to come down. . . .

Had I been wise, I should have taken the train at eleven o'clock : but I loathe the train and the boat as much as I love

the air, so I hoped for the best and made my way to Croydon—
and met my fate.

At half past twelve I spoke with the pilot himself.

" It's anyone's guess," he said, " but, strictly between you
and me, I would lay two to one that no 'plane will take off to-
day."

" What about to-morrow ? " I said.

" Perhaps. I'm not at all sure. If I wanted to get to Paris,
I'd take the train."

By now I had missed my connection—Paris to Pau. But
there was a day train to Pau—The Sud Express. This left Paris
at eleven and got in at nine at night. I decided to sleep in
Paris and take that train the next day. But I was extremely
cross—I always am, when I am unhorsed, so to speak, at the
starting-gate. In high dudgeon I sent some wires. Then I sent
for a car and returned to Town.

My train left Victoria at two, and I should have had time
for lunch—but for the fog. This was twice as thick as it had
been an hour before. But my chauffeur knew how to drive
and brought me up to the station with twenty-five minutes to
spare. I settled myself in my seat with ten minutes to go.

Nobody seemed to be travelling. I had the compartment to
myself. For this I was thankful. I am bad at luncheon-
baskets and at managing legs of chicken upon my knee. Besides,
I hate eating, when nobody else is eating.

And then, as the whistle was blown, came a rush of steps.
The door—my door was wrenched open, a suit-case was flung
on the floor and a man stumbled in. He turned and leaned out of
the window to pitch a coin. Then he dropped into a seat.

" Near thing, that," he panted. And then, " By God, it's
Pleydell."

I felt more cross than ever.

The last thing in the world that I wanted was to share a
compartment with Shapely for nearly two hours.

*　　*　　*　　*　　*

I shall always remember that journey.

It was a most curious experience and one which, I hope, I
shall never know again. There I was, boxed up with a man

whom I most firmly believed to have contrived the murder of one I had liked and respected for many years. I knew that he was in touch with the man who had committed the crime. I knew that he was being shadowed—that men would be waiting at Dover, to see if he took the boat : and that, if he did, a telegram would go to my cousin—for what it was worth. Yet Shapely had no idea—*and must have no idea*—that I knew anything. All that Falcon had told us was secret. The name of Tass had never appeared in the papers. . . . In a word, I had to play a most delicate game ; for, though I knew so much, if Shapely discussed the crime—and I was quite sure that he would—I had to pretend that I knew no more about it than what I had learned from the letter that he had read us and what had appeared in the Press. ' Pretend ' be damned. Neither by word nor look, must I give him the faintest impression of such a thing. The devil of it was that I could not remember how much was common knowledge, for since July, when Falcon's first letter had come, I had not troubled to note what the papers had said.

* * * * *

" It's Pleydell," said I, " because of this blasted fog. I ought to be nearing Paris."

" And I," said Shapely, " ought to be half way to Dewlap. I started home this morning by car, but the Dover Road's a nightmare ; so I threw in my hand and came back. They get the boat-trains through somehow. I'll lay we're not ten minutes late."

" Of course," said I. " That's very convenient for you. A four-mile drive, and the boat-train, whenever you please."

" It has its points," said Shapely. " But I prefer the road. By the way, you've left White Ladies."

" That's a fact," said I.

" You know what people are saying. They call it a sign of the times."

I shrugged my shoulders.

" We had no choice," I said. " We couldn't keep the place up."

" You're a generous lot. Why make it over to the nation ? I mean, it was yours—to sell. America would have paid you a fancy price."

" I know. But White Ladies is part of the History of England. We always felt that we were no more than trustees. Atlas saw our point and put up the money required. And now White Ladies is safe."

Shapely laughed.

" Like The Abbey Plate : now in the South Kensington Museum."

" That's only on loan ; but we felt the same about that."

" There's no accounting," said Shapely, " for points of view. Still, if it's only on loan, you can always sell that. But you must feel lost without White Ladies. What'll you do ? Travel ? "

" As a matter of fact we're building. Building a villa up in the Pyrenees."

Shapely stared.

" You're not ! "

I nodded.

" Not far from Lally. On the other side of the valley, as you come up from Nareth."

" What, not on Evergreen ? "

" That's right," said I. " Half way between Lally and Besse."

" I don't know Besse : but I slept at Lally once and the name ' Evergreen ' has always stuck in my mind. My God, what a site ! But you don't mean to live there, do you ? "

" All main services," said I. " I don't see why not."

" Main services *there* ? "

I nodded.

" Well, I'm damned. Still, it is a shade distant, you know. What's the idea ? Fed up with the wicked world."

" Let me put it like this," said I. " We like the vicinity and we feel the need of a home."

Shapely smothered a grin.

" You must admit it's funny," he said. " From White Ladies to Mountain View. I suppose that's where you're bound for."

" More or less. We're staying at Pau."

" D'you mean to say you haven't been back since I saw you ? "

I nodded.

" We should have been, but for the building. We naturally want to watch that. We're coming back for Christmas and the New Year."

" After which you'll leave England for good ? "

" Not for good." With that, I handed him a paper. " You had no time to buy one, and I had no time for lunch."

As I opened my basket—

" Do your stuff," said Shapely. " I'll talk as you go. Oh, and talking of White Ladies, I understand that Old Rowley was one of the trustees."

" Unhappily, yes."

" Why ' unhappily ' ? "

" Because he was our choice—and now he is dead."

There was a little silence.

Then—

" You saw the verdict—' Person or persons unknown ' ? "

With my mouth full, I nodded.

Shapely turned, to look out of the window.

" Between you and me," he said, " that verdict was false."

I emptied my mouth and stared.

" False ? " I said. " What do you mean ? "

Shapely lay back in his seat and crossed his legs.

" Oh, the jury was honest enough, and the coroner, too. They couldn't find anything else—on the evidence brought before them. But the police know who did it all right."

" Are you sure of this ? " said I.

" Of course I'm sure. They make no secret about it—between you and me."

" Then why not——"

" —say so ? " said Shapely. " Because they can't run him to earth, and they don't want to put him wise."

" Well, who did do it ? " said I.

" A fellow called Tass. Albert Edward Tass, a chauffeur by trade. And the funny thing is that I put them on to Tass. . . . But what's much funnier still is that your cousin, Mansel, gave me the line."

" What ever d'you mean ? " said I.

Shapely fingered his chin.

" D'you remember when last we met—in the *Place Royale*, Pau ? And how we spoke of the murder, and I read you my sister's letter and told you as much as I knew ? "

" Yes," said I, " I remember it very well."

" And Mansel said that it might have been done by a servant who'd been dismissed."

" Yes."

" Well, the moment he said it, I had a dreadful feeling it might be Tass. You see . . ."

He related what he had told Falcon and Falcon had written to us—how Tass had been dismissed by Old Rowley and how he had taken him on and how he himself had dismissed him at Luz Ortigue.

" And then," he went on, " in a flash I thought of the keys— the keys of the car and the garage. And I left you and went to look—to look in my dressing-case. *And the keys weren't there.*

" Well, I was in two minds whether to tell the police. When I saw that the keys were gone, I, so to speak, sensed the worst. I was damned sure Tass had done it. He was the brooding sort, and he used to burst out about Old Rowley, when he was with me. Work himself up, you know, and say ' If I'd got him here . . .' All the same, he'd been my man, and I felt a natural reluctance to put the rope round his neck.

" And then, when I got back, the police started asking about him . . .

" And so it seemed best to come clean. In my own interest. Supposing it had come out that I'd had the keys ? . . ."

" Myself," said I, " I can't see that you had any choice. Murder's never pretty, but this was a monstrous crime. All the same, the keys won't hang him. You've got to have more than that."

" They've got all they need—and to spare."

He told me how Tass had been traced—from Pau to Paris, thence to Dover, and back to Paris again.

" And there they lost him. He may turn up, of course, but the scent is cold. Quite frankly, I hope he won't."

I felt rather sick. I set down my luncheon-basket and shut the lid.

" That's a hope I don't share," I said shortly. " He damned well deserves to swing and I hope he does."

" Put yourself in my place," said Shapely. " Tass was my servant. For the better part of six months, he and I were alone—

with the caravan. And if they get him, I'm the principal witness
—I'm the fellow who's going to send him down."

" That wouldn't faze me."

Shapely leaned forward.

" Don't forget this," he said. " That by bumping off Old
Rowley, Tass did me a very good turn. Old Rowley had my
birthright. He controlled my mother's fortune—and allowed
me twelve hundred a year. Well, Tass washed out that outrage
and gave me my birthright back."

" I don't gather that's why he did it."

Shapely raised his eyebrows.

" I hardly flatter myself to that extent."

" In that case," said I, " the fact that the crime improved
your financial position is wholly beside the point—which is that
Tass did murder—vile and beastly murder—to ease a grudge.
Well, you know, there's a law against that."

Shapely leaned back.

" You're the wrong person to talk to."

" I think I am."

" You liked Old Rowley. I didn't. I make no bones about
that. If he had been nothing to either of us . . ."

" Yes," I said, " there's probably something in that. All
the same, one's a sense of justice. Pretend that Old Rowley
was nothing to you or to me—pretend that we never knew
him, except by name. Then consider how he was murdered.
D'you mean to sit there and tell me Tass oughtn't to
hang ? "

" I never said that," said Shapely. " I said that I hoped
they wouldn't get him. Damn it, man, I don't want to be
involved."

" I daresay you won't be," said I. " As you observed just
now, the scent is cold."

With that, I picked up a paper . . .

For perhaps two minutes, Shapely said nothing at all.

Then—

" You must admit," he said, " that Tass did his stuff well."

I laid down my paper and stared.

" What on earth d'you mean ? " I said.

Shapely laughed.

" Well, he's got the police beat. In and out of the country before they had time to turn round."

" It was pretty plain sailing," said I. " He banked on the French, and the French haven't let him down."

" It was well worked out," said Shapely. " You've got to hand him that."

" I don't hand him anything. He knew what he'd find and he found it. And then he got out. After that, it was a matter of luck. He might have been tapped on the shoulder at any time."

" The fact remains that he wasn't. He hasn't been up to now. No. You've got to hand it to him, Pleydell. He never put a foot wrong. And they say that a murderer always makes one mistake."

" That," said I, " is tripe. They usually make half a dozen— and bad ones, too. But that's beside the point. Tass was above mistakes. If what you tell me is true, he fairly blazed his trail. He simply banked on disappearance—and that came off."

" I'll take your word for it," said Shapely. " Weren't you in Treasury Chambers ? "

" Once on a time," I said.

" Did all your murderers make a pack of mistakes ? "

" That's ancient history," I said. " My memory's dim. I can only remember Crippen."

" ' Only ' ? " cried Shapely. " My God, you weren't in that ? "

" From beginning to end," said I.

" You helped to prosecute Crippen ? "

" I did."

This was perfectly true. And I was accustomed to excitement, whenever I mentioned the fact. After all, *R. v. Crippen* is a classic.

Shapely was leaning forward.

" Go on. Tell me about it. How many mistakes did he make ? "

I wrinkled my nose.

" In fact," I said, " Crippen made three. Three very bad mistakes. One was an error of judgment ; one was an error of knowledge ; and one was—well, just a mistake : he forgot to do something that he had meant to do."

Shapely settled himself in his corner and crossed his legs.

" Let's have the error of judgment."

" Well, you know what he did," said I. " He murdered his wife. Then he cut up the body and buried it in the cellar. Then he went about his business and, when he was asked where she was, he said that she had left him and he didn't know where she'd gone."

" And he got away with that ? "

" For about six months. Then somebody got suspicious and went to the police. . . .

" Well, the police didn't think much of it. The scent was cold. But they called on Crippen and told him that people were saying things. And they pointed out that it might be a good idea if he could locate his wife. Crippen entirely agreed, and arranged to advertise. And the following day he bolted—to Holland, *en route* for Canada.

" Well, there's the error of judgment. The moment they found he'd bolted, the police were perfectly sure that he'd killed his wife. And after a lot of labour, they found her remains in the cellar, where Crippen had laid them to rest."

" By God, what a fool ! " said Shapely. " And you mean, if he hadn't run, he'd have been alive now ? "

" That's my private opinion," said I. " I may be wrong." Shapely licked his lips.

" Let's have the error of knowledge."

" Well, before he murdered his wife, he took the precaution of buying a sack of lime."

" A sack of what ? "

" Lime," said I. " Quick lime. It's very ordinary stuff. But it's useful in an interment."

" Go on," said Shapely.

" Well, he murdered her, cut her up and then began to shove her into the grave. And each time he put a bit in, he put in a spadeful of lime. The remains were laid up in lime."

" Then how——"

" — were they discovered ? I'm coming to that. When he put the lime in, he slaked it . . . wet it with water . . . made it into slack lime. And there he made his error of knowledge. Though he posed as a medical man, he was unaware of the elementary fact that, while quick lime destroys, slack lime preserves. In other and better words, he did exactly the opposite to what he was intending to do. He proposed to destroy the remains : in fact, he took care to preserve them—to send him down.

" Well, there was his second mistake. And if he hadn't made that—well, he *would* have been alive now.

" And now for his third mistake . . .

" His wife had had an operation, and this had left a big scar. So he cut out the portion of flesh that bore the scar, intending, of course, to destroy it—in case of accidents. The scar was what passports call ' a distinguishing mark.' Lime or no, if the scar was not to be found, the remains could not be identified as those of his wife. When he cut up the body, he laid that portion aside. (This is surmise, of course, but it's probably sound.) And then, at the last, he forgot. Forgot he had meant to destroy it, and shoved it into the grave. He may have been startled, or something. The clock may have said it was later than he had thought. Anyway, in it went—the last piece of all ; for that was the first thing they saw, when they opened the grave."

" And that was identified . . . after a lapse of six months ? "

" Why not ? " said I. " He'd preserved it—by slaking his lime. The piece was in perfect preservation. I saw it in Court."

Shapely made to let down the window : but when he stood up, his knees gave way and he crumpled and fell at my feet.

I lugged him on to the seat, loosened his collar and opened the window wide.

The next moment he opened his eyes.

" Lie still," I said. " I'm sorry. It's not a tale for weak stomachs. Half a minute. I've got some brandy here."

He drank the brandy I poured, and then lay back.

" Weak stomachs ? " he said. " I don't know what you're made of. It's the most revolting story I ever heard."

" Damn it," I said. " You asked me."

" You don't leave much out, do you ? Have you got any more of that brandy ? I still feel sick."

So Crippen served my turn.

For nearly an hour, Shapely never opened his mouth, but lay

either sleeping or dozing, whilst I sat back in my corner and read a book.

At the end of that time I saw him looking at me.

" All right now ? " I said.

For a moment the man made no answer.

Then—

" The legal mind," he said.   " Trained in Treasury Chambers. You know perfectly well why I hope that they won't find Tass."

I looked at him very straight.

" What are you getting at, Shapely ? "

" All right.   Let's pretend.   And I'll tell you what you know. You know I don't care two hoots what happens to Tass.   Why the devil should I ?   The man was a blasted nuisance, and if I'd had any sense, I'd have fired him before I did.   But you also know that the very last thing I want is to be the principal witness at Tass's trial . . . because you know what Tass's reactions will be . . . when he sits in the dock and hears me swearing his life away."

" Do his—reactions matter ? "

Shapely sat up and swung his legs to the floor.

" They mattered a lot to Old Rowley.   Old Rowley had done him no wrong.   He'd every right to fire him.   But that didn't count with Tass.   Tass is the kind of —— who has it in for people who, as he himself would put it, let him down."

" You mean——"

" This," said Shapely.   " If I go into the box, I put the rope round his neck.   The moment I mention those keys, he'll know that he's sunk.   So he'll say, ' All right, I'm sunk : but I'll take the —— that's sunk me down with me.'   *And he'll say I gave him the keys*, to help him to do the job."

I raised my eyebrows.

" He can make what statements he likes.   It doesn't follow, you know, that they'll be believed."

" Be your age, Pleydell," said Shapely.   " Which of us two stood to gain by Old Rowley's death ?   He ' eased a grudge,' as you put it : but I got three-quarters of a million—and more than that.   That's something like a motive, and you know it as well as I.   And why stop at the keys ?   He won't.   He'll say

I fixed the whole thing—and promised him twenty thousand, provided he brought it off." He threw himself back in his seat, and mopped his face. " So now you see, if you didn't see it before, why I don't want Tass to be found. Would you—if you stood in my shoes ? "

I turned and looked out of the window.

" To be perfectly honest, Shapely, I don't think I should."

" Exactly. And, speaking as counsel, what would you give for my chances, if Tass went into the box and swore that I was behind him in all he did ? "

" Quite a lot," said I, " provided you hadn't paid him his twenty thousand pounds."

*   *   *   *   *

When I got back to Pau, I told Jonah what had occurred. When I had done—

" This is not for Falcon," I said. " In fact, as I see it, Shapely said nothing that Falcon ought to know. But, if you think he did, then you mustn't pass it on. I dislike the fellow intensely, and I shall always believe that he planned the whole of the murder and that Tass was no more than the weapon with which the crime was done. But he spoke to me as an acquaintance, and not as ' a copper's nark.' "

" I quite agree," said Jonah. " But, if you've left nothing out, he said nothing that could be used against himself." He hesitated. " Well, perhaps I shouldn't say that. He ' visualized ' a certain contingency. I mean, he told you the line which Tass, if he came to be tried, would certainly take. And if Tass does come to be tried and does take that line—well, the fact that he had foreseen it would not sound well. Never mind. I won't tell Falcon. But fancy his fainting like that ! I wouldn't have said he was squeamish. In fact, I don't think he is. I think it was fellow-feeling. Fellow-feeling for a man who did murder—and got caught out."

" You may be right," said I. " But it was a bestial experience. Shut up for two hours with the swine. I tell you I damned near died when I saw who it was."

" I can think of nothing," said Jonah, " that I should have disliked so much. And now let's forget the matter. I'm sure you'll be glad to hear that they've finished the excavation. In fact, the retaining wall is already eight inches high."

*   *   *   *   *

At eleven o'clock the next morning, I stood once more on the platform and looked at the mountains about me, lifting their lovely heads. The day was flawless. There was no cloud, no wind, and the sun rejoiced in an ocean of deepest blue.

A semi-circle of wall was rising against the mountain behind the house, and Joseph was laying out the stem of the capital T. On the cross of the T, no work was being done, for all the masons were busy on the semi-circular wall. To one side, lay a heap of tarpaulins, with which, every evening, the wall was carefully covered against the frost.

Joseph looked up and saw me.

He came at once to the platform, brushing the dirt from his hands.

" Well done, Joseph," I said. " You said you'd have something to show."

" To be honest, Monsieur, I did not expect so much. But Fortune smiled on us, and we have had weather like this to help us on."

We spoke for a little of my journey. Then we went to look at the wall. This did not touch the mountain at any point, and the gap between them was being packed with stones.

" The house must be dry, Monsieur. And so the foundations of this wall are rather deeper than those of the house will be. And we have built a gutter behind it, to slope either way : and then we shall build another gutter this side ; and of course the wall will be furnished with many pipes. So any water that comes from the earth behind will be caught and will flow away on either side of the house."

Just before mid-day I gave him a cheap dispatch-case containing his book.

" The case is nothing," I said. " But you are in lodgings up here and I think perhaps you have nothing which you can lock. And, since you are out all day—well, now you'll know that no strangers are turning the leaves of your book."

" Monsieur is more than thoughtful. I cannot bear my things

L

being touched. But Monsieur has not said what the book is
about." He weighed the case in his hands. " It must be a very
big book, to weigh so much."

" Open it when you get back."

" Monsieur has written my name in it ? "

" Yes."

And there the others arrived, with lunch in the car.

We broke our fast on the ledge, as we had so often done . . .
Joseph was standing before me, béret in hand.

" I have no words, Monsieur," he said. " Of all things that I
could have desired, Monsieur has chosen the fairest to give to me.
I never knew that such books as this were made. And on every
page, a picture. I opened it after my dinner—I made it wait
until then. I always rest for an hour : but to-day, when the
hour was over and it was time to return, the book was still
open before me. . . . And what shall I not learn from this book ?
It is a treasure-house. And now it is back in its coffer. See,
I have the key round my neck. But it must have been dreadfully
costly. Monsieur is very good to have spent so much money
on me."

" As long as you like it, Joseph."

" It is my Bible, Monsieur, from this time on. Full of lovely
pictures of lovely work. To-night I study those of foundations.
And this house will have the foundations which fine English
houses have. It is, of course, composed by a master. And,
thanks to Monsieur, I can now sit at his feet."

I found such gratitude upsetting. Anyone would. I had so
much, and Joseph had so little. And yet . . . I began to
wonder if he was not richer than I.

Half an hour later, perhaps, Jill and I walked up the road
towards Besse. As we came to the scarecrow meadow in which
the half-built cottage was rearing its ruinous walls, I saw that
labour of some sort was being done within.

When we came abreast of the doorway, I peered inside.

Two men were at work on the landslide—working with pick
and shovel, to clear it away.

One I knew by sight—he was living at Besse.

He saw me, came to the doorway and gave me good day.

" You see," he said, " I am following Monsieur's example. I am going to dwell in the country. This beautiful field is mine, and so is this handsome house. Soon it will be one of a row. That is the way to make money. Build, and then let to your neighbours. Monsieur should do the same : he has plenty of room."

"That's quite an idea," said I. "We shall have to think it over."

As we passed up the road, Jill turned a horrified face.

"But, Boy! A row of cottages? Their smoke right across the terrace, whenever the wind's in the west ! "

I slid an arm under hers.

"They'll never be built," I said grimly. "He's just ramming home the wisdom of buying his rotten field. And we shall have to do it. The sooner, the better, too : for he's sure to add to the price the cost of the labour he's putting into that house."

"But it isn't a house," cried Jill. "No one can ever live there."

"I know, my sweet. This is what is called ' big business '— by the people who win. The people who lose call it ' dirty work ' or ' blackmail.' And there you are. We're on a loser, all right. Never mind. It might be worse, for those stones will be very useful. We'll pull that ruin down and make something out of that meadow before we're done."

"If only," said Jill, "it was the field with the grotto. I love that meadow, Boy."

"So do I. But no one could build in that, so we've nothing to fear. And now I think perhaps we'd better get back. The others ought to know this, and I'd like a word with Ulysse."

As we turned about, Jill began to bubble with laughter.

"I cannot think," she said, "what Berry will say."

"I shouldn't try," I said. "It won't be fit for your ears." Nor was it.

CHAPTER XI

IN WHICH BERRY TAKES THE BIT IN HIS TEETH, AND JONAH CAPTURES A SPRING

WHEN Berry had calmed down, I led him back to the ledge.

As he took his seat—

" And where," he said, " does this skunkish slow-belly dwell? What vicinity does he defile? "

" Besse," I said. " I told you. But Ulysse says he'll be at the café from five o'clock on.

" In the Street of the Waterfall? "

" That's right."

" And you advise instant action? "

" Yes. We need rough stone—not for building, but for packing behind the semi-circular wall. We've enough for to-day and to-morrow, but after that we shall have to use quarried stone, which is wicked waste. That blasted ruin is built of stones from the river bed. Once it's ours, we've only got to push it, to knock it down : and there's ten loads of stone all ready to hand."

" And he was boasting on Friday that he would sell us that dunghill for five hundred pounds? "

" That's right. And somebody laughed and said, ' How much shall you give your aunt? ' And he shut up like a box and looked very grim."

The fellow's name was Saut. He owned the scarecrow field. But he did not own the ruin. This had been built by his cousin at his cousin's expense. Then his cousin had died and had left the ruin to his mother, Saut's aunt. This had nothing to do with whoever might purchase the field. But it deeply concerned Saut—for the more he received for the meadow, the more his aunt would demand for the ruin itself. But if he could sell the meadow . . . and could then be gone from Besse before his aunt was aware of what was afoot . . .

All this I had learned from Ulysse. He was a famous counsellor —because he offered no counsel, but only hard facts. He gave

me the straw, and left me to make the bricks. A wise, old man,
who worked all day for his living, and was content. But he had
no use for Saut. ' A man,' he said, ' who gets drunk during the
week . . .'

"All right," said Berry. "I'll fix him. I'll teach him to
handle blackmail."

"Don't you think," said Daphne, " perhaps de Moulin——"

"No," said Berry : " lawyers out of the ring. This is a personal issue. In fact, there's a good deal at stake. If we are to
live in this parish, we've got to have our neighbours' respect.
That meadow, put up to auction, would bring the man twenty-
five pounds. And he has publicly boasted that he will force us
to pay him just twenty times what it's worth. Well, either he
or we have got to go down the drain."

"Oh, dear," said Daphne, " I wish I hadn't come."

" My darling," said her husband, " don't worry. I'm not
going to hit the brute. I'm not going to have any row. I'm
going to have a drink in a café. And your brother is coming
with me. But Jonah will drive you two back. Unless I'm much
mistaken, we shan't be far behind."

Jill set a hand on his knee.

" I simply love you," she said, " when you take the bit in
your teeth."

*　　*　　*　　*　　*

The café was fairly full.

As Berry called for two brandies, I shot a look round. At
once I saw Saut, sitting on a bench by himself.

"Beside the pillar," I breathed. " With a red moustache."

Berry picked up his glass and stood his ground.

"Ah, Saut," he said, " I thought I might find you here."

The other rose, with a very unpleasant grin.

" Fancy that," he said, " that Monsieur should wish to see me.
Still, it is good that neighbours should know one another. And
would it be indiscreet to inquire what Monsieur desires ? "

An uneasy silence succeeded the fellow's words. Such mock
politeness was an insult.

" It would not," said Berry. " I want your aunt's address."

You could, as they say, have heard a pin drop. Saut stood

still as death and, mouth open, stared upon Berry as though he were not of this world.   All his assurance was gone, as though it had never been.

Berry continued easily.

" I know that she lives at Oris, but I am not sure of the house."

At the third attempt—

" M-monsieur desires," stammered Saut . . .

" Your aunt's address.   I propose to purchase her cottage— the one you are putting in order, by the side of the road to Besse."

The sweat was on Saut's forehead.

" But—but I am not sure, Monsieur, that my aunt will be willing to sell."

" Why should you be ? " said Berry.   " That is her affair— not yours.   And so I am going to see her.   That is why I want her address."

Saut moistened his lips.

" But, Monsieur, that paltry ruin goes with the field."

" I daresay it does," said Berry.   " I don't happen to want the field.   It's a worthless piece of land, and I have more than enough. But the cottage walls are well built.   I have only to finish the work which you have begun—or you can do it for me.   I'll pay you the same as the men who are working up at the site."

Saut swallowed.

" My aunt," he said, " is a very difficult woman.   Monsieur would be well advised to deal with me."

" But you don't own the cottage."

" If Monsieur should purchase my field, he would purchase the cottage, too."

" I have told you," said Berry, " I do not want the field. But the cottage will serve me well as a *conciergerie*.   It is right on the road and but two minutes' walk from my gate.   Come now—your aunt's address."

" I do not know it," muttered Saut.   " I have heard that she has left Oris."

Berry stared.

" But is she, then, unaware of your intention to finish and live in her house ? "

" I — I have written to her," said Saut.

" That's better.   Where did you write ? "

" I — I have not yet posted the letter, because I had no address."

" Well, I'll tell her," said Berry, " and that will save you a stamp. They'll know where she is at Oris. Of course, as you say, she may not wish to sell. She may prefer you as a tenant. You don't know what rent you're paying ? "

Saut started forward.

" Let me implore you, Monsieur—do nothing precipitate. My aunt is unconscionable. The instant she knows that Monsieur desires that ruin, she will determine to ask the eyes from his head."

" I am perfectly prepared," said Berry, " to pay her a very fair price. What reason have you for thinking that she will refuse an offer of fifty pounds ? "

Saut clapped hands to his mouth, to smother a squeal.

" I know her, Monsieur. She is a rapacious woman. But fifty pounds for that eyesore—that undistinguished hovel ! I beg that Monsieur will listen. My field is for sale."

" I do not desire your meadow. I do not wish to be burdened with such an ill-favoured waste. To remove those briers and nettles——"

" Monsieur will see reason. The meadow contains the ruin."

" What ruin ? " said Berry.

" The ruinous cottage," screamed Saut. " The verminous huddle of stones, on which to-day I have nearly broken my back."

Berry frowned.

" Let us call it," he said, " the *conciergerie*."

With bolting eyes—

" As Monsieur pleases," said Saut. " The meadow contains the *conciergerie*. If Monsieur buys the meadow, the—the *conciergerie* must go with it. That is the law."

" But I do not want——"

" Patience, Monsieur, I pray you. Monsieur does not want the field. That is understood. But still it might come in useful. One never knows. It is always land, and one might make a depot there. So Monsieur, to gain his cottage, will purchase the field from me. It is just the same and will save a journey to Oris. I mean, I have the right. That is the law— that the building goes with the freehold."

" Of course, but——"

" Consider, Monsieur. I am asking next to nothing. For two hundred pounds——""

" Two hundred pounds ! " cried Berry. " You're out of your mind. If I deal with your aunt, I pay fifty—and get what I want. If I deal with you, I am to pay four times as much for a ragged, worthless strip from which a goat would retire. No, no. I do not want it. I prefer to purchase only the *conciergerie.*"

Saut writhed.

" But I will sell this to Monsieur. It goes with the land. I am in the happy position——"

" Then sell it," said Berry. " I have said I will pay fifty pounds."

" For the—the *conciergerie*, Monsieur. But what of the field ? "

" But I do not want the field. Why should I pay for something I do not want ? "

" But think of the advantages, Monsieur. The *concierge* will have a fine garden, which he can till."

" Have no fear he will trespass," said Berry. " Give me your aunt's address."

" No, no," screamed Saut. " I will not show Monsieur the way to a den of thieves. That woman will victimize Monsieur— a most disgraceful thing. At my own expense I prefer to save the family name. I will sacrifice the field as it stands for one hundred pounds."

Berry shook his head.

" I prefer to visit Oris and pay the half of that sum." He tossed his brandy off and gave me the glass. " Have you any message which I can give to your aunt ? I shall, of course, tell her of your offer—to save the family name."

Saut drew himself up.

" I cannot permit it, Monsieur. My conscience says no. That dirt of a woman will take advantage of Monsieur. It is painful to me to speak ill of a relative. But she is untrustworthy, Monsieur. There ! I have said the word. I cannot agree that Monsieur should make her acquaintance. I have my pride. And so I shall make the following sacrifice. I will give my meadow to Monsieur for eighty pounds."

Berry fingered his chin.

" With immediate possession ? " he said.

" If Monsieur so desires."

" So be it," said Berry. He turned to me. " Give me some *papier timbré.* We'll get this down."

I produced a sheet of stamped paper, and someone produced a pen. Then and there, on one of the liquor-stained tables, we drew the Agreement up. And Berry and Saut signed it, and then Ulysse and I subscribed our names.

Then we stood drinks all round and, after a few minutes' chatter, withdrew to the car.

As I set the key in the switch, a head came in at the window.

" Monsieur will not go to Oris."

" No," said Berry, grimly. " I'll let you break the good news."

I heard the man catch his breath.

" How soon does Monsieur think we can sign the Deed ? "

" I'll tell you to-morrow," said Berry, " at two o'clock."

As the car slid out of Lally—

" Monsieur Saut," said I, " is proposing to disappear. His aunt won't see one penny."

" Yes, she will. His aunt will see twenty pounds. I had a hundred in mind, so I took the precaution of beating him down to eighty. As soon as the Deed has been signed, under de Moulin's advice we shall pay the balance to her."

So, thanks entirely to Berry, all fell out very well. We became the owners of the last of the ' dangerous ' fields—and that, at a fair price : we got ten loads of stone of which we were very glad : Saut, whom Besse detested, was seen no more : his aunt —I need hardly say, a highly respectable widow—travelled to Pau to present us with two most excellent ducks and, on meeting Berry, insisted on kissing his hand : best of all, as Berry had predicted, once for all the air had been cleared. So far as we were concerned, the peasants now knew where they stood and that, while we were prepared to be generous, we knew how to deal with blackmail. As for Berry's personal stock . . .

" But, what a man ! " breathed Joseph. " Ulysse was ravished. He would not have missed it, he said, for twenty thousand francs. To see the wicked reduced ! And the one full of sound and gesture, and the other as quiet as death. But that, I have always heard, is the English way. Yours is a great country, Monsieur. I do not wonder that England leads the world."

* * * * *

On Wednesday, the fourth of November, the weather broke. That night the heavens were opened, and it rained so hard the next day that we did not visit the site. On Friday, at ten in the morning, one of the brothers, Henri, telephoned to the flat. " There has been a little accident, Monsieur, up at the site."

Instantly, I thought of the *ruisseau* which we had piped. An immense amount of water must have been coming down, and if the pipe had been choked . . .

" No, no ; it is not the *ruisseau* : a piece of the excavation has given way."

" Right," I said. " We'll be there within the hour."

While Carson ran for the Rolls, Jonah and I got into our overalls, and Jill put on what she called her ' service dress.' Fifty minutes later we reached the site.

It had almost stopped raining now, and patches of blue were showing between the clouds.

As I drew on my rubber boots, Joseph came up to the car.

" I am very glad to see Messieurs."

" Is it very bad, Joseph ? "

" No. It is very, very trying, but it is not a catastrophe. But let me waste no words. Its best that Miladi and Messieurs. see for themselves."

We climbed to the back of the platform as fast as we could. . . .

Swollen by the downpour, a spring had broken behind the great wall of earth. Always the spring had been there, and often enough had been swollen, because of heavy rain : but then it could not break out of the mountainside, for fifteen feet of soil lay upon it, to hold it back : so all it could do was to thrust its way down the mountain, deep under ground. But now we had taken twelve of the fifteen feet, and the three feet left could not hold it and so it had broken out—twenty feet above where we were standing . . . and had done, in two or three hours, what twenty men could not have done in two or three days. Some fifteen tons of soil had broken away from the face of the excavation and had fallen over the wall that was being built.

With pick and shovel, men were already at work, loading the soil into trucks, to be taken away; and others were shoring up the face of the excavation, in case there should be more rain and another fall.

"The first thing to do," said Jonah, "is to capture that blasted spring. Then we can school it to the gutter, and, after that, it can flow with what force it likes."

His counsel was good, as always.

A spring is an underground river, a tiny thing: but when it breaks out above ground, it knows no law. This one had made for itself a ragged delta: the face of our excavation was running with threads of silver, each one of which was eating into the soil. Unless the spring was captured, this erosion was bound to continue until enough earth had fallen to lay bare the spring itself. And that was unthinkable.

"How far in is that spring?"

Joseph spread out his hands.

"Monsieur," he said, "I have taken the men's opinion, and they say between two and four feet. I have asked how they would capture it, but all they can say is 'With stones.'"

My cousin shook his head.

"Good enough to save a meadow, but not a house. We've got to have masonry here. I think the thing to do is to sink a well."

"Ah!"

"A well, say, eight feet deep. They make wells now of sections of ferro-concrete, all ready to sink. We place one section directly above where we think the spring has broken, and dig out the earth within it until it sinks; then on goes another section, and we dig out the earth again, until the two have gone down. And so on. And when we are eight feet down, we shall capture the spring. And after that we can pipe it wherever we please."

"It shall be done, Monsieur. The sections will be here this evening, and I shall construct the scaffold this afternoon. I think that by Sunday evening we should have the spring in our hands."

Had the clouds returned, we should have had a bad time. But, by the mercy of heaven, we had fine weather until the work was done. The men worked all day Sunday, and Jonah and I, with Carson, remained at Lally until the danger was past. From Friday to Tuesday, the three of us laboured full time, from seven o'clock till five. (Carson had driven Jill back and had returned with our things. And we had done very well at the little hotel.)

Our labour consisted mainly in shifting earth. The soil which was dug away from within the well was cast on to the heap below, and from that heap below to the heap below that ; that heap in turn was shovelled into the waiting trucks and the trucks were run down a terrace and tipped straight on to the mound which had supplanted the gully of other days.

Early on Monday morning we captured the spring. This was seven feet down. It rose three feet and then stopped. That meant it had done its worst. Gravity was against it, and, now that it was confined, it found itself compelled to resume its underground course. As a result of a cloud-burst, it might rise another two feet, so we set in an overflow pipe a foot from the top of the well. That made assurance sure. Then we cleared away the loose soil between the well and the wall : and the moment this was accomplished the masons set to work. Their job was to raise the wall as fast as they could ; and while the wall was rising at this particular point, stones from the ruinous cottage were packed where the soil had been.

By Tuesday afternoon the wall at this point was nearly five feet high, and the wound which had been gaping above it, whose sides had been shored with planks, had been plugged with hundreds of stones from the river-bed.

There was still much soil to be cleared from the platform side of the wall, but now, though it rained to glory, no harm could befall.

As we bade Joseph good night—

" It has been a great honour, Messieurs, to have you and Monsieur Carson in the *équipe*. You have set a great example which no one will ever forget. And let us not count this a setback. For me, it is well that it happened. Sooner or later, you see, that spring would have had its way. And it is a hundred times better that it should have broken now than that it should have broken after the house was built."

And that was a true saying. Had it broken the following winter, it would have been awkward indeed.

* * * * *

Another two days went by before all the earth that had fallen had been removed : but even when that had been done, Joseph would not proceed with the house, for fear of another fall. He concentrated, instead, upon the semi-circular wall and set the few men that were left to digging the large recess which should house the septic tank. This was to lie beneath the lower of the terraces running to the west of the house. The bath- and sink-water would pass by a separate drain which did not enter the tank, but, after threading a grease-trap, would slant down under the meadows, to meet the *ruisseau* a few feet above the road. (Such a meeting had been foreseen, and when the *ruisseau* was piped, a branch had been left all ready, plugged and carefully housed.) At the opposite end of the site, the Lally water had now been led into our ground, and the plumber's men were working upon the pipes which would lead it up to the house. That the pressure should not be embarrassed there were to be no corners, but only curves, and, before the trenches were cut, the pipes were laid in their order upon the turf. They were then lightly screwed together, branches and all, when Felix Arripe, plumber, desired us to say if the line was such as we wished.

With Joseph, we inspected the lay-out and found it good.

Joseph addressed his uncle.

" You will plug the main line, if you please, but set stand-pipes at the ends of the branches without delay. Such action, I mean, will be very convenient for me. I can then have done with the *ruisseau*. Moreover, by means of a hose, I can see if the pressure will reach the roof of the house."

" All this I will do," said the other, " when you have interred my pipes."

On the sixteenth day of November, the Lally water was running upon the site—and Joseph had tested the pressure and found it would force the water as high as the roof. And the semi-circular wall was nearly done.

We had, indeed, a great deal to be thankful for.

* * * * *

" Three weeks from to-day," said Jonah, " we are going to leave Pau for England, where we shall spend a month. I think that, before we go, we should choose an electrician. You may think I'm looking ahead ; but so I am. I hate knocking walls about. Arripe is in touch with Joseph and keeps him posted regarding the holes he must have. I think we should have an electrician, to do the same."

" Why not ? " said everyone.

We found one almost at once—an excellent man, called Carol, and Daphne and Jill and Berry were soon absorbed in a pile of catalogues.

" Now here's what I want," said Berry. " Here's what I want. I shall have it beside my bed. You see it in the ' big business ' films. You just breathe your requirements into it, and everyone hears what you say all over the house."

" I don't believe it," said Daphne. " Any way, it's the very last thing you're going to have. I can think of nothing more frightful."

" Of course I shall have it," said her husband. " It's what I've been needing for years. Take a case in point. I'm short of shaving-cream. Well, it's very hard to remember to buy a cosmetic like that. But if I'd had one of these gadgets, everyone in the flat would have been aware of the truth. And if I'd rammed it home, somebody would have remembered to buy me a tube to-day."

" If you get one of those," said Daphne, " you'll live in the house by yourself."

Berry sighed.

" Well, do remember," he said, " that I'm short of shaving-cream."

Jonah and I were more concerned with cables and screwed steel joints. We visited Carol, when he had studied the plans.

" How will this do ? " said I. " The main lines run into the garage right at the foot of the site : and there we have the meters—in a cupboard which we can lock. From there the cables go under ground to the house, and pass by the side of the water into the furnace-room. Your main switch-board is in the garage. You have two subordinate switch-boards, one on the ground floor and one on the floor above. All the fuses are presented on these two boards, and each board will have a main switch, to cut out that floor. The boards to be hung head high, and so within reach."

" I shall be happy," said Carol, " to do as Monsieur suggests. But I see there will be an attic which covers the whole of the house. Also an underground chamber some twenty-eight metres long. I suggest a miniature switch-board for each of these. It will not cost very much, and the lights outside the house can be controlled from the *cave*. So the whole house will be sectioned. I have some good fuses here. They are very new. Monsieur observes the little red spot upon each ? But that is not a spot. It is a little red peg which is sunk in the porcelain. And if a fuse should go, the little red peg will shoot out. One glance at the switch-board, therefore, and Monsieur cannot help seeing of all the fuses before him, which one must be replaced. And he has, of course, several spare fuses all ready to hand."

Remembering the many occasions on which I had stood upon ladders, checking fuse after dust-laden fuse in the sweat of my face—and one very special occasion, when Berry met two hundred volts and dropped the one torch we had, and then lay down in the dark and demanded an iron lung—remembering these things, I felt that the house was worth building, if only for the sake of the fuses which Carol was proposing to use.

" And now for the rooms. I cannot bear to do damage, and I shall do my best to follow the plumber's pipes. But my tubes must nowhere appear. So before any tiling is done or floors are laid, Messieurs will please decide exactly what lighting they want and where they would like the switches and the plugs for the light and the power."

" We'll see to that," I promised. " We propose to have indirect lighting throughout the house."

" I am glad of that," said Carol. " It is the best light in the world : and I have a plasterer here who will fashion the fittings for that to your own design—at less than half the price which the great houses charge. Which reminds me, a new radiator has just come in. It has behind it a fan, which drives the sultry heat all over the room. I have taken the liberty of sending one round this morning to Monsieur's flat—for Miladi and Madame to try, and to use as much as they like. It is nice in the bedroom, you know, when Madame is dressing for dinner. Her maid can switch it on five minutes before she comes up . . ."

It occurred to me that if Carol was as good a workman as salesman, we should, indeed, have little to worry about.

*　　*　　*　　*　　*

Right at the end of November, the coping was laid on the semi-circular wall.

"And now we are free," said Joseph," to build the back of the house. Upon that we must concentrate, for we must catch up with the front. The two must arrive together at the point where the ground-floor ceiling is to be laid. For this will be another platform—less solid, of course, but almost exactly resembling that upon which we stand. It will gird the whole house together and will give every room a ceiling which nothing on earth will crack.

"And here I take the occasion to raise an important point. Raise it I must, before Messieurs depart for Christmas, because, I think, when they return, it may be too late. It is the height of the ceilings. The plans tell me less than three metres. I find that terribly low. I would have said four metres—four metres for a château like this."

The French believe in high ceilings. We had arranged for ceilings of nine feet six—nine feet six exactly above the floors. And Joseph was commending ceilings of thirteen feet. I knew that to argue was hopeless. But nothing this side of hell would have made me give way.

"It's an English fashion, Joseph. Refer to ' the Bible.' You'll find we're not very far out."

Joseph smote upon his thigh.

"Of course," he said. "But I am still concerned with the doorways and walls. I have not got so far as the ceilings. And Monsieur means to say that all these fine houses in England have ceilings as low as that ? "

" Some have higher ceilings, Joseph. But only a mansion to-day would have ceilings thirteen feet high. And no one is building mansions."

" But this is a mansion," said Joseph.

I shook my head.

" It would have been lost in White Ladies, the home we have given up. There were fireplaces there which would have accepted a car. And the Royal Chamber was twenty-two metres long "

" *Mon Dieu*," said Joseph.

" A book's being made about it. One day I will show you a copy. And that reminds me. Don't forget the niche you are going to leave in the wall."

" Monsieur need not remind me. Monsieur le Major talks of that niche every day. And he is perfectly right. He desires that, when he is bathing, the soap shall be within reach. But neither he nor I——"

" I don't mean the soap-niche," said I. " I mean the secret recess which is to be left in a wall."

" Ah! I know now. I remember. Depend upon me, Monsieur—that shall be done. I have the dimensions here." He tapped his breast. " Monsieur is going to have a canister made ? "

" That's right. I'll get it made in London. And in it, with other things, we'll put the White Ladies book."

" That idea attracts me," said Joseph. " I think it is very nice—that this house should wear in its heart the picture of its great predecessor, now full of years."

* * * * *

Two days before we left Pau, with one consent we visited Paradise.

It was a perfect day, and though the beeches were bare, thousands of firs were still clothing the mountainsides. Above them, the snow-clad peaks seemed stuff that dreams are made of—against the blue. The astonishing brilliance of the sunshine, the steady thunder of the torrent, the cool, sweet air and the absence of any being except ourselves seemed to proclaim with one voice the paramount excellence of Nature, compared with

M

Art. Great London seemed cheap and sordid beside such things :
her finest buildings, vulgar beside those time-honoured walls :
the roar of her traffic tuneless, beside such harmony.

Our pool had disappeared. Twelve feet of water were raging
where we had lain beside it three months ago. But the meadow
was at our disposal, smooth and gay and secluded—a true
Horatian lawn. As I have hinted before, the oaks and the
hedges about it gave it an English air, and, late in the year
though it was, a lizard was sunning himself on the slates of its
jolly barn.

Jill and I strolled past this, while the others were arguing
where we should eat our lunch.

As we looked up at the heights—

" Shall you ever forget that day when young de Moulin got
stuck ? "

" Never," said Jill. " We nearly went home that day. I
suppose we didn't really. I mean, ever since then we've had
such a glorious time. The house and the site and those three
months at Lally, and the thought that we're going to live there
. . . You must admit it smacks of some future life."

" It does," I said. " But I think that's because we've walked
out of the world we know. The world we know's gone down
hill. Once it was very fine, but now it's—well, meretricious.
Nothing but money counts. Love and beauty and genius—they
all take second place. And manners are dying out. And we
have left that world and stumbled on Arcady. Well, of course
we find it heaven. Remember that picture you took—of the
threshing-floor above Mose, and the three men standing there
with flails in their hands ? "

" Very well. It was the most perfect evening I ever saw."

" I've a print of that in my note-case. I'm going to show it
to them when they pull my leg at the Club."

" ' As they did in the golden world ' ? "

" Well, you should know," said I. " That's where you
belong."

That, I think, was true. Yet those of the golden world belong
wherever they go. When, exactly five days later, I found my
small cousin at the top of St. James's Street, discussing Walt
Disney with an Inspector of Police and looking ' a million dollars '

and more than that, I stopped to suggest that she should join me for lunch.

" At your Club ? I'd love to. This is my cousin, Inspector. Boy, Inspector Randal agrees with me. That Walt Disney should do Æsop's Fables. And isn't it funny, his mother was born at Brooch. And he used to go and stay there when he was a little boy."

We spoke for a minute or two before some traffic confusion returned the Inspector to duty and cut the acquaintance short.

Having seen Jill into the Annexe, I passed through into the Club to see what letters there were. On my way through the hall, I stopped to look at the tape. As I turned away, Jonah strolled up to my side.

" Read that," he said.

' That ' was a telegram which had been forwarded from Pau.

Aunt Mary left Dover for Paris this Sunday afternoon.

In silence I handed it back.

" It doesn't really matter," said Jonah. " We couldn't have done anything. But did you tell Shapely that we were coming home ? "

" Yes," I said. " I said we'd be back for Christmas."

Jonah nodded.

" I thought you must have," he said.

CHAPTER XII

IN WHICH DAPHNE COMES BY HER OWN, AND PARADISE IS
LOST

BEFORE we returned to France, Falcon dined at the Club, with Jonah and me.

After dinner we sat in the silent smoking-room.

" Shapely returned," said Falcon, " two days ago. He's been away exactly three weeks. That he has met Tass in that time, I have no shadow of doubt. But I can do nothing about it, but watch and pray. The Home Office is furious. One of His

Majesty's Judges wilfully and wickedly murdered, yet no arrest ! But the French are adamant. Had we dreamed that they'd stick in their toes, we should have acted first and asked afterwards : but now that we've asked their permission, and they have refused, we cannot take that line— in case they should discover that we're going behind their back."

" You're perfectly sure that Tass doesn't write to Shapely ? "

" I don't think so," said Falcon. " God knows what it's costing to watch his correspondence, but he never gets a letter that hasn't been read."

" Accommodation address ? "

Falcon shook his head.

" He's watched incessantly."

" Banking Account ? "

" He has an account in Paris : we can't check that."

" What I don't understand," said I, " is how Shapely can count on Tass not to let him down ? Of course he's warned him on no account to write. But Tass has got his address ; and a man like that might easily get fed up and write a letter which he thought was quite all right."

" He hasn't so far," said Falcon. " If we could produce such a letter, the French would give way."

" My cousin," said Jonah, " is right. Sooner or later Shapely will have trouble with Tass. I don't know what form it will take, but one day it will dawn upon Tass that he's had a raw deal. And then the balloon will go up. Till then, you can do nothing— except what you're doing now."

" I'm afraid you're right," said Falcon. He leaned back and covered his eyes. " I never saw such a case. All the cards in our hand, and we can't play one. And Time's against us, you know. Suppose that after a year Tass takes the bit in his teeth. And we get him—and Shapely, accessory after the fact. I'm not at all sure that a jury would send them down. Juries don't like cold murder. And witnesses are less certain. And think of the play that defending counsel would make with the lapse of time."

" All that you say," said Jonah, " is painfully true. But you're up against one of those walls that no one can climb. It's the damnedest misfortune, Falcon . . ."

" I wish you could have seen the Chief, sir."

" So do I. But I couldn't have done any good. If I could have, I would have waited. You say he'll be back next week ? "

" I think he's sailing on Friday."

" Well, give him my compliments, Falcon. And my address. You never know."

*   *   *   *   *

That night, when I was alone, I thought over what Falcon had said. Only one thing stood out, and that was the length of time that Shapely had spent away. Three weeks, Three days would have been sufficient, if he had gone to meet Tass. And then I perceived that Shapely had done no more than take ordinary care. He had almost been caught in September, and that had shaken him up. No more flying visits for him. A fortnight at Pau, playing golf and bridge and doing as visitors do. And one or two drives perhaps, to look at the countryside. Then, perhaps, a visit to Biarritz of three or four days. And so to Paris and England . . . Yes, that was how it was done. All the same, I was perfectly sure that his meeting with Tass had been anything but cordial. Lying low is a rotten business, and the standard of life by Orthez is very much lower than that of the English countryside. Shapely could give him money, but what was the use of that ? You cannot spend money, when you are lying low. I felt it was a question of waiting. Sooner or later, Tass would lose patience and let the two of them in.

*   *   *   *   *

We reached Pau at eight in the morning—a really beautiful morning, all blue and gold. And we were all at the site before mid-day.

Great progress had been made. The whole of the ground floor was finished—the walls, I mean. And the tiles had been delivered. And so had the baths and basins and things like that. These were all stored in what we had come to call ' the guardroom '—that is to say, the great chamber under the house.

The stem of the T had been floored with six inches of concrete : this, of course, was resting upon the soil.

Around the stem of the T, between the house and the semi-circular wall, ran a passage four feet wide.   This was floored with concrete and very slightly sloped, to carry surface water away.

" You've really done wonderfully, Joseph."

Joseph bowed.

" Madame is very kind : but the weather has helped a great deal.   Only two days of snow.   And now they foretell a mild spring.   We have much to be thankful for."

" And the damp-course ? " said I.

" I wish that Monsieur could have seen it.   It went against the grain to cover it up.   Such a course has not been laid in the Basses Pyrénées.   Three inches of asphalt, Monsieur.   Applied all smoking hot.   Not one centimetre escaped.   Exactly according to the pictures in Monsieur's book.   Madame need have no concern—her house will be dry."

" When will you start the ceiling ? "

" To-morrow morning, Monsieur.   The wood and the steel are here and the tiles are to come."

(In fact, the tiles were not tiles.   They were made of clay, as are tiles, but they resembled nothing that I have ever seen. They were roughly the shape of a flat-iron, the handle of which is bent sideways, to form a crook.   So they could be hung in a row on a rod of steel.   That was, of course, their function.   Except for the cut for the stairs, the whole of the ground floor was to be ceiled with wood.   Upon this wood the ' tiles ' would be laid in rows, until the wood was hidden beneath a great sheet of tiles. Then the steel would be laid and tied across and across : but certain rods would be run beneath the crooks of the tiles.   When all was ready, thin concrete would be run in ; and, once this concrete had set, those tiles would hang there for ever and nothing would make them move.   Then the wood would be taken away, and the ground-floor would have its ceiling, and the first floor would have its floor—water-proof, fire-proof and sound-proof —a good idea.)

" All will be ready, then, by the end of this week ? "

" Before then, Monsieur.   Say Friday.   But when we can run in the concrete, I cannot say.   That will depend on the weather. It is, of course, the platform over again.   But the risk, for obvious reasons, is very much less.   For one thing only, the job can be done in one day."

That night, in our flat after dinner, we discussed for the last time certain documents. All things considered, it was likely that, if indeed they were ever discussed again, such discussion would not take place for several hundred years.

The first was a skin of parchment which I had had engrossed. The statement it bore ran as follows:

THIS HOUSE was built in the years of our Lord one thousand nine hundred and thirty-seven and thirty-eight :—
(1) to the order and under the supervision of
Bertram Pleydell, J.P.,
Daphne, his wife,
Jill, Duchess of Padua, his cousin,
Jonathan Mansel, D.S.O., his cousin,
and Boy Pleydell, M.C., his cousin and brother-in-law, all late of White Ladies in the County of Hampshire and all British subjects by birth :
(2) by Henri and Jean Lafargue, builders and contractors of Pau in the Basses Pyrénées.
Their foreman, Joseph Condé, was directly responsible for the construction. He built well and knew his mystery.
The plumber was Felix Arripe, also of Pau.
The electrician was Jean Carol, also of Pau.
The tiler was Georges Lavarini, also of Pau.
And many lesser men, especially masons, contributed to the excellence of the work.
'Except the Lord build the house, their labour is but lost that build it.'

The second was a copy of *The Times* containing an account of His Majesty's Coronation.

The third was a copy of *Punch's Almanac*.

The fourth was a menu of the Savoy Hotel for New Year's Eve.

The fifth was an advance copy of *White Ladies*—a dignified tribute to what had once been our home.

And the sixth was that remarkable production the catalogue of the Army and Navy stores.

I need hardly say that the last was Berry's idea. He was, of course, perfectly right. Few things will be of more interest a thousand years hence.

When we had finished, we put them into the canister which had been specially made.

As I fitted the top—

" Where exactly will it lie ? " said my sister.

" To the right of and above the front door."

" And it's going in to-morrow ? "

" As soon as the men have gone : at a quarter past twelve. Joseph and the master mason will do the job. No one else knows anything about it. I shall take it to the garage to-morrow and under my eyes the lid will be soldered on. Joseph has some tar at the site, and, before it goes in, it will be coated with tar. I can't think of anything else."

" That price list will fetch them," said Berry. " I mean, when the canister's found, five million years hence. It'll rank with the Rosetta Stone."

" But they're sure to have others," said Daphne. " Not many, perhaps. I think it's a brilliant idea. But some museum will have one."

" There won't be any museums," said Berry. " When the world catastrophe comes, all the museums will go. Destruction will be the watchword. But this house'll take some destroying. And no one will know that there's anything valuable there. And so the list will survive—to illumine a happier age. Antiquarians will be transported. Fancy knowing what a sink-basket looked like before the Sphinx was designed ! "

" I suppose," said Jill, " I suppose they'll know what it is. They may be so far advanced that they'll think it's a book for children. I know I used to love it when I was very small. In fact, I love it now."

" Let them think what they like," said Berry. " Any way, if Christies put up a hoop belonging to William Rufus, America'd buy it for a hundred thousand pounds."

" We might," said Jonah, " have put in a dictionary."

" Let them do a spot of work," said Berry. " We mustn't spoil the brutes. Damn it, we're presenting them with something which is above all price. The least they can do is to set up a monument to us. Perhaps we'd better suggest it. An outsize pyramid would do—with our names in six-foot letters about the base."

" Let us," said Daphne, " leave it to their good taste. Besides,
I should hate to think that my name was plastered up somewhere, for everybody to read."

Berry smiled.

" It won't matter then, darling," he said.

I was half undressed that night when Berry came into my room.

" I have here a trifle," he said, " which might go into that box.
I don't really want it read, until the box is opened in eighty-nine
twenty-two. But you'd always be uneasy, if you didn't know
what I'd said. So read it, and shove it in. But for God's sake
keep your mouth shut. I'm not in the habit of wearing my heart
on my sleeve."

As the door closed behind him, I opened the envelope.

The words had been written by a master—on parchment ten
inches by eight. Blue and gold and scarlet lighted the lovely
thing. The initial letter alone must have taken two days to
produce.

THE LADY OF THE HOUSE.

*DAPHNE PLEYDELL would have distinguished any age.
A famous beauty, she steadfastly refused to allow any picture of
herself to appear in the public prints. As the hostess of White
Ladies, as of her London home, she displayed an efficiency,
dignity and charm seldom encountered severally, never together.
Her servants worshipped her ; men, old and young, were proud to
sit at her feet ; all women bore her goodwill. She was all things
to one man—her husband. Gentle in fair weather, gallant in
foul ; gay, resolute ; honest, wise and kind, she was for all time
a model of excellence.*

When I had read it through twice, I put it back in its envelope
—thoughtfully. Then I opened the canister and slid the envelope
in. . . .

The next day this was immured, and its lodgment was sealed.

*   *   *   *   *

As Joseph had said, the ceiling was ready on Friday ; and on
the following Monday the concrete was run in. Mild, wet weather
subscribed to the enterprise ; and before the end of that week,
the masons were building the walls of the floor above.

Because of the rarefied air, all masonry dried very fast. I do not mean to say that it dried too fast for its health ; but a wall which in England would have taken three months to dry, would dry upon Evergreen in roughly a third of that time. This was more than convenient. Before the first floor was finished, the floor and walls of the ground floor were being tiled.

With the exception of the furnace-room, the floors of the stem of the T were to be wholly tiled. All white tiles would be used, with an edging of blue. And, except for the servant's hall—and, of course, the furnace-room—all the walls of the stem of the T would be hung with glazed tiles to six feet above the floor.

" Strength through joy," observed Berry, watching Lavarini at work.

I need hardly say that we all watched Lavarini at work. It was a fascinating spectacle. The tiles were bedded on sand and actually laid in cement. A very fine cement was washed over the area done : this filled in the joints : the surplus was washed from the tiles, before it could dry, and the tiles were then laid with saw-dust, soon to be brushed away. It seemed to us, looking on, that Lavarini worked largely by eye. Any way, the result was perfect. I believe that you could have played billiards on any one of his floors. His walls were just as flawless. All his corners were rounded, and so was every angle, where wall met floor.

Perhaps I should have said that, before Lavarini began, the plumbers and electricians had laid their pipes.

Meanwhile the house was rising.

The weather could hardly have been more favourable. Mild, damp day was succeeding mild, damp day, and the tell-tale buckets of water never froze. Still, Joseph was taking no risks ; and every night the masonry done was covered, in case of accidents.

Built of concrete blocks, the inside walls took next to no time to raise, and before the month of March had come in, all was ready for just such a ceiling as had been hung below.

So we surveyed the floor on which we should pass our nights.

We had no spare room. (' Guest-room ' is very lovely, but ' spare room ' is English and, therefore, ' spare room ' will serve.) But it would have been very expensive to build an extra room, and it was not to be expected that all of us five would be together in residence all the year round. So the room of whoever was absent would serve the guest.

In all the house, if you do not count the larder, only five windows looked north, and two of those were only lavatory lights. Daphne and Jill, I think, had done very well.

Three days later the first-floor ceiling was run in.

" You're hurrying, Joseph," I said. " I'm terribly glad to see it, but tell me why."

Joseph smiled.

" I have talked with Ulysse," he said. " This is an unusual year—of weather, I mean. He remembers just such a year before the last war. He cannot read or write, but he notices things."

" He can sign his name," said I.

" Yes. He was taught to do that. But he has no idea what the letters mean. And because he has had no education, he is unearthly wise. Monsieur, the harm that is done by this education! These fools of politicians who would not know wisdom if they saw it and keep on bawling that all men must have the same chance. What chance are they speaking of ? A chance to make money ? No happiness came that way. A chance to learn slick talk and bamboozle your fellow men ? Perhaps that is what they mean. Who are the agitators ? All of them ' educated ' men. The uneducated are too honest—too honest and much too wise. More. They are content, Monsieur. Yes, and these prating idiots would ' educate ' Ulysse—Ulysse whose little finger is thicker than all their loins. He was educated, Monsieur, before they went to their schools. Ulysse is seventy-seven and never in all his life has he been as far as Pau. And yet, I tell you, Monsieur, Ulysse is very much wiser than you or I. But there ! I get heated. Politicians have to live. And fools will keep them in office, if they commend the destruction of all that counts."

" I wholly agree with everything that you say."

" I thought that Monsieur would, for Monsieur has eyes to see. He builds this house in the mountains, because he is sick of the world. He seeks to withdraw himself—to spend what time he has left among things worth while. And I am the same. I

could go to Paris to-morrow—and earn three times the money
that I am earning here.   And have my ears battered with nothing
but communist talk.   But here we can see.   Always there must
be rich, and always there must be poor.   It is a law of Nature.
But both can be well content.   Give me this house, Monsieur,
and I should be miserable.   I shall come to see Monsieur, of
course, in the years to come.   We shall walk and talk together,
as we do now.   But Thérèse and Monsieur Carson will be my
hostess and host.   Ah, well, I have talked too much.   But old
things go by the board, and the new are nothing worth.   Besides,
I find it sad to see the world being fooled by a parcel of knaves.

" And now for Ulysse.

" He believes that April and May will be very wet.   And
that then we shall have a hot summer—almost a drought.   And
so I must get the roof on.   Once the roof is on, it may rain as it
likes.   But the frame of a roof is of wood, and I do not want
that soaked."

On the first of March, the concrete was run in, and the first
floor had a ceiling that nothing would ever move.

The framework of the roof was ready—it had been built at
Pau.   The tiles had been coming up for the last ten days.

On the tenth of March we drove up, to see the framework in
place and the flags of England and France at either end of the
ridge-pole which ran from east to west.

The tradition was gratefully honoured.   Berry, with Joseph
beside him, gave every man two days' pay.

Then the tiles began to go on—in summer weather.   You
never saw such a thing.   Indeed, it might have been August,
but that the sunshine was cold.

" What about the garage ? " said Jonah.   " I think it's time
we brought the electricity in."

" And the telephone," said I.   " It'll save a second trench."

On the 25th of March the last tile was nailed into place, and
two days later the foundations of the garage were laid.

*   *   *   *   *

Before the end of the month the brothers requested us to visit
their carpenters' shop.

" The back staircase is made, Messieurs, and this we should

like you to see before it goes up to the site. And we have some shutters and also some window-frames. These we should like you to pass, before we proceed with the rest. A door also. And one or two other things. One morning perhaps. Of course, if Madame and Miladi would care to come . . ."

I did not say that nothing would have kept them away.

The shops were impressive : I had not known that there were such workrooms in Pau.

First we were shown the staircase, which had been roughly erected—I think for ' Mesdames ' sake.

This was all of old elm and made as fine a back staircase as ever was built.

" But where," said Jonah, " did you get such very fine wood ? "

The brothers smiled.

" Monsieur is a connoisseur," said Henri. " Whenever I hear that an old house is to be pulled down, I visit the scene myself and examine the beams. And if they are sound, I buy them." He fondled the newel. " This came out of my favourite. I had been keeping that for something worth while. My masons are proud of the work they have done on your house. My carpenters' one idea is to equal the work they have done. Such rivalry is good, Monsieur. It is good for you and for me, and it is good for the men. If you knew the pleasure, Monsieur, of building for some-one who cares."

We passed to the shutters. These were all of oak and were very well done.

" All seasoned oak," said Henri. " Neither sun nor snow will move it—that I will guarantee."

We could find no fault at all with the oak window-frames. But the sample door was too thin.

But for that, it was an excellent door. It was a plain sheet of oak—not solid, of course. Two sheets of oak had been ' applied ' to a frame. Every door in the house was to be made like that.

" Thicker, still ? " said Henri.

" Seven centimetres," said I.

(That is two and three quarter inches. I like a door you can feel.)

" It shall be as Monsieur says."

The library was to be panelled. We did not like the moulding and promised to provide a design.

" And the front door ? " said Jill.

" I await the oak, Miladi. I am not yet satisfied. Be sure I shall find it. And when it is made, four men will scarcely be able to lift it up. Such a house deserves such a door. Miladi will come and see it when it is being built."

" If I shall not be in the way, I hope to visit your workshops many times."

" They are open to you, Miladi, whenever you please to come."

" That's very kind of you."

Jill never said a word that she did not mean.

In the next two months, she spent more time in the shops than anyone else. It was she who designed the moulding and saw it cut. It was she who chose the door-handles and had the happy idea of doing away with locks on the bedroom doors. Instead, they were fitted with ' buttons,' a bolt which you shoot by hand when you are within the room. A miniature door-handle. Very unobtrusive. To be found in lavatories.

*   *   *   *   *

I shall always remember Saturday, April the third.

That day we determined to visit Paradise.

On the way, we picked up a puncture just short of Mirelle.

Mirelle has a marble mill ; and, whilst Carson was changing the wheel, we walked to the office and asked if we might be permitted to see the mill at work.

The foreman was most obliging.

The torrent provided all the electric power—a fact which made me envious. If we had had but half such a head of water, we could have had turbines installed and had as much power as we pleased.

We saw the saws at work and then the primitive polishers, doing a lovely job. No doubt the methods were old-fashioned, but I have yet to see more perfect results.

As we took our leave, very much wiser—

" There is," said the foreman, " a great deal of waste in this place. Many bits and pieces of marble are thrown away. If

Messieurs desire any ash-trays, it will be a pleasure to make them
—in my spare time. I have a platter here . . ."

It was a beautiful platter—and would have been sold in London
for two or three pounds. He asked us seven shillings and would
have taken less.

We ordered a dozen ash-trays and promised to give him the
pattern next time we went by.

It was as we were leaving that Berry let out a squeal.

" What on earth's the matter ? " said Daphne.

" Marble," said Berry. " Marble. That's what I want to
floor the soap-niche with. Of course it's ideal. Marble. I'll
do a little design and bring it next time we come. Yes, you may
laugh, if you please : but you don't know how to live. You
can talk of ferro-concrete and stairs of elm. But who ever
heard of a soap-niche floored with marble ? Joseph and Lavarini
will be beside themselves. Can't we go up by the site ? I'd
like to break the good news."

We declined to go up by the site and proceeded to Paradise.

The pool would be out of the question—as it would be out of
sight. A frantic river would be raging where it had been. But
there was always the meadow—the little, English meadow, locked
in the arms of France.

We passed the Customs' control and told them that we would
be back in two or three hours : we climbed the curling shelf that
led to Spain : and then we slid off to the left and down the
shadowy ramp, that left the road for the valley we knew so well.

A furious head of water was coming down, lashing the rocks
till they shuddered, filling the chasm with thunder and snaring
a precious rainbow in one of its clouds of spray.

For two or three minutes we watched it, standing upon the
bridge. Nature was giving battle and setting forth her standard,
as decent captains should.

And then we turned to our meadow . . .

This had been straitly fenced, since we saw it last. And two
notice-boards were blaring their ugly news.

PROPRIETE PRIVE
DEFENSE D'ENTRER

We stared upon them in silence.

"Oh, well," said Daphne, at last. "I suppose we were trespassing."

My brother-in-law was less lenient.

"Thrombosis of the spleen," he said shortly. "The lousy, black-livered skunks. They've lain in watch and observed the very great pleasure we had of that pretty field. And that was enough for them. What harm did we ever do? We never left any traces, we always shut the gate. But they saw that we enjoyed it—and that was enough for them."

Jill was half way to tears.

"But it's so gratuitous. Of course we'd have asked, if there'd ever been anyone here. But there never was."

"They didn't appear," said Berry. "All right. Let them have their meadow. I wouldn't set foot in it now for a thousand pounds."

Whilst Carson was turning the car, I walked up round the meadow to look at the little barn. Even this was padlocked. Whoever owned the meadow was determined to hold what he had.

There are people like that—in England as well as in France. We had invaded no privacy: there was no privacy to invade. Neither had we done damage: there was no damage to do. All the same, we had done trespass. And the owner had every right to warn us off. It was very childish of us to take offence. Still, we were disappointed. Paradise was lost.

CHAPTER XIII

IN WHICH WE WATCH MAGIC MADE, AND JILL HAS HER HEART'S DESIRE

ULYSSE was right.

On the fifth of April the rain began to come down, and we hardly saw a fine day before the middle of May. But, since the roof was on, the work within the house proceeded apace. The work without was not stopped, but it was much interfered with for those six weeks. All the same, we could not complain, for at every critical moment the weather had seen us through.

Since spring was now in, we began to think of the garden. The first thing we did was to sow the long, low barrow which lay where the lower half of the *ruisseau* had run. This, with good, meadow grass, which would not only clothe the soil, but would hold it in place. Then we planted the great slope of soil above the semi-circular wall. This we planted with baby, ever-green shrubs; for seed scattered here was sure to be washed away, but the roots of the shrubs would go down and would grip the soil. Then we turned to the terraces. The loam was rich, but the number of stones it kept was unbelievable. And Daphne and Jill were relentless. The stones must go.

One thing, at least, we were spared, and that was transporting the stones to some desert place, for the terraces had to have paths. I will swear that those paths will last as long as the house, for all their beds are of stone—some eighteen inches thick. So the Romans built their roads. Later on they were to be paved.

The middle terrace on the east was to be our lawn : all the others would be reserved for flowers. But you cannot manage a garden, when you dwell some twenty-five miles from where the garden lies. So we did no more than prepare it, against the day when we should return to Bel Air. Besides, we had plenty to attend to, if we were to have the house as we wished it to be.

The plumbing was far advanced before April was out. Before the roof had gone on, a monster tank had been hauled up to the attic, and pipes were leading from this all over the house. This tank received the main water from Lally's source. (The water which ran in our pipes never saw the light of day until whosoever required it opened a tap ; for the fountain from which it came was snared under ground. Indeed, by Roger's advice, we never drank it at once, but allowed it to stand for a moment and so to breathe.) A mighty hot-water cistern stood in the furnace-room. By Arripe's advice—I should say, at his earnest desire—we had decided that the furnace should be fed upon oil.

" The advantages, Messieurs, are great. True, it will cost more to install : but, once it is in, it is clean, it requires no labour and it controls itself. And the fuel is no more expensive than anthracite. If Messieurs agree, Monsieur Carol and I will set up an apparatus which you can forget.

" Let us take the hot water first. You must always have

constant hot water. Very well. That will be maintained by means of a thermostat. When the water begins to grow cold, the furnace will spring to life. Six baths running will make no difference at all. No question of stoking arises. The furnace will supply what the thermostat may demand.

" And now for the central heating. This Messieurs will only require when the winter is here. But this house is very well placed. There will be many days in the winter, when it will be full of sun. So the heat must be regulated. Very well. We install a clock—an electric clock, which will always keep perfect time and will do as you say. To this clock you will give your orders ; and the clock will see that the furnace carries them out. For instance, at six in the morning, the heat will begin to come on. But at ten o'clock in the morning the sun will begin to grow hot : so at ten o'clock the furnace will go off duty. But at four in the afternoon, it will resume its labours, which it will pursue, say, till mid-night, by which time you will have retired. Now this is all very well. But supposing you have bad weather and see no sun. For that, a switch is provided—I think that it should be fixed on the library wall. A touch upon that, and you over-rule the clock. More or less heat, exactly as you desire. And the clock will pick up your ruling and do as your finger says."

" Such a system will suit me," said Berry. " Can I have another switch in my bedroom, in case I feel cold at night ? "

" But why not, Monsieur ? I find that a good idea."

Berry looked round.

" You know," he said, " I'm going to like this house. It's going to prolong my life. And I like obedient gadgets. You haven't got any taps that know their names ? "

* * * * *

Our decision to use an oil-burning furnace meant that we must have a tank in which the oil could be stored—just as petrol is stored in the tank of a car. The comparison is really exact. So a tank like a submarine was sunk in the terrace which was to be our lawn. This terrace was of the level which the engine required, but the lawn would not be disfigured, for two feet of soil would lie upon the top of the tank. There was certainly a man-hole, but that would be covered by a flag. To fill this tank was simple. A pipe was run down underground to where the garage apron would lie. The waggon would run on to that and would then connect its pipes and pump the fuel up.

Meanwhile Lavarini continued to lay and to hang his tiles, Carol continued to run his screwed-steel pipes, the carpenter's-shop was making shutters and doors, and Daphne and Jill were discussing washable paints.

The back stairs were hung in April. These led up to a landing, as I have said. And from the landing, a smaller flight led to the attic, now being lined and floored. This made a spacious apartment. The pitch of the roof was steep, in case of snow, and so there was headroom to spare. There was but one window, and so its recesses were dim, but electric light was there, and a plug for a radiator, in case it was very cold. In fact, the attic covered the whole of the house. There was ample room for our luggage and things like that, and wires were stretched from the beams that clothes could be hung to dry. With such a place and 'the guard-room' we should be very well served, for the latter would make such a workshop as many employers of labour would be very glad to have. And neither attic nor guard-room had cost us a penny-piece. They were incidents of building. The guard-room we owed to the mountains—that I admit. But I must confess that in more than one modern house, that I have explored, the attic has been a quarter one tries to forget. It seems to be in the tradition that attics should be approached through a hole in the floor—an inconvenient method, as anyone will allow. Often enough, they are neither floored nor lighted —two things which work together against their habitual use. And so all that room is wasted. . . . But then we were heretic. We had no architect.

Early in May the fireplaces began to go up. I say 'go up,' because they were built by an expert with little toy bricks. Very delicate work it was, but, so far as I saw, he never made a mistake. The recesses to hold the wood were framed in oak. Plate glass was cut, to lie on each mantelpiece. Between this and the brick would lie mats which the girls and Thérèse would adorn. These sheets of glass were inlaid : that is to say, the bricks on the edge were laid a fraction higher than those within ; so that, once the glass was in place, it could not move.

And then came the day when the marble stair was hung. The brothers had advised us beforehand.

Henri spoke for them both.

" Specialists, of course, will do it : but it is an operation which should be observed. Mesdames and Messieurs will enjoy it. Myself I have seen it three times. But I shall be there on Wednesday, because it takes me by storm."

That we all paraded on Wednesday, I need not say.

The three lowest steps had been laid. They had no support. Risers and treads simply jutted into the semi-circular wall. They were five feet long, and they jutted into the wall to the depth of an inch. They were set in with plaster : and plaster joined together the risers and treads.

The fourth riser was fitted. We saw it laid. Then the specialist chipped out his niche, and his helpers lifted the fourth step and guided it into place. The specialist plastered it in. It took him, perhaps, two minutes to do this work. He adjusted it to his liking and wiped the spare plaster away. And then he walked up the stair *and stood on that step*.

I do not expect to be believed, but we all of us saw him do it. He must have weighed thirteen stone, but the step never budged. And the step itself must have weighed a hundredweight.

" But why doesn't it collapse ? " said Daphne, putting a hand to her head.

The brothers, Jean and Henri, laughed and laughed.

" Madame, we cannot tell you, and we are builders ourselves. It is an art beyond ours. But the specialist only smiles and talks about stresses and strains."

" But it doesn't look safe," said Jill.

" Yet I have seen one such in a block of flats at Paris. It was the common staircase which everyone used. It had to carry four or five people at once. And pianos were carried up it. And yet it moved no more than if it had been cut from the living rock."

" And the balustrade ? " said Daphne.

" That is nearly ready, Madame. It looks most charming. Madame's design is really exquisite."

" I copied it," said Daphne. " The credit must go to a smith who died many years ago. I don't even know his name, but he knew his job."

This was the truth.   Daphne had found a picture of an elegant balustrade that once had guarded a balcony belonging to Bloomsbury Square.   How or where she found it, I do not know.   But she had reproduced it with great success.

The stairway was done the next day, and two days later the gallery had been paved.

The roof was now on the garage : but the timber had been soaked in the process, and Joseph would not put up the ceiling until it was thoroughly dry.   Neither would he render the walls of the house itself.

" What's he mean—' render ' ? " said Jill.

" ' Cover with a skin of strong mortar.'   The whole of the house and the garage are going to be rendered twice.   We don't want hot weather for that : but we musn't have heavy rain. A Scotch mist would be ideal."

" I like the stone.   I'm sorry it's going to be covered."

" It won't be covered on the terrace—the front of the house.   At least, the ground-floor won't.   The ground-floor is going to be pointed and stay as it is.   But the skin is a great protection.   A house which is really well rendered will never be damp."

Strangely enough, the weather changed the next day and before the week was out, the house had been rendered once.

Next week it was rendered again and the moment the mortar was dry, the carpenters arrived with the shutters and window-frames.   These had already received two coats of paint.   The third would be administered, when they had been set in place.

As soon as the frames were in, the windows were glazed : and the moment the glass was in, men came from a neighbouring town to lay the floors.

The house began to look like a house : and the rooms began to look huge.

The ' service ' steps which ran from the house to the drive— to the left of the house as you faced it—were now in use.   There were eighty-four, and the last twelve made you think.   They passed by the guard-room door, and here was a pleasant landing, on which, if you pleased, you could rest.   This was really, a miniature terrace, and a balustrade was to guard it—a balustrade of wrought-iron, like that of the stair within.

Joseph was determined to lay the front steps himself.

"They are most important, Monsieur. The 'service' steps are nothing. The peasants are well accustomed to climbing the side of a house. But Madame and Miladi are not. Their ascent must be made as easy as ever we can. The steps must be broad and low, and the flags must be perfectly laid. No rain must rest upon them. That is why I shall do it myself. And while I am doing that, the masons will build the parapet of the terrace. So, though I shall be engaged, I shall still be at hand and so shall be able to see that the work is properly done."

As he said, so he did.

He laid the front steps in ten days. He had two men to help him but every single step he adjusted and laid himself. They ran down straight to the foot of Hadrian's Wall: there was a little landing, as on the other side : and then they curled down to the garage to splay out on to the apron beside a waiting car. They were low and most easy to tread, and I cannot understand to this day how he managed with ninety-three. It sounds a great many, of course. It is a great many. But the effort required to climb them was really extremely slight. Even Berry admitted this.

"He's laid more than steps. He's laid a hell of a ghost. I don't see how he's done it, but that is beside the point. That flight might have been a nightmare. I don't pretend I'm not glad to get to the top; but I'm not exhausted. I haven't even perspired. And he's managed to give the swine a certain allure. You feel inspired to climb them. . . . Not so with the 'service' steps. We shan't be troubled with hawkers. And I'll lay the butcher leaves the fish in the drive."

The parapet surrounding the terrace was nearly done. Its actual height was decided by Berry himself. It was to be coped with specially chosen flag-stones, three inches thick ; and one of these was brought up and laid on the unfinished wall. Then Berry leaned upon it and looked at the lovely view.

"Too low," he said shortly. "Another two inches, I think."

The flag was removed and another two inches were added to the height of the parapet. Then the flag was put back.

Berry tried it again.

"One more inch," he said.

The procedure was repeated.

" Now that's just right," said Berry. " On that you can lean at your ease. It's just right for the folded arms. Ideal for meditation." He glanced at us, standing behind. " No protrusion of the buttocks, I trust ? "

" You won't be arrested," said Jonah, " if that's what you mean."

Berry turned to Joseph.

" My cousin, the Captain, mocks me."

" And that, without cause," said Joseph. " Myself, I wholly approve the trouble which Monsieur has taken to get the height right. After all, the parapet will be there for a thousand years ; but this little exercise has taken a short half hour. Before buying a pair of shoes, Monsieur will take the precaution of trying them on. And what is a pair of shoes, beside this parapet ? "

" And the soap-niche ? " said Berry.

" It is justly famous already. Lavarini can talk about nothing else. The marble floor, so scooped, was a great idea. I had thought and thought—to no purpose. But Monsieur arrived. I see Miladi smiling—and so I have to smile, too. But Monsieur mocks himself. He mentions only his soap-niche. He does not mention the appointments throughout the house. It is he who has measured himself exactly where each shall go. Every light, every mirror and shelf ; it is he who has judged and measured and marked the spot : servants' quarters and all, that all may be just as it should be for everyone. Miladi's pier-glass, for instance, will hang two inches lower than that of *mon Capitaine*. But there ! I can never declare the joy that I have had in helping to build this house. No detail has seemed unimportant in Mesdames' and Messieurs' eyes. They have stood not behind, but beside me in all I have done. And when I am very old, I shall always remember that."

The parapet was not completed. Its wings were built and, roughly, four-fifths of its length—that is to say, the length of Hadrian's Wall—but a gap was left in the middle, because the scaffold was there which led to the crane. When we had done with the crane, then the gap would be closed.

On the second day of June we had left Pau for Bel Air, and

though we were leaving a really luxurious flat, we were more than happy to sleep among the mountains again. In the last twelve months we had spent so much time in high places that, when we went down, we missed them, body and soul. Of this there can be no question. Mountains can be compelling. They can get hold of a man, as can no other country I know. After all, the old gods lived there ; nymphs inhabited their groves ; Artemis hunted in their forests ; and Amaryllis' footprints embroidered the dew that overlaid their lawns. That lovely lease is up : horn and laughter and echo are heard no more : but tenants like those must have larded their haunts with magic and have magnified the mansions that lodged them, when earth was young. For proof of this, match me the silence of mountain-tops. It is not of the world : it passes all understanding : it is, for me, the presence . . . And I think that those who have felt it will bear me out.

*   *   *   *   *

The furniture in our flat had shown that it was well made of seasoned wood, and we had visited the factory and had placed the kind of order which factories like to receive. We needed beds and bedding : we needed a dining-room table and dining-room chairs ; we needed dressing-tables and chests of drawers. Every piece was made to our order, of oak or walnut or rosewood, just as we said. For such wood and such workmanship, the price was remarkably low, and we were very much tempted to order more than we did. But we did not want to live with nothing but modern stuff : so we bought what we had to have, proposing to furnish slowly, looking for things in the sale-room and gradually acquiring some things that cannot be made to-day. The goods that we had in England were being sent out ; and, with them, the linen and silver which we had kept.

So I come to the balusters, which once had graced Waterloo Bridge.

Their arrival had been greeted with rapture. Daphne and Jill had embraced me, Jonah had made me a present and Berry had sworn to remember me in his Will. But when it came to deciding where they should stand . . . For six months they had waited by the garage, because we could not agree where they would look best. The question was raised on an average twice a week, and discussion grew more bitter as time went on.

" They should go with grass," said Jonah. " You can't get away from that."

" Your mind's diseased," said Berry. " They've gone without grass for over a hundred years."

" Jonah's quite right," said Daphne. " On the bridge it never mattered, because they were part of a scheme. But we've only got six. And we can't possibly build upon them : they've got to stand by themselves."

" That's what I say," said Berry. " Turn them into sundials and shove them about the place."

" You can't have six sundials," said Jill. " Besides they shouldn't be scattered."

" I quite agree," said I. " The eye should run from one to the other."

" And what about the nose ? " said Berry. " Where's that going to run ? All over them I suppose."

" You really are filthy," said Jill.

" It isn't my fault," said Berry. " I've not been the same since I slept in that *wagon lit*. You know. When I had that blanket that somebody'd been——"

" You would bring that up," said Daphne.

" Don't confuse me with my predecessor. Incidentally, I'm perfectly sure that that was a ramp."

" What was ? " said Jill.

" The, er, magic blanket. I gave the conductor ten francs to give it to somebody else. Well, there's an income there. He can probably count on fifteen francs a night."

" I should like to see them," said Daphne, " along the edge of the lawn. But they wouldn't show up from below, because from that angle you'd get the wall behind them."

" What wall ? " said Berry.

" The wall of the terrace above."

" They should stand against green," said I. " And, if we can do it, on green. Three would look very charming, planted about the ledge at the foot of the bluff."

" I know they would," said my sister. " But what of the other three ? "

With a fine inconsistency—

" You can't possibly split them," said Berry.   " They'd better all stand in a ring—to the west of the house.   A little, alfresco temple, in honour of that fine old English god, Siwian."

" Siwian ? " said Jill.   " I never heard of him."

" Oh, you must have," said Berry.   " Macaulay's *Brays of Home*.

> *For Ferro loves the concrete,*
> *And plaster loves the lime,*
> *And Siwian loves the septic-tank*
> *And runs there all the time.*

" Of course, just as Woden's Day has become Wednesday, so Siwian's Day has become Sewage Eve.   That's when they used to play grab-griffin and sardines in the good old style.   I remember, when I was Nell Gwynne, Sam Pepys bet me a silver warming-pan——"

" Quite so," said Daphne.   " And now supposing we returned to the balusters.   For some reason or other, the idea of a temple to drainage doesn't appeal to me."

" Then do as I said at first and range them all in a line by the side of the road."

" But," cried Jill, " they wouldn't mean anything there.   If they carried lamps or something, that would be different : but just in a row they'd look silly."

" What would they mean if you shoved three round the ledge ? "

" There," said I, " they'd suggest a belvedere.   I don't suppose you'd get it ; but that would be the impression on those who had eyes to see."

" How rude," said Berry.   " Besides, what slobbering tripe ! Why the whole damned place is a b-blasted b-belvedere."

" What if it is ? " shrieked Daphne.   " It doesn't look like one.   Don't you want our home to look nice ?   Considering it can be seen for about five miles . . .   We've got to do landscape-gardening."

" She's perfectly right," said Jonah.   " We can have a bed of violets, because they give us pleasure : but the lay-out here has got to be good to look at. I hold that to be our duty. We can't let such scenery down."

" Then plant trees," said Berry. " You'll get a damned sight further with two or three blubbering elms than with half a dozen swag-bellied pedestals, short of their funeral urns."

This slander provoked indignation, and we were all dealing with Berry who was, I need hardly say, invoking his blue-based baboons, when Thérèse appeared and stood waiting for the tumult to die.

" And I tell you this," said Berry. " They'd know what to do with those bird-stands. They'd tell you where to put them. Yes, Thérèse ? "

" Someone is asking for Monsieur. It is the Sarrats of Besse. He is the burly roadman—Monsieur will have seen him about."

As Berry got to his feet—

" What do they want ? " he said.

" I do not know, Monsieur. I have no idea at all. But they are a decent couple. They have no children and they keep very much to themselves. Madame will remember the girl— a very pretty creature, who always smiles."

" Of course," said my sister. " We had a long talk one day. She comes from Argèles."

" Madame is right. That is she. And she has such a pretty garden—the best in Besse."

I followed Berry on to the terrace.

Sarrat spoke haltingly.

" Monsieur will forgive us, but we were wondering if Monsieur would care to purchase another field."

Berry smiled.

" To be perfectly honest," he said, " I think we have bought enough land."

The man looked down, and his wife took up the running on his behalf.

" Monsieur knows best, of course. But we do not ask very much. It is not a very valuable meadow—we know that well. Still, it is pleasing to look at and will be no discredit to Monsieur's property. Besides, it lies next to the meadows which Monsieur purchased first. It is the one touching the road, with the old, stone trough which is fed by the grotto above."

The elegant meadow . . . which Jill and I so much desired.

" It is very pretty," I said. " The water keeps it so green. But what are you asking ? We honestly had not thought of buying another field."

" That is understood, Monsieur. The thing is this. We have already three meadows—very useful fields on the road above. My husband is always busy, mending the roads ; but I can deal with them and they suit us well. And in the summer he helps me, when he has finished his work. But this meadow is far from them, and I cannot manage it, too. And so we let it each year— let it for next to nothing, for half the price of its hay. And that is unprofitable. If Monsieur would care to have it, to round his property, we will sell it to Monsieur for fifty pounds."

It's market value was thirty. But this was the fairest dealing which we had met. Though I could not help liking the Sarrats, I remembered de Moulin's words. Had we sought to buy that meadow ten months before, I was sure that they would have asked us two hundred pounds.

I looked at Berry and nodded.

" All right," he said. " If we can have immediate possession. You see, we're arranging to have the property fenced."

" Monsieur can enter to-morrow. We had sold the hay to Lafitte, but now he cannot cut it, and so it is back on our hands."

" Very well," said Berry. " My cousin will bring some stamped paper, and we'll make the Agreement out."

I fetched a pen and stamped paper and wrote out the vital words. I was getting quite good at such things. Then we all four signed the sheet and Berry called for wine.

" This year's hay," he said, " should belong to you. D'you think you can manage to take it ? "

" Monsieur is very gracious. We shall be very glad."

We parted on the crest of goodwill.

Then Berry and I returned to the sitting-room.

" What did they want ? " said Daphne.

" I think they'd heard us talking," said Berry. ' They came to, er, offer a solution of that very engaging problem which we were in fact discussing when they arrived."

" What on earth d'you mean ? "

Berry looked at me.

"Am I right?" he demanded.

"Brilliantly right," said I. "Green behind them, green beside them, and the eye running——"

Jill had hold of my arm.

"Boy, I can't bear it. Please tell me what you mean."

"Sweetheart," said I. "They've just sold us the meadow we love."

"No!"

"They have, indeed. Grotto and trough and all. And because, with all his faults, that mountebank sitting there has eyes to see, he saw in a flash that the Waterloo balusters should run from the ledge to the grotto, in an elegant curve around the base of the bluff."

Jill ran to Berry and kissed him. Then she came back and laid her cheek against mine.

"Come up and look at it, Boy. There's still enough light."

*　　*　　*　　*　　*

Jonah and I were strolling in what had been Pernot's field. It was the eighth day of June—the anniversary of Old Rowley's death.

"Ancient history," said Jonah. "The warrant will stay on the file till the writing fades."

"Looks like it," said I. "And Shapely is staying put. No more visits to Tass. At least, you've had no wire."

"I know," said Jonah. "I don't quite understand that. Falcon would surely have written, if the Home Office had decided to throw in its hand. And so we must assume that Shapely is still being watched. Which means that he hasn't seen Tass for exactly six months."

"I can't construe that," said I. "Tass is dangerous. Dangerous to Shapely—damn it, he said as much. Well, if I were in Shapely's shoes, I shouldn't try to forget him."

"Nor I," said Jonah. "D'you think he got him out of the country, when he came over last time?"

"You always say the French are very hot on their ports."

"So they are," said Jonah. "If I was wanted in France, I'd never try to get out."

"Oh, I give up," said I. "What's the good? If Tass was arrested to-morrow, he'd never swing. The jury wouldn't like it. The murder's cold."

Three days later we had a letter from Falcon.

SECRET

June 9th.

DEAR CAPTAIN MANSEL,

Sir Steuart Rowley

The Home Office has thrown in its hand, and all measures we were taking have come to an end. If Tass should return, he will, of course, be arrested—for what it is worth.

Yours very sincerely,

RICHARD FALCON.

CHAPTER XIV

IN WHICH JILL AND I FIND LAVARINI AT HOME, AND CARSON FETCHES SOME LIME

IT took us exactly a fortnight to set the balusters up. We did the work ourselves, with Carson to help. I suppose it seems a long time, but it must be remembered that each of the six was given a base of concrete on which to stand, and that more than four days went by before we could perfect the curve which they were to take.

The balusters must have weighed three hundredweight each, and to carry such a weight up a mountain entails the kind of effort one seeks to forget. We set them up in a curve, blocking them into position with stones and pieces of wood: and when the last one was up, we called down to Daphne and Jill who were sitting by the side of the road.

"What does that look like?" roared Berry, wiping the sweat from his throat.

We could not hear their reply, and Berry slid down towards them, to hear what they said.

"Nothing on earth," shrieked Daphne.

"Give me strength," said Berry. "What d'you mean—
'Nothing on earth'?"

"What I say. Come down and look for yourself."

We all went down and looked up.

My sister had not exaggerated. Our work appeared to be that
of some drunken giant. And that was how we began. As soon
as we got three right, the fourth threw the rest of them out.
And when we had got those right, the fourth was wrong. Then
we began again. And we were not moving ninepins about a floor.
We were shifting pillars of granite that took three men to hold
them upon the mountainside. And all the time two charming,
but merciless critics sat in the road below.

"You see what I mean. If you bring the second one forward
and lift the third one up . . . And it might go back a trifle.
The fourth one, I think is all right. But when you've moved
the third one, I'll let you know."

And nearly an hour later—

"Yes, that's much better. But the fourth will have to come
down. I think, perhaps, if you lowered the first a little . . ."

"The first?" screamed Berry. "You're raving. Move the
first, and you're sunk. Besides, it's the heaviest."

"Now don't be silly," purred Daphne. "You know as well
as I do we want to get them right."

"I don't," said Berry mutinously. "I don't care what the
swine look like. And I wish to God we'd been beaten at
Waterloo. Then there wouldn't have been any blasted bridge."

And nearly an hour later—

"That's terribly good. The third's still a shade too high, and
the second should come back a little. I think the fourth's all
right, but if you'll put up the fifth, we shall see in a flash. Of
course, if we moved them all a shade to the left . . . But let's
get the fifth one up."

"You hear that?" said Berry. "'Let's.'" He laughed
wildly. "Of course we're all insane. Shoving a lot of cromlechs
about a lop-sided field. And you two Pharaohs loll there and
talk about 'Let's.' You come up and shift them a shade to the
left. You come up and mix it with half a ton of granite on a
gradient of one in one."

Daphne and Jill accepted the invitation—not to move the

pillars, but to climb up to where they stood. They expressed concern, when they got there, at what they called the way we were cutting the field about.

" Can't you be more careful ? " said Daphne. " I mean, I know they're heavy, but look at that gash."

Berry gave an unearthly shriek and lay down on his back.

" I won't," he mouthed. " I refuse. It was very different when I was the Gadarene Swine. I didn't care then. I had no object in life. I admit that trough's suggestive, and this is a very steep place. Oh, and that reminds me—we mustn't forget that trough. We'll do it on the way back. If we push it back six feet and then drop it two, they won't be able to see it from Nareth. But we'll have to take off our trousers. We mustn't scratch that road."

Still, as I say, the Herculean labour was done at last, and, when it had been concluded, the balusters looked very well. I think it likely that, given the requisite labour, a landscape-gardener would have done it in half the time : but the site must have troubled him, for he could not describe a circle, because of the bluff behind.

*   *   *   *   *

Whilst we were thus engaged, the plasterers were busy within the house. The carpenters worked with them, sometimes preceding them and sometimes following on. All the staff-work seemed to be very good. Lavarini had finished his tiling. The floors were done.

The flags were being laid on the terrace and experts had arrived to put the awnings in place. The steel frames of the awnings had to be fixed to the house, and the master-mason himself cut the holes that had to be made. He was surprised, as was Joseph, to find the masonry already so very hard.

" I would not have believed it," said Joseph. " It is, of course, the climate. And if weather like this goes on—and Ulysse declares that it will—the plaster will dry very fast. That will advance the painting. Monsieur will sleep in his bedroom before the month of August is out."

" And the garage ceiling," said I. " You won't forget that ? "

" Last of all," said Joseph. " The timber is dry, of course.

But it did get wet, and since it does not press, we may as well leave it exposed until the end of this week. The crane will come down on Monday, and on that day we shall finish the parapet. The next day we begin the drive—the drive and the garage apron. And I think we should reinforce the dry stone wall which is running beside the road. Only for the length of the drive. It was built to hold back a meadow, but not a drive which petrol-waggons will use."

"There's one coming up next week. Your uncle is anxious to try the central-heating, and he can't do that without oil."

"That is so," said Joseph. "I have said it must come on Monday : otherwise, it will interfere with our work on the apron and drive. Has Monsieur seen Lavarini ? "

"No," said I. "What does he want me for ? "

"That is his secret, Monsieur. If Monsieur will excuse me, I go to find him at once."

Two minutes later, the tiler stood before me, twisting his cap in his hands.

"What is it, Lavarini ? I thought you'd done."

"There are odds and ends, Monsieur. And plasterers make a mess. I shall stay here for two or three days, to see that all is all right." He hesitated. "Mesdames and Messieurs have been very good to me, and I have made them a present. Nothing much : I have done it in my spare time. It is a fountain. Perhaps it could stand on the terrace that is to become a lawn."

"But, Lavarini, that's very kind of you."

"No, no. It is nothing. It is now at my cottage, two or three miles from Pau. But I would like Monsieur to see it, before it comes up. And if it is not to his liking, then I shall make another."

"I never heard of such a thing. Of course we shall like it— and be very proud to have it. All the same we shall be very happy to visit your home. When will that be convenient ? "

"Whenever Monsieur can honour me, I shall be there."

"What about Sunday evening ? Say half past six."

"With very great pleasure, Monsieur. I live in *La Vallée Heureuse*."

"I know that well."

"My cottage stands by itself, on the left-hand side of the road

—perhaps two hundred paces beyond the private drive of the château that stands to the right."

" We shall find it, Lavarini, and thank you so very much."

Jill and I found it on Sunday at a quarter past six.

It was a perfect evening.

The valley lay in the foot-hills, and the sun was slanting over the swell of the woods, to fill the meadows with splendour and print long, clear-cut shadows of poplars upon the green. All was most still, and the only sounds we heard were a great way off—the low of a cow, I remember, and the regular stroke of an axe.

We were before our time, and the cottage was locked : and so we left the car and leaned on a meadow's gate, regarding such an order of haycocks as Nursery Rhymes were made of—in other and better days. At its farther end, the meadow ran up to the trees which were thick with leaves ; and as we were looking, a man trotted out of the wood, with a child upon either side. The children, a boy and a girl, were running and laughing beside him, and each had hold of one hand, and their mother came running behind them, as though she were driving the team. Dancing in and out of the haycocks, they made the prettiest picture of simple happiness, and, though they were poor, as we call it, they were richer than many I know.

Jill and I slid out of sight, before they knew we were there, and when the four reached the gate, we were sitting on the step of the car.

It was, of course, Lavarini. . . .

" Miladi and Monsieur have been waiting ! Oh, I am more than sorry. We thought to amuse the children by taking them into the woods."

" We're early, Lavarini. It isn't yet half past six."

" All the same, I should have been here."

He presented his wife, a glowing girl of not more than twenty-six, with very English features and gentle eyes. The children, aged five and six, had very charming manners : they came and shook hands gravely, and then returned to stand by their mother's side. Then we all passed through the cottage and into the little garden that lay behind.

The fountain was far more handsome than we had any right

to expect. Its basin appeared to be held by the weathered
boughs of an oak and might, indeed, have been fashioned of oak
itself. In fact, the whole thing had been made of ferro-concrete,
most beautifully made and modelled from Nature herself.
Within, the basin was tiled—a miniature crazy pavement of
blue and gold. ' Bits and pieces of Monsieur's tiles, for which I
could find no use.' (The gold was not ours—we had not risen so
high.) No pipes were visible—they were concealed in the
boughs : the inlet rose through one and the overflow sank
through another, without any fuss. The whole thing stood four
feet high and the basin was three feet across.

Jill and I were quite overcome. Had such a thing been
ordered in Paris, it would have cost forty pounds—and been
inferior. But this was given to us out of sheer goodwill.

Lavarini's humility shook us.

" If Miladi and Monsieur like it, Monsieur Joseph has said that
a lorry shall carry it up. But if they think it unworthy——"

" But, Lavarini," cried Jill, " it's superb. It is the most
lovely present I ever saw. We shall be most awfully proud
to set it in the midst of our lawn. And the birds will come and
drink there. They'll know no fear, for it looks so natural."
She turned to his wife. " Your husband is a true artist—as well
as a very nice man. And now take me back to the children. I
want to make their acquaintance. I had two babies once."

Lavarini and I discussed the virtues of the fountain over a
cigarette. After ten minutes we made our way through the
cottage and back to the Rolls. Madame Lavarini was sitting
behind. Jill sat in front with a child upon either side. The
boy, of course, was ' driving.' Every now and again he sounded
the horn. . . .

As we said goodbye—

" We are simple folk, Miladi. This has been a great day for
us all."

" It's been a great day for me. And you're all coming up next
week to see the beautiful work which your husband has done.
And François and Helène are going to visit my grotto."

To our great distress, Madame Lavarini began to cry.

Jill was out of the car in a flash, and the two went into the
cottage and out of sight.

Lavarini was by my side.

"Monsieur must forgive her," he said. "She is overwrought. Miladi's kindness has been too much for her. We are not accustomed to this. To be perfectly frank, I am very near tears myself."

Ten minutes later, we said goodbye again, and the Rolls stole down the valley, much as a punt steals down the reach of a river after the sun has set.

We were nearing home, when I remembered something.

"The garage ceiling," I said. "It never was done. We all forgot it. Damn it, I knew we should. It doesn't matter, of course. They can send a plasterer up."

* * * * *

I was at the site the next morning at half past nine.

"Ah," said Joseph. "Monsieur need not say it. I remembered it yesterday evening. And now I am paying for my forgetfulness."

I opened my eyes.

"Paying? But what do you mean? There's no hurry about the garage ; and the ceiling can be done in a day."

"Monsieur is right," said Joseph. "But I have always found that errors breed errors. Make a mistake yourself, and others will catch the infection. That is why I try so hard not to make a mistake."

"So far as I know, it's the first thing that you have forgotten ; and, as I say, it is of no consequence."

"Of little," said Joseph. "That I freely admit. But now see what has happened. I forget the garage ceiling and let the plasterers go—two on Friday evening and the rest on Saturday. On Sunday I remember. So early this morning I leave a note at the office to send a plasterer up. He will be here any minute : he has come by the eight o'clock 'bus. I saw it across the valley, five minutes ago. 'Very well,' I say, 'we will have things ready for him.' So I tell Pepito to take the slats to the garage as well as other things including a bag of lime. I take these precautions, Monsieur at half past seven o'clock. At five and twenty to eight Pepito comes running to say that there is no lime. That I decline to believe and I hasten to the guard-room myself. The thing is true. Cement, yes. Forty or fifty bags. But not one bag of lime. I send Pepito post-haste to the telephone. But when he gets on to the office, the plasterer has left for the 'bus. ' Then send a lorry,' says Pepito, exactly as I had told him, ' to bring us three bags of lime. If he leaves in half an hour, he will be here before the 'bus has arrived.' Well, that is all right : the plasterer's ' bus-fare has been wasted, but that is all.'' He raised his eyes to heaven. " This is my bad day, Monsieur. You see, it was not all. The lorry arrived, sure enough, but twenty minutes ago. *And it brought three bags of cement.* No lime, at all. Cement. Of which we have already some fifty bags. I tell you, Monsieur, I could have struck the man. The clerk in the office is good : I have never known him make a mistake. And this son of a dog admits that ' he may have said lime.' But when I say, ' Go back. You will pay for the petrol, yourself ; but you will go back at once and fetch me the lime I require '—when I say that, he says he is sick of his stomach and cannot drive.'' He shrugged his shoulders. " I think it is true. He is lying behind the garage : and Pepito has gone to the chemist's to get him a dose. And of the other three lorries, one is being repaired and both the others are out. And the one that brought us this morning by now is nearing Bayonne.''

" Let Carson get it," said I. " Here's Captain Mansel coming. I'm sure he'll agree.''

Joseph's face lighted up.

" Oh, if Monsieur Carson will do it, I shall be deeply obliged. And while he is gone, the plasterer can put up his slats. Monsieur must not think that I make a fuss about nothing. This plasterer is in the midst of another job. At my request, Monsieur Henri has let me have him just for to-day. I cannot have him to-morrow, and he is a very good man.''

I explained the position to Jonah.

" But of course," he said. " Carson has gone to the post, but he'll be here in a quarter of an hour. He'll be delighted to go. Where does he report ? At the office ? ''

" It will be quicker," said Joseph, " if he goes to the depot direct. It will save him at least ten miles. He turns at Louvie and takes the Oloron road. After five miles that joins the road from Pau, and two miles farther on the factory is on his right.

Monsieur Carson will not pay for the lime. As soon as they see the lorry, they will give him as much as he asks. But three bags will be more than enough."

"Consider it done," said Jonah. "He'll be back long before noon."

"*Mon Dieu,*" said Joseph. "Was ever a man better served?"

And that was that. Twenty minutes later Carson was gone for the lime, and Jonah and I were at work.

As I have said, a grille had been set where the *ruisseau* entered its pipe—a very substantial grille, to arrest all foreign bodies on their way down. Throughout the winter it had done its work very well: next to nothing but water had entered the pipe. But we had observed that, at the time of the deluge—that is to say, when the spring at the back of the house had caused so much earth to fall—the grille itself had been very nearly choked with the stones and the wood and the refuse which the force of the water brought down. And so we had decided to build another grille some forty feet higher up. Its mesh would be very much coarser than that of the grille below: but it would trap the big stuff and, in the event of a spate, would certainly save its fellow from being choked. And so we had made five posts of ferro-concrete. These would be driven into the bed of the rill, and would then be linked and bridged by a cross-bar of ferro-concrete, running from bank to bank.

The day was hot, and I well remember how very pleasant the cool of the water was: and I felt sorry for Carson, who was to have worked with us, but, because of a fool's mistake, was driving a pounding lorry for forty miles.

Berry was in the house, supervising the fixing of mirrors upon the walls. Daphne and Jill were planting a bed of violets at the foot of the bluff. The crane was being dismantled—Joseph was seeing to that. And the scaffold which led to the terrace was coming down. And masons were filling the gap in the parapet.

We had set up our posts in the *ruisseau* and had begun to shutter the line which the cross-bar would take, when Carson made his appearance just before noon.

"Ah, Carson," said Jonah. "Did you get the merchandise?"

"Yes, sir. Three sacks. I've handed them over to Joseph."

"Good. Well, now you get back to lunch. We'll have this shuttering done before we go ; so if you're back before us you might start mixing some concrete."

"Very good, sir," said Carson. He hesitated. "A curious thing happened, sir. It's very slight and it's nothing to do with me ; but I think that I ought to tell you, for what it's worth."

Jonah threw down his hammer and wiped the sweat from his face.

"Tell me, Carson," he said. "And leave nothing out."

"Well, I found the factory, sir. It was just where Joseph had said, standing a little back from the Pau to Oloron road. I drove the lorry into the yard, and then I walked into the office, to ask for the lime. It was very dim in there, for the shutters were to, but after a moment I saw there was no one there. Just as I turned to go out, a little, fat fellow comes in, by the door I had used.

"'Ah,' he cries. 'So it is you. You have come for your change. It has been in my desk for months.' Then he peers at me very close. And then he bursts out laughing and lays his hand on my arm. 'Excuse me, my friend. I have mistaken you for somebody else. For another Englishman. He came here—oh, last summer some time, and purchased two bags of lime. At thirty francs apiece. And he had a hundred-franc note, and I had no change. And his forty francs is still waiting to be redeemed. I thought it was strange, his coming in a lorry belonging to the brothers Lafargue. He had a wonderful car— a kind of caravan . . .'"

I looked from Carson to Jonah and put a hand to my head.

"Lime," I cried. "Lime ! Shapely was purchasing lime. And he fainted when I talked about Crippen ! By God, Jonah, I've got it. Why did he faint like that ? *Because he had slaked his lime. Because he had made the mistake which Crippen had made.*"

My cousin had me by the arm.

"Boy," he said, "you've got something. You've picked up the scent. And now let's get this straight."

I tried to keep my voice steady.

"Look at it this way," I said. "Shapely collected Tass's suitcase at Tass's request. That was 'last summer some time.'"

And then he went to meet Tass.   And on his way—for the factory *was* on his way—he purchased the lime.   What did he want lime for ?   *Because he knew that Tass was going to be killed.*   Tass was dangerous—Shapely admitted so much that day in the train.   So Shapely met him—and killed him . . . not very far from Orthez . . . on September the first last year.   No wonder he paled, when Falcon asked him how he had spent his time : for he'd spent it murdering Tass and shoving him under the sod. *And why did he have to have lime ?   Because Tass was short of an eye* . . . and so the body could be identified.   But lime destroys . . . quick lime . . . And that's why they can't find Tass. Because he's dead and buried—and has been dead and buried ever since September last year."

"Murder and burial ? " said Jonah.   " All in the light of day ? "

" In one of those woods," said I.   " He took a risk, of course. But it was even money that anyone would come by.   And apparently nobody did."

"That's right," said Jonah.   "And when he came back in December——"

" — he came back to put things right.   I'd put him wise, in the train.   I'd shown him the fatal error which he had made. He'd slaked his lime—like Crippen.   I remember using these words—' Quick lime destroys, but slack lime preserves.'   And so he came back in December, to put things right."

" When we were out of the way.   But how could he put things right ? "

" I don't know.   I can't answer that question.   But I'll lay that's why he came.   It does fit in, Jonah.   This purchase of the lime . . .   Seven hours to himself by Orthez, in which to do the job. . . .   He faints when I tell him of Crippen's fatal mistake. . . .   And then he comes back in December, when he knows that we're out of the way."

" To put things right," said Jonah.   " Now how would he put things right ? "

*   *   *   *   *

Carson finished the grille.

For, all that afternoon, Jonah and I were composing a careful letter—a letter to Scotland Yard.

It was not addressed to Falcon, but to someone greater than he.

Some of it will bear reproduction.

Well, there are the facts. Now for the speculation. But let me insist that this is not your affair. If a man is murdered in France, that has nothing to do with you. And you have importuned France to look for Tass alive : you can hardly ask them now to look for Tass dead. And we are not going to look. There are acres and acres of woods in the region concerned. Still, it is right that you should know that my cousin has picked up the scent. I mean, you never know. Any day, for instance, the body may be discovered. In which case, as soon as we hear, we shall get in touch with the police, and Falcon ought to come out as quickly as ever he can. We ourselves may stumble on something else. I hardly think that's likely, but we do seem doomed to be mixed up in this affair. So, will you stand by—just in case ?

As regards the date. Carson, who is no fool, tried to pin the manager down. But he stuck to ' last summer some time,' with which we must be content. Well, September the first was ' last summer ' . . .

I had not meant to tell you of my cousin's conversation with Shapely, when they were in the train. You see, it was off the record. But now I feel bound to tell you as much as I have . . .

And now, to sum up.

First, what did Shapely want lime for ? What does any man want lime for, when he is en route for a port, at which to embark his car ? And quite a lot of lime—two hundredweight.

Secondly, why did he faint, when my cousin related the details of Crippen's crime ? I would not have said he was squeamish : and, even if he is squeamish, people don't actually faint, when presented with details like that. It may make them feel sick. It may put them off their food. But I do not believe that they faint. But a shock will make a man faint. And if my cousin is right and Shapely had made the very same ' error of knowledge ' which Crippen made, the sudden realization of the truth that he had in fact preserved what he meant to destroy would have been a considerable shock to any murderer.

Thirdly, where is Tass ?

Fourthly, why did Shapely's last visit to France coincide with our visit to England ? There may be nothing in this, but the fact remains.

Fifthly, six months have gone by, but Shapely has not visited France. Why ?

My cousin has always maintained that an English chauffeur like Tass, who, as Shapely himself volunteered, ' disliked foreign parts,' would soon become impatient of the business of lying low in the French countryside. Who so aware of this as Shapely, whose servant Tass was ? And any show of impatience would be very dangerous—not only to Tass, but to Shapely, as accessory after the fact. So Shapely had a first-class motive for putting Tass out of the way.

Well, there we are.

I have told you certain facts, as well as the construction, which my cousin has put upon them. With that construction I agree. I tell you these things that you may be forearmed. I can hardly believe it, but we might have another break. We shall not go after it ; but we didn't go after this. If we should run into anything concrete, we shall have to inform the French police. But, in such an unlikely case, I am sure you would see the wisdom of sending Falcon out—on a private visit to us. And then he would be on the spot, to hold a watching brief.

I seem to be repeating myself, so I'd better stop . . .

Five days later, my cousin had a reply.

July 1st.

DEAR JONAH,

We are profoundly interested by all you say. More than interested—moved. I firmly believe that you and your cousin are right. But, as you say, we can do nothing. Oh, of course you are right. The thing sticks out. If only it had happened in England ! With you, I can hardly believe that you'll get any further than this. But once one has picked up the scent, one never knows. Any way, you have only to wire, and Falcon shall leave at once. I know I can trust you there. In such a case, much will depend upon your liaison between the French police and him. His position will be irregular, and you will have to regularize it somehow. If you don't think you can do that, then you must not wire.

I need hardly add that, if Falcon had had his way, he would be with you now. But this, of course, I cannot permit. We must not get wrong with the French, and, as you have pointed out, this is—and must be—their show.

Yours ever,

———.

* * * * *

It is not too much to say that, but for the house, Jonah and I would have been obsessed by the crime. It was not our affair, but, as Jonah had said, we seemed fated to be involved. And now the case had been re-opened—after a space of six months. This, out of the blue, as they say : by the merest accident. We should not, I think, have been human, if we had not dwelled upon the matter day after day.

" It's no good," said Jonah, one evening. " We're up against a brick wall."

" Say a locked door," said I.

" Locked door, if you like," said Jonah. " But where's the key ? "

" I have a feeling," I said, " that the key is lying concealed in the action which Shapely took ' to put things right.' He came out in December to do that, and we must presume that he did. But—what—did—he—actually—do ? Dig a deeper grave ? Get more lime—which he did *not* slake ? I don't think those are the answers. The woods were bare in December, and he might well have been seen. But I do feel this—that he may have done something desperate. And desperate acts are the acts that let a man down."

CHAPTER XV

IN WHICH DAPHNE SURVEYS HER HOME, AND WE ARE MADE A PRESENT OF A VULLIAMY CLOCK

IT was Berry who had insisted that the drive should be made, as roads are made, with metalling, large and small, and cold tar and chips above.

We thought this extravagance and said so. But Berry was adamant.

" If we do it like that," he said, " we shall never have to touch it for fifty years. No wear, no weeds, no pools of water ; and so, no maintenance. And it will always look nice."

That Joseph supported him goes without any saying. Only the very best was good enough for ' the property.'

And so it was done. And then the garage apron was laid, at the end of the drive. When the whole was finished, it certainly looked very well.

The balustrades had gone up, within and without the house, and the carpenters had the interior to themselves. To help the plaster to dry, all the windows stood open the whole day long, so that the brilliant weather could play its part.

On Monday, July the fifth, Lavarini's fountain arrived. God knows what it weighed, but it took seven men to carry it up to the terrace which was to become a lawn. There it was bedded on concrete, lest it should sink : and Carol and Lavarini arranged the run of the pipes. Flags were laid about it, because of the splash—a labour which Lavarini insisted on doing himself. Its play was controlled by a tap by the side of the porch.

On Tuesday, after breakfast, Jill and Jonah and I were walking up to the site, when we saw a little crowd in the midst of the way. It was usual enough for strangers to stop as they passed and look up at the house : but the peasants were used to it now and, if they stopped at all, it was only to shout a greeting to someone working above. But this little crowd was composed of peasants alone.

" What is it ? " said Jill. " D'you think something's happened ? I mean that something's gone wrong ? "

"I don't think so," I said. "I can't think what it can be. Any way, we shall know in a minute."

So we did. And we stood and looked with the others—before we went up.

Lavarini's fountain was playing.

The pressure was high, and a lovely plume of water was rising out of the basin and casting its lovely burden into the sunlit air. The dazzling shimmer of the flourish against the green was really beautiful, and we all cried out with pleasure the moment it met our eye.

"It is a surprise, then, to Monsieur?"

"Yes, indeed," said I. "We had not seen it at work. It is Monsieur Lavarini, the tiler, who has made us a present of this."

"He is very valiant. And he has given Monsieur a present which we shall all share. For myself, I could stand here all day."

I need hardly say that Jill was in ecstasy.

I tore myself away and made for the library. This was now being panelled, and called for meticulous work. . . .

That afternoon, I remember, the telephone was installed.

Without the house, not much remained to be done. These walls had to be coped, and those reinforced. Iron gates had to be hung at the mouth of the drive. The property had to be fenced—more against cattle and goats than anything else. Jonah, Carson and I were at work on the scarecrow field. At present this was an eye-sore. Now that we were its owners, we were determined that it should not let 'the property' down. Daphne and Jill spent all their time on the garden. Berry stayed in the house, supervising the fitting of cupboards and the hanging of doors.

The time was now approaching when the call for our supervision would come to an end. At the end of the week, the carpenters would have finished, and two days later, the painters would enter the house. The walls would not be touched till the week after that, but there was a great deal of woodwork which had to be done. The electrical work and the plumbing had been finished the week before. Joseph was still in charge and held the keys of the house, which he opened himself every morning and closed himself at night. He was a jealous warden. Every shutter was fastened by his own hand.

Berry was consulting his diary.

"We should be able to enter on August the tenth. The furniture at Asen is all ready : they want twenty-four hours' notice, to send it up. The stuff that's coming from England will leave the last week of July. One large van will accept the whole of it—luggage and all. It ought to be here on time ; but we can't go in till it comes, for it's got all the plate and linen, as well as the china and glass."

"Fuel ? " said Daphne.

"The oil-tank is full, and fifty loads of wood will be delivered next week."

"Fifty ? " cried everyone.

"Foresight," said Berry. "Wood is going up. Fifty loads will last us two years—and more than that. I did the deal through Guillaume, the bloke at the marble-mills ; and once it's stacked in the guard-room, you'll hardly know that it's there. You'll live to thank me all right. All oak, too—a metre in length. We cut it in half as we need it—one of us does. I'm not too good with a saw."

"I suppose we're wise to have an electric range. Eugène is not enthusiastic."

"If Eugène had had his way, we should have the kind of range that they used at Windsor Castle when Henry the Eighth was King. It'd burn a ton a week, and you'd want a fireman's kit to enter the kitchen at all. As for the dirt . . . But he'll be converted all right. After one week of electricity, there'd be a riot, if you suggested coal. Any way, the chimney is there : and if the cooker's a failure, we've only to hand it back and get in a stove."

"About August the tenth, then ? "

"Yes. And since we can do no more, I suggest that we go to Freilles for three or four days. Change is good, and a bathe in the Bay of Biscay would tone me up."

"I must be here," said Daphne, "before they begin the walls. The paint will have to be mixed, and then we're going to try samples, to see how they look."

"The walls will not be started until the week after next. They can't go wrong with the woodwork. Let's go to Freilles on Monday for three or four days."

After a moment's hesitation—

" Right oh," said everyone.

We had spent a week at Biarritz in April, and, whilst we were there, we had taken a look at Freilles. This was a little resort, some twenty miles north of Bayonne. It was sunk in the pine-woods, on the edge of the roaring surf, and it was being very well done. I say ' was being,' because it had not been developed. Freilles was in existence, but it was hardly known.

That evening I telephoned to a tiny hotel . . .

* * * * *

My sister laid a hand on my arm.

" Freilles on Monday," she said. " D'you know—before we go, I'd love to see over my home. Quite quietly, you know. When nobody else is there. Could we get up early on Monday, just you and I ? "

" Very early," said I. " The painters will be here by seven."

" What about six ? "

I sighed.

" I wouldn't do it," I said, " for anyone else."

I thought it best to tell Joseph.

" That is right and proper," he said, " that Madame should consider her home, with nothing to distract her—no workmen, no noise, no movement. . . . The house to herself. All shall be ready, Monsieur, on Monday at six o'clock."

" But you'll be at Pau," said I. " You must leave me the keys."

" No, Monsieur : I shall be here. I shall not be seen, of course ; but I shall be here. From now on, I sleep in the guard-room. It is my will. Till Mesdames and Messieurs enter, I shall not leave the house."

" You're very good. Joseph," I said.

" It is my pleasure, Monsieur."

" And I am going to Freilles, to lie on the *plage*."

" That is as it should be, Monsieur. But I shall be happier here. To be honest, I slept here last night : and I stood on the terrace this morning and watched the dawn get up. It was a famous experience. Believe me, I shall be sad when my tenancy comes to an end."

" We'll be back on Friday, Joseph. I'll ring you up each day at a quarter past two."

Joseph inclined his head.

" And I shall be ready and waiting to listen to Monsieur's voice."

* * * * *

Daphne looked up at the house.

" Why everything's open," she said. " And the awnings are down."

" Yes," I said ; " that's Joseph. But nobody will be there."

" What a dear he is," said Daphne. " He has the most charming nature. How can we ever repay him for all he's done ? "

" I don't think we can. We can only keep up with him and make him welcome here whenever he comes."

As we came to the entrance-drive—

" Don't think me foolish, Boy ; but I've a whim to enter the house by the terrace."

" Splendid," said I. " We'll go by the little footpath we've made through the scarecrow field. That'll bring us up to the garden ; and then we can walk along and take the terrace steps."

We passed through the dewy meadows, glanced at the *ruisseau* thundering through its grille and into its pipe, and, taking the upper terrace, approached the house from the west.

As I have said, the stone terrace proper was seven feet longer than the house : so we could gain it, without passing through the house : this, on the west side only, but that was the way we had come.

We passed up the three broad steps and moved to the parapet. . . .

And there lay a bouquet of flowers.

The dew was still upon them. They must have been growing in their garden a short half-hour before.

The scrap of ribbon that bound them was threading a battered card.

Je présente à Madame, avec mon plus profond respect, l'assurance de tout mon dévouement.

JOSEPH.

My sister read the card. Then she picked up the bouquet and put it up to her face. . . .

With one accord we entered the library.

Facing us was the door, with book-shelves on either hand. These rose to the ceiling : below them ran a series of cupboards, each of which could be locked. To our right stood a wide brick fireplace : on our left, two large French windows, now open wide, were commanding the sweep of the valley and the road running up towards Besse. Behind us, three ' door-windows,' as they are called in France, gave to the sunlit terrace we had but that moment left. The panelling looked very nice. It was not the ' linen-fold,' which we had known all our lives : it had not that lovely colour which only age can bring ; but it looked very fresh and pleasant, and the moulding which Jill had designed was a great success.

I opened the plain oak door and we entered the gallery.

The morning sun was lighting it half way down, just reaching the foot of the semi-circular stair, which rose to our left. The doors of the rooms were shut, and their plain sheets of oak looked well. It was all very simple, but it had dignity.

Immediately on our left, the flash of blue and white tiles declared the lavatory. In the telephone booth, by its side, a broad, oak shelf accepted the telephone : by this lay a pad and pencil, and, just to the right, within reach, was the switch for electric light. The shelf was low, to stand to ; but a stool had been made at Asen, so that whoever was speaking could take his seat. Lesser shelves had been hung above the first, for hats and gardening gloves. All the dimensions had been worked out by Berry, and all three walls were sound-proof—that I knew.

I opened the service door, the next on the left.

At once we saw the beauty of Lavarini's work. The floors were tiled and the walls were tiled head-high. It was fresh and gay and effective. No dirt could lie here. On the right was a spreading switch-board : every fuse upon it was well within reach. On the left was a long row of hooks, on which coats could be hung. Above the hooks hung the only bell in the house. This consisted of two polished, tubular, gongs which, when struck, rendered different notes. One was reserved for the front door and the other for the first floor : if anyone rang from the ground floor, both gongs would sound. (Berry had written to America for this very attractive toy. For some strange reason, it had been sent post free and had cost considerably less than any ordinary bells which we could have purchased in France.)

Daphne tapped with her toe on the floor of the servant's hall.

" D'you think they'll be cold ? " she said. " We'll have to give them a rug."

" There's a plug," said I, " for a radiator. And, of course, they've the ordinary heating."

" Tiles make the feet cold," said Daphne. " Besides, they'll love a rug. And the shelf ? "

" For the wireless," said I. " Your husband again. A set is waiting in Pau. Observe the plugs, if you please. One for the power, and one, combined, for the earth and the aerial. We've the same in the library."

The scullery looked very smart. An electric ' washer ' took up some of its room.

" I hope it works," said Daphne. " Thérèse is mad to try it. If it does, she says, we needn't send anything out."

As did the other two rooms, the kitchen looked to the west—over Pernot's field and the depths of the valley below. Another, ground-glass window gave to the north. The electric range was in place. All along the length of one wall ran a broad, tiled slab. And there were two fine cupboards from ceiling to floor.

Beyond the kitchen, the lavatory looked very fresh.

Opposite was the larder. Two large, tiled shelves were offering ample space. An electric refrigerator was waiting. A cage, or bin, for bottles stood at the end. And one side was nothing but cupboards, again from ceiling to floor. The open windows faced north and were carefully screened.

" If Eugène complains," said Daphne, " then he can go."

We turned and came back to the pantry, facing east. As in the larder, one wall was nothing but cupboards. The sink had been hung at a height which Thérèse had determined, ' for most,' she said, ' are either too high or too low.' The draining-board —eight feet long—was made of some special wood. Berry, Thérèse and the brothers had seen to that.

We passed to the furnace-room.

" Make it work, Boy," said my sister. " Just for fun."

To be sure that the water was running, I turned on a tap. Then I pressed the master switch . . .

There was a moment's hum, and then, with a roar, the furnace sprang to life. I made my sister come down and I opened the furnace door. A gigantic tongue of flame was licking the special bricks.

"It's very wonderful," said Daphne. "When I think of all that stoking, and Holly who got up at five to rake the clinkers out." She pointed to the furnace switch-board. "And now that clock up there will do the whole thing."

I shrugged my shoulders.

"They call it progress," I said. "I expect they're right."

We climbed the old-elm staircase and turned to the left.

The servants' rooms were all exactly the same, except that Thérèse had a pier-glass. Berry had seen to that.

Each had a built-in wardrobe, six feet long. One half was for hanging clothes, and the other was full of shelves. All could be locked and all had different keys. Each room was central-heated, and each had a pleasant basin, with hot and cold running-water, and a looking-glass hung above. The glass and the basin were surrounded by blue and white tiles. Three rooms looked to the east, and two to the west.

We passed to the servants' bathroom. This had been very well done, in blue and white. The bath was encased. But, instead of a basin, there hung a capacious sink. Hand-washing could be done there. The lavatory stood by itself.

We turned at the end of the passage and made our way back. On our right, the *lingerie* made an attractive room. One side of it was all cupboards. The shelves were open or slatted, to let pass the heat which would rise from the pipes beneath. This, again, was Berry's idea. It was he who had carried it out. An electric 'ironer' was awaiting experiments.

The *lingerie* looked to the west.

We let the attic go, and passed across the landing, through the service door and into the gallery. As was its fellow below, this was full of sunlight and sweet, fresh air.

Immediately on our left, the bathroom door was open, and the bathroom itself was alight with the morning sun. This, of course, was Daphne's

All powder-blue and white, it filled the eye. The floor and the walls were blue, and the bath and the basin were white. It was an ' apron ' bath and it looked as though it had been moulded out of some gleaming stone. The sponge- and soap-niche beside it were almost too good to be true. On either side of the basin, a looking-glass hung. Over each had been placed a shaded electric light. The window was naturally recessed. Beneath the window was a shelf, all tiled in blue. And beneath the shelf were cupboards. . . .

It was the finest bathroom I ever saw. And Berry had done it all. And when I say that, I mean it. No one had dared to interfere.

A second door from the bathroom led into his bedroom and Daphne's.

On the left were two windows, admitting the morning sun. Between them was a built-in wardrobe of vast capacity. In front, were two more windows commanding the south. Between these hung a pier-glass. On the right was a pleasant fireplace, fashioned of brick. A second door led into the gallery.

Next to their room, facing south, were two rooms exactly the same. These were mine and Jonah's. Each had a built-in wardrobe, a fireplace of brick, and a pier-glass between the two windows, which Berry had placed.

Then came Jill's room. This was a lovely chamber, with its private bathroom beyond. The bathroom again was all blue, but the bedroom was to be white. The bathroom faced west, and a door gave out of that to the end of the gallery.

There we turned, to face east.

On our left two capacious cupboards delighted my sister's heart. Then came another bathroom, Jonah's and mine—again hung and floored with blue tiles. And then, all at once, we came to the head of the stairs.

Down these my sister passed. . . .

Turning to the left, we came to the massive front-door. This was open wide, and standing there we could hear the fountain playing some twenty-five paces away.

Immediately on our right was the morning-room. Here two large French windows gave to the east, commanding a glorious view of the Pic de Fer. Two more ' door-windows ' gave to the terrace without. Another fireplace in brick had been built in the western wall.

Between this and the library lay two smaller rooms—first a withdrawing-room—for Jill and Daphne alone, and then the dining-room. Both opened on to the terrace, but nowhere else.

The whole of the front of the house was lit by indirect lighting. Because of the daylight, we could not prove it now, but the plaster bowls, within which the reflectors lay hid, were very good-looking, yet inconspicuous. (I call them ' bowls,' for lack of a better term. They resembled bowls cut in half and then applied to the wall.) They were of course, to be painted with the same colour as their walls. Berry had sited every one with the greatest care—as well as every plug, for the day would come when we should have reading-lamps.

It was all very simple and direct. There were no frills. We had our quarters in the cross, and the servants had theirs in the stem—of the capital T. The whole house was full of light. It was certainly labour-saving—no doubt about that. And it was very convenient, and had been very well built.

We walked back up the gallery and out of the great front-doorway into the porch beyond. The front-door was facing north, but the porch faced east. We left the porch and turned right, to descend the ninety-three steps.

" I'm very lucky," said Daphne. " Little more than a year ago, I was accepting the fact that never in all my life should I have a home again. And here I have a new home—a very beautiful home, much nicer than I deserve. Boy, you know, we've a lot to be thankful for."

Be sure I agreed with her. White Ladies belonged to England. But here was ' a foreign field ' that belonged to England, too.

*   *   *   *   *

From Lally to Freilles is roughly one hundred miles.

You can go by Pau and take the *route nationale*. Or you can strike across country and go by Oloron. If we went by Oloron, we should be traversing the region which Shapely had seen fit to visit on September the first.

The others took the Rolls and travelled by Pau. But Jonah and I took the Andret and went by Oloron.

The country was more than handsome. The foot-hills were
in all their glory. The river, the Gave d'Oloron, was very plainly
rejoicing to run his course. Hill and dale, meadow and wood-
land made up a panorama fit for the gods. We met a little traffic,
but not very much. Often enough, we seemed to have the world
to ourselves. We passed any number of by-roads and scores of
tracks, many of which led into the heart of the woods. If I was
right, and Tass lay buried here, his body might as well have been
sunk in the ocean itself. That is to say, so far as any search was
concerned. Of course, someone might stumble upon it . . .
might . . .

To prove our case to the hilt, we chose a track at random and
drove slowly into the wood which instantly swallowed it up.
After two hundred paces, the track seemed to come to an end.
We left the car and looked round. Except for the flutter of birds,
there was no sign of life. There was not even a footpath ; but
some aged stumps of trees showed that the track had been used
for hauling wood. Without losing sight of the car, a man could
have dug at least twenty several graves, not one of which, had
he been careful, would ever be found.

I began to wonder why Shapely had taken the trouble to buy
any lime . . .

After a little, we backed the car down to the road and went on
our way.

Freilles was certainly attractive. The *plage* was one of the
finest I ever saw. It could have held at least two thousand
bathers. That first afternoon I counted seventy-one. Every
day we lunched and dined in the open air. This, at our little
hotel : but we spent the whole day on the *plage*, which was ten
minutes' walk. The sun was very hot and the sea was delight-
fully warm. There was no wind. Had Daphne not brought
some oil with her, we should have been badly burned.

But Freilles by night was transformed. It became like nothing
that I have ever seen—except upon a stage. It was theatrical.
The moon hung like a lantern—three times its size. The pines
might have been properties, they stood so still. The sand was
white. The whole was scenery. There was not a breath of
wind, and music from the casino floated out into the woods to
wander at will. The ceaseless thunder of the rollers hung upon

the air like a back-cloth to lesser sounds, and the world was all black and silver, and still as death.

"It can't be real," said Jill, as we strolled down a shadowy road.

"We know it is," said I. "But Nature is showing Art how to do her stuff. Critics would turn this down, if you shoved it on to the stage. They'd say it was overdone. And I don't know that you could blame them. No one who hadn't seen it, would ever believe."

We wandered past elegant villas, standing well back from the road, and surrounded by pines. As far as I saw, no tree that could be spared had been cut. All windows and doors were open everywhere. You could see right into the rooms and observe the furniture.

The contents of one of the villas took us by storm. Standing in the shadows, we identified more than one piece.

"Look at that candlestick, Boy. What a lovely thing."

"What about those corner-cupboards? I'll swear they're Chippendale."

"That chest's Italian. I know it. There used to be two at Irikli. And look at those two stalls. They came out of a church in Spain."

"Mademoiselle," said a voice, "is perfectly right. Three hundred years ago they stood in a church in Seville. Please come and look at them closely. The chest I found in Verona a year ago."

"You're very forgiving," said Jill; "but we couldn't dream of such a thing   I am so very sorry. We didn't mean to be rude."

"Mademoiselle has no need to tell me that. But I am an *antiquaire*. All these things are for sale. So please come in."

We followed our invisible hostess into the house.

As we took our seats—

"You see," said a very smart lady, " I have a shop in Paris : but this is my holiday home. Every year I come here for three months. But it is furnished from my shop, and if it is all sold to-morrow—well, then I shall get some more down, to take its place."

" But it all looks so lovely," said Jill. " I mean, it would be such a shame to break it up."

" Madame," said the other, " *antiquaires* have to live. And if they are true *antiquaires*, they have to learn to harden their hearts. I am now past the stage of hating to part with nice things. All that concerns me is that they go to a proper home, where people will care for them as I have and show them as they should be shown."

It was perfectly clear to me that, while ' *antiquaires* have to live,' it would not be this lady's fault if she failed to survive.

As though to confirm this impression—

" And now," she said, " I shall leave you and take my small dog for a run. Customers like to look at things by themselves. I shall be back in ten minutes, and then I will answer whatever questions you please. But you must come back to-morrow, for things look different by day."

Before we could protest, she was gone.

" Oh, Boy," breathed Jill. " Those stalls . . . in the gallery . . ."

" Those corner-cupboards," I said, " in the little drawing-room."

The best thing there was a set of tapestry chairs. These were not in use, but stood in a little chamber beyond two wrought-iron gates. Outside a museum, I had not seen such a set. They were not, of course, for us ; but when I had looked upon them my heart sank down. Madame Yvonne Martigny—the name was on one of her cards—was one of the great *antiquaires*. You had to have money to deal in such pieces as those.

I was still looking at them, when our hostess returned.

" Ah, Monsieur observes my set of tapestry chairs. I should not have them here really. They make the house smack of the shop. But there is no money in Paris, and they have cost me so much that I cannot hold on to them long."

" What do you ask for them, Madame ? "

" Eight hundred pounds."

" I don't think that's dear," I said ; " but they're not for people like us."

" Of course they are not. Who has eight hundred pounds to spend in such a fashion to-day ? If I sell them at all, they will go to America. But in fact they are not expensive. Eight years ago I could have sold those chairs for two thousand pounds."

" I love those stalls," said Jill.

Madame Martigny smiled.

" You should not have told me so. I would have let those go for thirty pounds. But now that I know that you like them, I double the price."

" Oh, dear," said Jill.

" Mademoiselle—I refuse to call you ' Madame '—I was but showing you the tricks of my trade. They are yours for twenty-five pounds. But do not sit in one ; for, if you do, I shall give them to you for nothing. Your beauty against that background . . ."

I began to have great respect for the great *antiquaires*.

We purchased the stalls and the chest—and promised to return the next day.

So we did—after tea . . . with the others. Berry ran riot, as I had known he would. Madame Martigny and he got on like a house on fire. But if she was a business woman, he was a business man. Honours, I think, were even. But he made us all feel ashamed. When she asked ten pounds, he smiled and looked into her eyes and offered her four. But she smiled back and said ' Eight '—and he paid her six.

" I don't say they're not worth it," he'd say, " but put them up to auction and see what you'd get."

" Monsieur is telling me."

" Very well then. I am offering more than the market price —and a great deal more than you paid. No, if I buy all this, you must help me out."

I think we both did very well.

We bought the corner-cupboards, as well as the candlestick. We bought a pair of tallboys—a very rare thing : rare, because they were really period stuff. We bought a binnacle—a fine old fellow that had weathered some wicked seas. And we bought a fine *chaise longue*—the only comfortable one in which I have ever sat.

" And now," said Berry, " to show that there's no ill will, if you'll let me telephone, I'll do my very best to sell those chairs."

" What do you mean ? " said Daphne.

" Van Heusen's at Biarritz.   I saw it in the paper to-day.   I met him two years ago, and he's mad about tapestry chairs." He turned to Madame Martigny.   " I don't know what you're asking, but that's a very fine set.   Shall I say thirteen hundred pounds ? "

" I will let them go for that."

" I bet you will," said Berry, and picked up the telephone . . .

We did not see Van Heusen.   He visited Freilles on Friday ; but we had already left.

On Sunday a letter arrived.

> *Friday evening.*
>
> DEAR MONSIEUR PLEYDELL,
>
> *My chairs are sold.   Monsieur Van Heusen has bought them for twelve hundred and fifty pounds.   The things which you bought have been very carefully packed and will leave here to-morrow, travelling by road.   I have written to Paris to send you an English tall-case clock.   It is by Vulliamy, and keeps most excellent time. This with my compliments.   Consider it, please, a token of gratitude.*
>
> *Cordially yours,*
> YVONNE MARTIGNY.

There was no harm done.   Van Heusen's income was two million sterling a year.

CHAPTER XVI

IN WHICH WE ENTER GRACEDIEU, AND JONAH AND I ASSIST AN UNFORTUNATE DOG

THE painting was over and done, and the floors had been scraped.   And now they were being oiled, before they were waxed.   And when those things had been done, we could enter in.

All the service cupboards were white.   They had been painted, while we were away at Freilles.   The walls of the offices were white, except for the kitchen's : these were done in pale blue—

to discourage the flies. The servants' bedrooms were yellow, woodwork and all. Jill's bedroom was painted white, but all the others were painted powder-blue, woodwork and all. And all the rest of the house took its tone from the marble stair. The galleries were done in a lighter shade than the rooms. To describe this particular hue is very hard. I think perhaps ' peach ' is as near as I can get.

For all of this, the credit was Daphne's alone. And few, I think, could have chosen so very well. For the whole of one day she sat in the gallery, while sample after sample was painted upon the wall.

" Add a little white," she would say, " and the merest trifle of blue."

And ten minutes later—

" No. That's not right. We shall have to start again. Now this time . . ."

The thing is she knew what she wanted and knew that what she wanted was right. The result was admirable. Till then I had never perceived that a house can be made or marred, according to the colour in which its walls are hung.

" The day after to-morrow," said Berry. " I wasn't far out."

Nor was he. He had planned for August the tenth, and to-day was August the ninth.

" Nothing from Bordeaux ? " said my sister.

" Not a blasted word. I shall have to wire again. The stuff from Freilles is in the guard-room, waiting to be unpacked. The tall-case clock is at Nareth : Carson is going to get it this afternoon. The stuff from Asen is coming to-morrow at ten o'clock. The stuff from England ought to be here by noon."

" Will the floors be ready ? "

" Yes. It takes no time to oil them. That will be done this morning. And the men will begin to wax them this afternoon. They've got four men to do it, which means that they should be through to-morrow before mid-day."

The fence about the property was up ; the cars were standing in the garage ; and all that Joseph could do was almost done. His staff had shrunk to five. Four of these were clearing the mortar which had fallen down from the scaffold to the foot of Hadrian's Wall. When this had been done, fine earth would be strewn there instead, and presently sown. Joseph himself and Pepito were up on the roof, replacing four or five tiles, which had been cracked by the hammer, when they were nailed into place. . . .

At six o'clock that evening Bordeaux replied.

Your telegram not understood no van received from England for your address.

We wired to London the next morning at eight o'clock.
The post arrived at nine—with a letter from Bordeaux.

August 5th.

SIR,

We have the pleasure to inform you that we are holding at your disposal one large furniture-van and contents. On receipt of your esteemed instructions, this will proceed to Pau by road. There it will pick up three packers from the Maison Barouche, afterwards proceeding to your address at Lally.

We should appreciate twenty-four hours notice, not only for ourselves, but for the Maison Barouche, by letter or telegram.

We beg that you will accept the expression of our most distinguished sentiments.

Société des Organisations Internationales.

" God give me strength," said Berry. " When was that letter posted ? "

The post-mark showed that it was posted on August the ninth.
" Written on Friday, posted on Tuesday and denied by wire the same day. How the hell this country survives, I do not know."

London's reply arrived at eleven o'clock.

Van received by Société des Organisations at Bordeaux on July thirty-first

Another violent wire was sent to Bordeaux.

Reference your letter numbered K/351 dated August 5th. posted August 9th. stop so carry out your orders that the van reaches Pau to-morrow at ten o'clock stop it must be here two hours later stop if the van is not here by mid-day I shall inform London and advise them to cancel your agency stop acknowledge.

This telegram was not acknowledged and the van was not at Lally by noon the following day. Nor was it there at one. Nor at two.

At a quarter past two we telephoned to Bordeaux.

Berry spoke and I held the spare receiver.

" Is that Bordeaux ? " said Berry.

" You are mad," said a voice. " I am not wanting Libourne. I have cancelled——"

" Blast what you've cancelled," said Berry. " Is that Bordeaux ? "

" You are on the wrong line, Monsieur. Kindly get off at once."

" Is that the Société des Organisations ? "

" Yes. But——"

" Don't argue with me. Refer instead to your letter K/351 dated August the fifth."

" Have you finished ? " asked the Exchange.

" No, I haven't," roared Berry. " At this rate I shan't have finished for half an hour. Are you there, Société des Organisations ? "

" Kindly replace your receiver. I do not want Libourne. In any event, I shall not pay for the call."

" This isn't Libourne," yelled Berry. " Will you refer to the letter I mentioned just now ? "

" What letter ? " said the other.

" K/351," howled Berry, " of August 5th."

" Patience, Monsieur. I shall connect you at once with the department concerned."

" Have you finished ? " asked the Exchange.

" No, I haven't," screamed Berry. " I'll let you know when I have. I'll tell you what I'll do. I'll let you into the secret. I'll put the receiver back. And when you find I've cut off, you'll know that I've done."

" Is that Libourne ? " said a voice.

" My God," said Berry. " I didn't know there was such a place."

" I have been trying to get you, Libourne, for three hours."

" Get this," said Berry. " I am not Libourne. I never have been Libourne, and, by the grace of God, I never shall be Libourne.

I am speaking from Lally in the Basses Pyrénées. My name is Major Pleydell."

" Oh, yes. Enchanted, Monsieur. About your van. We have no news of it yet. I wired you yesterday."

" But it's there," yelled Berry. " You've got it. You've had it for days."

" Monsieur is mistaken. We await the van with impatience."

" Refer to your letter K/351. In that you admit——"

" Have you finished ? " asked the Exchange.

" God in his heaven ! " cried Berry. " No, I have not. Can you construe the negative ? NO ! "

" We have no such letter, Monsieur, upon our files. For that I can vouch. The fault is no doubt with London. The moment——"

" Look here," said Berry. " That letter was signed by you. It reached me yesterday morning at nine o'clock. I immediately telegraphed you, ordering you to arrange that the van should reach Lally not later than noon to-day."

" The wire is before me, Monsieur. But the van is not here."

" Then why did you say that it was ? "

" Have you finished ? " asked the Exchange.

" Not yet, sweetheart," said Berry. " When you hear me vomit, then you can cut me off."

" How long," said a voice, " am I to wait for Libourne ? "

" Several weeks, I hope," said Berry. " Will you refer to that letter, you black-livered fool ? "

" Patience, Monsieur. What letter ? "

" The letter I referred to, you idiot. In which you declare that the van is awaiting my instructions."

" Monsieur, I have before me your very clear telegram. To that I replied on Monday——"

" I'm going to read your letter. Listen to this."

" Have you finished ? " asked the Exchange.

Squinting with emotion, Berry mastered his voice.

" Not yet, Goo-goo," he sighed. " Don't rush the rising gorge."

With that, he read the letter.

" Well, what about that ? " he demanded.

" Is that Libourne ? " said a voice. " I have tried to receive Libourne for——"

" For your information," said Berry, " your call to Libourne was cancelled some time ago."

" But that is absurd," said the other. " And who are you ? "

" By the time I'm through with you, you'll know who I am. And I hope and believe you'll shortly be eaten of worms."

" Of what ? " shrieked the other.

" Of worms," roared Berry, " you flat-footed, blue-based baboon."

" I am not a baboon," howled the other. " Much less blue as to my seat. You describe yourself, Monsieur. I will not endure——"

" Is that Libourne ? " said Berry.

As the choking scream died away, Berry rang off.

He was wiping the sweat from his face, when Jill's clear voice rang out.

" It's here ! It's here ! It's turning into the drive."

We ran through the library and on to the terrace beyond.

A large, yellow furniture-van was proceeding towards the garage : Joseph was backing before it, beckoning it on.

* * * * *

That night we slept in our home—twelve months and a half since Berry had ' turned the first sod.' It was a great experience. Things were not straight, of course : but the linen was aired, and the china and glass were washed. So we lay in our own beds and drank our morning tea from the service we knew so well. Everything worked very well, down to the bells and the fountain, which, because we forgot all about it, was playing all night. Is was not a very long night : except for the servants, no one wat in bed before two. But even Berry was down to breakfast at nine.

One great adventure was over : another was about to begin.

" Monsieur," said Joseph that morning, " behold ! I have had my reward. Many a time at dawn I have taken the Nareth road, to observe the house from the opposite side of the valley. One always likes to see how one's building looks. And last night, at eleven o'clock, I took that same road again. You see,

I knew it would be lighted : and, as it was very warm and you had so much to do, I thought that perhaps the shutters would not be closed. Well, they were open, Monsieur, and every light was on. I can never tell you, Monsieur, of the splendour that met my eyes. It made the most lovely picture high up on the mountainside. I could not leave it, Monsieur. I stood there for more than an hour. Mesdames and Messieurs must drive out one night to see it ; else they will lose the pleasure that others take in their home."

Two days later we said goodbye to that good and faithful servant, who had done all things well.

It was Jill who spoke for us all.

With his hand in hers—

" We shall miss you terribly, Joseph. You see, you belong to the house. And so you always will, as long as we're here. But you must come and see us, whenever you can. We shall always feel it natural to see you here, because it is thanks to you that we have such a lovely home."

* * * * *

Tea was served on the terrace on Sunday afternoon.

" Is anyone," said Daphne, " thinking of going to Pau ? "

" Where is Pau ? " said Berry. " My feet are still off the earth."

" You're hopeless," said Daphne.

" I shall never leave here," said Berry. " I should like to be buried on the ledge at the foot of the bluff. I'm through with pomps and vanities. I told Nobb so yesterday morning. And he said he quite understood."

" Nobb ? " said his wife. " D'you mean you've been talking to Nobb ? "

" Why shouldn't I talk to Nobb ? He's made me damned good shoes for thirty-five years. Besides, he's a friend of mine."

" You actually rang up London, to order a pair of shoes ? "

" Two pairs," said Berry. " And what's the telephone for ? We had a long talk. There he was in St. James's Street, and here was I in the heart of the Pyrenees. I could hear the taxis passing. And then I knew I had chosen the better part. And that reminds me. I'm not sure I'm going to die. I may be

translated. So if you can't find me one day . . . And I rang
up the Army and Navy. They've got some things to lie on, out
in the open air. The assistant was most understanding. He
doesn't know this part, but he's been to Tours."

" Of course we shall be ruined," said Daphne. " Still, I may
as well contribute. I'll ring up Helen to-night."

" There's a beautiful creature," said Berry. " Give her my
love. And tell her I've found the way. You know, that soap-
niche has it. I can hardly get out of the bath. But, as Joseph
says, I deserve it. You can't get away from that."

" I can go to Pau to-morrow," said I.

" I've got to," said Jonah. " I've got to choose some trowels."

" We'll go together," said I. " What does my lady want ? "

" Samples for curtains," said Daphne. " We'll have to have
curtains up before October comes in. Jill and I and Thérèse
can make them, but we must get hold of the stuff."

" Tell me where to go," said I, " and I'll do the job."

" That's right, be mundane," said Berry. " And, by the way
I want some writing-blocks. Can nobody think of a name for
this heaven on earth ? "

" I know," said Jill. " *Gracedieu.*"

And Gracedieu it was. I ordered the dies the next day.

*   *   *   *   *

The next day.

I think I shall remember it always, Monday the sixteenth of
August. . . .

Jonah and I had done our business in Pau. We had had our
lunch. We were more than half the way home. We were, in
fact, about to emerge from Bielle, a little village some five or
six miles from Nareth, when we saw before us a flurry in the
midst of the way.

Two cars had stopped and a dog on a chain was standing upon
its hind legs by the side of a ten-foot wall. Dancing about it
was a man in a shirt and plus-fours—the most enormous plus-
fours I have ever seen. They were of bottle-green and they fell
very near to his ankles. His shirt was canary-yellow ; his
flowing tie was red. In a word it was Caratib—whom we had
flung out of our flat six months before.

What had happened was plain—and there was no time to be lost.

The dog, a powerful mongrel, had been chained up in a garden behind the wall. The level of the garden was higher than that of the road. The dog had leaped or had fallen over the wall. But his chain was not long enough for his fore-feet to reach the ground. For a time no doubt, the poor beast had saved his neck by standing upon his hind legs against the wall; but now these were giving out and he was in imminent danger of being hanged.

Caratib rushed towards us, as we fell out of the car.

"Messieurs, I implore your assistance. This poor, dumb beast. When I have tried to release him, he tries his best to savage me with his jaws. He does not, of course, understand. Oh, my God, what shall I do? To see a poor creature dying and yet be unable to help. And the people are out, and the garden gate is fast locked and is covered with spikes."

Jonah ran to the dog, but though it was nearly done it tried to spring at his throat.

Somehow I got my hands on the top of the wall . . .

And then I was up and over and in the garden beyond.

The chain was long—too long, of course, but that is beside the point. It did not run straight to the wall, but first to a heavy stone roller, beneath which it now was jammed.

Putting forth all my strength, I hauled the roller aside . . .

As I did so, the chain ran forward and then went slack. I heard a shout from the road. And when I looked over the wall, there was the dog on four feet and Caratib hugging Jonah who looked extremely annoyed.

Then Caratib saw me and rushed to the wall.

"Hero!" he shrieked. "Hero! You have done the impossible thing. Behold your protegé. Already he moves his tail. Come down and let me embrace you. All your unkindness is forgotten and washed away."

"Shake hands, instead," said I, leaning down from the wall.

Caratib seized my hand, clapped it to his lips and mouthed it.

"Accept my homage," he cried. "You have saved a fellow-creature. For me, I adore the beasts. I have at home four cats, all of which are clean in the house."

" Listen," I said. " That poor dog will want some water.
Perhaps, at that house over there . . ."

" Of course. Dolt that I am ! "

As he rushed down the road, I saw my cousin coming with
a pail in his hand. Still, it was plainly my chance. So I made
my way back down the wall and ran for the car. I had no mind
to be hugged by Caratib.

The dog was recovering. After drinking a little, he lay down
in the shade of the wall. But he would not let Jonah touch him :
he had no use for strangers ; he was a *chien de garde*.

" We can't do any more," said Jonah. " The people next door
have promised to tell his owners who have gone to Pau for the
day. They're happily fond of him, and thought to make his
life pleasant, by giving him a long chain. Idiotic, of course.
But I've made that clear."

Here Caratib returned with a very small saucer of milk.

As he made to lay it down, the mongrel rose in his wrath ;
and Caratib recoiled and the milk was spilt.

" Ingrate ! " cried Caratib, wiping his green plus-fours, with a
purple handkerchief. " Never mind. You are not yourself."
He rushed to my side. " Monsieur, believe me, I owe you as
much as that dog. Had he not been saved, my holiday would
have been spoiled."

" You're on holiday, then ? " said I, as Jonah slid into the
car.

" Alas, it ends to-day." He pointed to his car and to what I
now saw was a trailer, standing behind. " I am a family man.
That is my wife sitting there." We raised our hats and she
bowed. " And my four children behind. We have been in the
mountains. Behold our tent in the trailer. We have no use
for hotels. Always we do the same. Does Monsieur know
Luz Ortigue ? "

" Yes, I know it," I said. " A lovely spot."

" We return from there at this moment—after as fair a fortnight as man could ask. Consider the dawn there, Monsieur.
The dew on those perfect meadows, the early mass of the birds,
the sumptuous music of the torrent and the clouds snared on the
summits, caught in a net of gold. And people will talk of
Biarritz. Monsieur, I spit upon the *plage*. Is man but vermin

that he must make one of a herd? But I made a mistake this year. Oh, it is done now. But this year we went too late. My wife persuaded me. Last year we went in June—the first fortnight in June. And had the place to ourselves. Fifteen days, Monsieur; and never a human being, to break the spell. But that woman there said it was cold. 'Later,' she said. 'In August.' And like a fool, I gave way." He approached his face to mine. "Four other parties, Monsieur. And two had brought gramophones." He flung up his hands. "The peace of sundown was murdered. The atmosphere was destroyed. As an artist, Monsieur, I tell you, it seared my heart. And last year, in June, not a soul."

Jonah leaned forward.

"A caravan," he said. "For three or four days."

"No, Monsieur. No one at all. Not even a caravan."

"But——"

"I am telling you, Monsieur, that Luz Ortigue was ours— our private pleasance for fifteen flawless days. A passing peasant, perhaps: but no visitors. And certainly, no caravan."

"Are you perfectly sure," said I, "that you've got your dates right?"

"But certainly, Monsieur. It was the first fortnight in June. I shall never forget it. The year before, the same time: but then it rained." He wagged a finger. "But I prefer the rain to two poisonous gramophones. My God! Shall I ever forget? Up there I walk all day. I commune with Nature, Monsieur. She gives me ideas for my bath-rooms. And when I come home, I am tired. I desire to sleep. But no! Till long past midnight, Monsieur. *Yes, we have no bananas,* and filth like that."

He paused to wipe the foam from his lips.

"But last year you're perfectly sure there was nobody there?"

"Monsieur, I swear——"

"No blue car—half-car, half-caravan?"

"No," screamed Caratib. "Nothing. I have had the world to myself for fifteen days."

I started the engine up.

"Well," I said, "we'll have to be getting on."

We had to shake hands again, and Caratib held my right hand in both of his.

" Our misunderstanding is forgotten.   From this time on our relation is white as snow.   Ah, *mon brave*, I shall never forget your action."

" Nonsense," said I.   " You'd have done it before we got here, if you could have managed that wall."

" My homage to Miladi and Madame."

" Thank you."

" And I shake the Major's hand."

" I'll tell him.   *Au revoir.*"

I let in the clutch . . .

" And now what ? " I said.

Jonah had a hand to his chin.

" We drive up to Cluny and ask to have a look at that book. He may have got his dates wrong.   If he hasn't . . ."

" We're on to something, Jonah."

" I think so, too.   Though I'm damned if I can see what. Where was Shapely, if he wasn't at Luz Ortigue ?   And why did he say he was there, if he wasn't there ?   That he was up above Cluny there can be no doubt.   The Customs had his passport. Well, that alibi's good enough.   Why should he lie about where his caravan had rested ? "

" That," said I, " is the second unnecessary lie.   He said that I saw him on Tuesday, when, in fact, it was Wednesday I saw him, taking in petrol at Lally."

" When was the murder ? " said Jonah.

" On Monday," said I, " at eleven o'clock at night."

" Well, he couldn't have done it," said Jonah.   " He may be many things ; but he's not a blasted magician.   No man born of woman can be in two places at once."

We whipped through Nareth, swung to the right at the cross roads and flung up the sounding gorge.

Ten minutes later, we sighted the village of Cluny rising up like a gate-house about the mountain road.

Its street was very narrow, and I laid the car as close as I could to the kerb.

Then Jonah got out and I followed him into the office . . .

A sergeant looked up.

" Ah, good afternoon, Messieurs.   I recognize you at once. You were with the English Inspector, when he asked questions last year. He has not, I suppose, run the malefactor to earth ? "

" Not yet," said Jonah. " Would you be so very kind as to let me look at your book ? "

" With pleasure, Monsieur. The book, I surmise, for Class Three ? "

" I think that's right. For those who camp in the mountains."

" That is quite right, Monsieur. They have to produce a passport, and that we hold in this office against their return." The book was laid open before us. " There you are, Messieurs. Examine it as you please."

Jonah turned over two pages . . .

1937

EXIT on June 1st. at 2.30 p.m. car and trailer black No. ST 541/P ; passengers six—husband and wife and four children ; passport X3552 Caratib.

RE-ENTRY on June 15th. at 10.30 a.m. ; all present ; passport returned.

" No doubt about that," said Jonah, and gave the book back. " Where do people camp, if they don't camp at Luz Ortigue ? "

" In all sorts of odd places, Monsieur. Some go up above Jules : but the valley widens there, and the trees are few. Besides, if a car breaks down, they are too much cut off. Luz Ortigue is the spot which most of them patronize. That is sheltered and only five miles from here. There is, of course, Echelle, which is closer, still. But few, I think, go there. For from there you cannot walk, but must be prepared to climb."

" Echelle," said Jonah. " I don't think I know Echelle."

The other rose to his feet.

" I will point it out to you, Monsieur." We followed him to the wall. " This is a copy of the Cadastral Plan. Now here is Cluny, and there, higher up, is Jules." His finger returned to Cluny, and then began to move. " Here we leave Cluny and at once we cross the bridge ; then the road turns to the left. So for two miles, and then there is a ramp on the left. It is steep and not inviting, unless you are sure of your car. So you come down to the gorge, and there you can leave your car and climb down to the river-bed. Very well. That is Echelle. But it is, as I say, more for mountaineers than . . .

But I had no ears to hear what else he said.

Echelle was the name of the spot which we had called 'Paradise.' *And that was where Shapely had camped.* Not Luz Ortigue. *Paradise.* Not above Jules, for Tass had walked to Cluny to catch the 'bus. And who ever heard of a chauffeur walking a good ten miles in the heat of the day?

I glanced at Jonah. His face was set, and his eyes were fast on the map. He seemed to be trying to read some secret it held.

At last he turned to the sergeant.

"I know Echelle," he said. "But not by that name. I have lunched there more than once. There's a little meadow there. I see that it's numbered here."

"That is so, Monsieur. I know the field you mean. But it is of small account. It is awkward for a peasant to get at, though they say that the grass is fat."

Jonah spoke very slowly, with his eyes on the other's face.

"It is nice to picnic in. At least, it was. But when last I went there, in April, the meadow was straitly fenced . . . and the barn was locked."

"That would be the new owner," said the other. "I heard that it had been sold. Though why he should be so jealous I cannot conceive. I mean, there are no beasts there, to ravage his hay."

After a long silence—

"I . . . find it strange, too," said Jonah, and turned on his heel. "May I leave the car where it is for half an hour? I want to go for a stroll . . . and I may want to telephone."

The officer passed to the door and glanced down the street. Then—

"Certainly, Monsieur. No one will touch it there. Stroll as you please. My men will keep their eyes on it, till you return."

In silence, we left the guard-room and crossed the bridge.

"We've got it," said Jonah. "We've got all the pieces now; but they won't fit in. It's only a question of patience. I never was so excited in all my life."

My brain was unruly—fighting against the bit.

" Let's sit down on that bank," I said, " and sift the grain from the chaff."

As we took our seats—

" Shapely camped at Echelle," said Jonah, " and not at Luz Ortigue. He, therefore, knew Echelle for a lonely place."

" I know, but——"

" Wait a minute. On one thing we both agree—that when Shapely came out in December, he came out ' to put things right.' But we could not think how he could do it. You said yourself, ' Find out what he actually did, and we'll have the truth in our hands.' Well, now we know what he did. In ten minutes' time I'm going to ring up de Moulin and ask him to find out at once *who bought that field*. That, as a matter of form ; for we both know that Shapely owns it . . . and why it's fenced."

I caught his arm.

" The barn," I cried. " The padlocked barn, Jonah ! "

My cousin struck his hand on the bank.

" Of course. In the barn. Well done. We're getting on. I'll lay a monkey he buried Tass in that barn. And then, in fear and trembling, because you had shown him the awful mistake he had made, he came back here in December and bought and locked the place. . . . We ought to have thought of that. That was an obvious way ' to put things right.' And now we go back to the murder—the murder on September the first."

There was a little silence.

" He had eight hours," I said, frowning. " He left Pau at half past ten and never got to Orthez till half past six."

" Just nice time," said Jonah. " An hour to pick up the lime and then go on to meet Tass. Another hour to get to Echelle. Four hours in which to kill and then bury his dead. And then two hours in which to get to Orthez. And now we come to the jump. How did he get through the Customs ? If he and Tass passed out, but he alone came back . . ."

" Tass must have been dead ? " said I. " And his body concealed in the van."

" But what a risk ! " said Jonah. " They always look into all cars. And a caravan like that might very well have been crammed with contraband stuff. Besides, who takes a van for an afternoon trip ? Oh, no : we're off the rails there. Of course he could have changed to a car, but then what about Tass ? "

There was another silence, while both of us thought very hard.

" We're right so far," mused Jonah. " I'm sure of that. You see it explains his lie—that he was at Luz Ortigue."

" No, it doesn't," said I. " He hadn't bumped Tass off, when he told that lie."

Jonah looked at me sharply. Then he caught my arm.

" Wait a minute. *What if he had ?* The fellow who sold the lime, kept saying ' last summer some time.' Well, June was last summer all right. We've always looked at September. *But what about June ?* "

My heart was hammering. Once again, I was sure that my cousin was right.

" June," I said. " Now let's go over the dates. Tass murders Old Rowley on Monday—Monday night. He reaches Paris on Tuesday and travels to Pau that night. At eight on Wednesday morning he puts his suit-case into the cloak-room at Pau. Well, he could have been here by ten, if he'd taken the early 'bus. And Shapely didn't leave here till five o'clock. That means he had seven hours in which to kill Tass and bury him in the barn. Say six, to be sure. And six was more than enough. But once again, how the hell did Tass pass the Customs ? "

" I can't answer that question," said Jonah. " But I'm sure that somehow he did. He left Shapely and came back to Shapely —and Shapely did him in. He'd bought the lime beforehand— before they came here at all. And he probably dug the grave, while Tass was away."

There was another silence. Jonah had his eyes shut and a hand to his head. And I stared up at the cliffs which were looking down on Echelle. The sun was . . .

And there, as I looked upon them, the contact was made.

I must, I think, have cried out, but I cannot be sure. But Jonah was shaking me and crying, " What do you know ? "

" One second. Let me go back. Tass shoves his suitcase in the cloak-room and catches the early 'bus. *But he doesn't travel to Cluny : he travels to Lally, instead.* And then he walks over the mountain, by the path which Shapely has shown him— past where we found young de Moulin, down to Echelle."

Jonah started up to his feet.

" By God," he cried, " you've got it ! And it's been lying under our nose for more than a year. From what de Moulin said, to walk from Lally to Echelle would take no more than five hours. Tass reached Echelle, exhausted, at three o'clock— exhausted . . . an easy prey. Shapely met him, heard his report and killed him. He had the grave all ready. All he had to do was to add his lime and cover the body up."

" Quick work," said I, finger to lip. " Shapely passed through the Customs at five o'clock. And I'll lay any money Tass didn't arrive before four. A chauffeur walking over the mountains ? "

" Don't pull your case to pieces. I'm sure you're right. But what's the matter with us—that we never saw it before ? And now come and ring up de Moulin. Quick work or no, we have the truth in the bag. Tass's body is in that barn. We'll have to make sure, of course. But the moment we *know*, I'll wire for Falcon to come."

We walked back to Cluny and entered the little hotel.

Two minutes later, de Moulin was on the line.

Jonah made his request.

" With pleasure, Monsieur. What is the number again ? "

" It's numbered 534 upon the Cadastral Plan. I want to know the name of the owner and when it changed hands."

" I shall know within the hour. It is now just four o'clock. I will ring you up at five—at your beautiful house."

" If you please," said Jonah.

We left the hotel and made our way back to the car.

As we came up, a Customs Officer smiled and put a hand to his hat.

" The sergeant has gone off duty ; but he commended to me the care of Monsieur's excellent car."

" Why, it's Jacques," said Jonah.

" That is right," said the fellow, grinning. " It was I who was sent for when Monsieur the Inspector was here."

" I remember. You picked out two photographs."

" That is quite right, Monsieur. I was the one, you see, who saw the murderer."

" ' A poor man, with one eye.' I remember. But you haven't seen him since."

" Alas, no, Monsieur, although I have strained my eyes. Once I was sure that I had him. A man came by in a car. My God, if I was excited. He had his features. I could have sworn it was him. And he bowed his head, as though he would not be seen. But when I had run round the car—well, it was not he. Alas, he had two eyes, Monsieur ; and the murderer had but one. And yet, you know, I was sure I had seen him before."

Jonah stood very still.

" At last," he said quietly. " I think that was in December."

Jacques recoiled.

" It was just before Christmas," he said. " But how does Monsieur know ? "

" Common sense," said Jonah. " And don't forget this, Jacques. *A man may wear a patch. But it doesn't follow, my friend, that he hasn't two eyes.*"

With that, he entered the car and took the wheel.

I followed him in, and he turned the car about.

As we slid out of Cluny—

" We're so many fools," said Jonah. " Falcon and all. Shapely purchased the lime before he came up to Echelle. He came up on June the fourth. On June the fifth he reconnoitred the path which he knew existed, which led to Lally on the other side of the hills. He told you in the train that he had known Lally for years. He killed Tass the following day. And buried the corpse in the barn. The next day he put on Tass's eye-shade and Tass's clothes, collected Tass's passport and took the 'bus to Pau. He travelled to Paris and Dover and did Old Rowley in. He had the keys, of course, and he took the family car. And he left in the car a packet of cigarettes, upon which were Tass's finger-prints—very ingenious that. He returned to Paris ; and there he took off his patch and changed out of Tass's clothes. So Tass disappeared in Paris. That night he travelled to Pau, shoved Tass's case in the cloak-room and caught the 'bus to Lally arriving at ten o'clock. Then he walked over the mountain and back to the caravan. And you recognised him in Lally at half past five that day. Damn it, the thing's too easy. To judge from those photographs, he's not at all unlike Tass. And who would ever look further than the patch on a fellow's eye ? We didn't. No one did. That patch in itself was a passport. . . . But he had to get rid of the suit-case, for men who are living don't leave their luggage unclaimed. And so he came back in September and picked it up. As like as not he chucked it into the *Gave*. The *Gave d'Oloron*. Weighted it first, of course. But that is why he was round about Navarrenx. And there we have the whole thing. I know I'm right."

So did I.

There was no more doubt about it.

Everything fitted in.

*　　*　　*　　*　　*

At five o'clock precisely de Moulin rang up.

" The owner of that field, Monsieur, is one of your compatriots. A Monsieur F. C. Shapely. He purchased it in December, and the sale was registered in January this year."

" Thank you very much," said Jonah.

" One moment, Monsieur. That is what the register says. But it will not say that very long, for the sale and the registration are going to be revoked."

" Revoked ? "

" Revoked. I cannot explain just now, but this evening I leave for Lally for two or three days. Will you come to my villa to-morrow that I may give you the facts ? "

" With pleasure," said Jonah. " What about half past ten ? "

" That," said the lawyer, " will suit me admirably."

CHAPTER XVII

IN WHICH JUSTICE IS DONE

THAT evening we laid our plans.

So far, we could *prove* next to nothing. We never should be able to *prove* that F. C. Shapely, his stepson, had put Old Rowley to death. But, provided that Tass's body lay in the barn at Echelle, we ought to be able to prove that Shapely had murdered Tass.

That the body was there, we had not the slightest doubt.

But we dared not wire for Falcon, until we knew. Well, that was easy enough. We could visit the barn and see. But, if the body was there, then, without any delay, we should have to inform the French police.

We decided to visit the barn the next morning at eight o'clock. An hour should be time enough for us to discover whether it held a grave. If it did, we would stop at Cluny on our way back and send a wire requesting that Falcon should leave at once. We would then return to Lally, to keep our appointment with de Moulin at half past ten. And when we had heard what he said, we would tell him what we had found and the whole of the truth.

The thing was this. Even though the body was there, the murder was old. Shapely would be arrested and extradited and tried. But an able counsel might very well get him off. And we did not want him to get off. We knew that he had murdered two innocent men. One of these was our very good friend. It was a cruel and barbarous double crime—for which it was right and proper that Shapely should pay the price. Yet, unless the case was carefully handled, he would not pay the price. If the French police would not hear us, handled the body roughly, declined to take photographs and other precautions like that, then Shapely would be acquitted, when he came to be tried. But de Moulin was sympathetic and very shrewd. He had authority. When he heard what we had to tell, he would see in a flash the importance of moving with very great care. More. He was a just man. The crimes would provoke his indignation. And he would do his best to see that justice was done.

* * * * *

We ran into Cluny the next morning at eight o'clock.

As I slowed up for the Customs, the sergeant came out.

"Ah, good morning, Monsieur. And how can I help you to-day?"

Jonah smiled.

"Only by letting us pass. We're going to have a look at Echelle."

"Proceed, then, Monsieur. But if you go climbing, be careful. The cliffs are dangerous."

"Not to-day," said Jonah. "We shan't be very long. We've got to get back."

Ten minutes later I brought the Rolls to rest at the foot of the ramp.

Perhaps because it was early Paradise seemed more lovely than ever before. Since it was summer, the water had put off its wrath and, though a decent head was still coming down, it was tumbling cheerily and leaping as though at play. Beneath the oaks in the meadow, the long grass was bright with dew, and the cliffs beyond hung like a giant back-cloth, down which two threads of silver were making their lively way.

"Reconnaissance, first," said Jonah. "We want to be sure we're alone. You stay with the car, Carson. If anyone enters the ramp, just touch the horn."

We crossed the little bridge and walked round about the meadow and back to the barn. And saw not a soul. We had the place, as usual, all to ourselves.

Jonah drew a screw-driver out of his coat.

"Get the things, will you?" he said. "I don't think Carson should leave the foot of the ramp."

The padlock was securing a hasp. By the time I was back the staple was hanging free.

And then we were in the barn, and the door was shut.

Jonah lighted his torch and I laid the things I had brought against the wall—a pick, a diminutive shovel and two steel rods.

Foot by foot, we examined the floor of earth.

As we reached the end of the barn, Jonah picked up a pinch of something between his finger and thumb.

"Lime," he said quietly. "This, of course, is the obvious place. Oh, yes. Look. That's where he piled his earth. Damned careless workmanship: but then he never expected a light to be lit in this barn. I imagine the body's lying against the wall. Yes, that's right. You can see the marks of his rammer. He must have used a mallet. . . . Give me the pick, will you? You hold the torch."

The earth was soft. Once the crust had been broken, we had little need of the pick. Sixteen inches down, we came to the lime.

Jonah laid down the shovel and put on a pair of gloves. . . .

Two minutes later we had the awful proof that a human body was there.

"Poor wretched fellow," said Jonah. "God rest his soul."

My cousin replaced the lime and most of the soil. Then he took the shovel and beat the earth tight.

As he got to his feet—

"Thank God that's over," he said. And then, "It might have been worse."

It might, indeed. Very much worse. But slack lime devours the gases which a body puts off.

Ten minutes later, the staple was back in its place, and we were, all three, in the car.

Jonah had his telegram ready, and we stopped for a minute at Cluny, to send it off.

Send Falcon immediately stop strongly suggest Aunt Mary has day and night nurse.

Then we drove back to Gracedieu and bathed and changed.

* * * * *

"Let me explain," said de Moulin. "The meadow was sold and purchased in perfect good faith. All, in fact, was in order, except one thing. Monsieur Shapely does not happen to be a Frenchman by birth. No one but a Frenchman by birth may own or lease land which stands within twenty miles of this frontier of France : and Echelle is within that limit by nearly four miles. The lawyer should have observed that the title could not pass : but he does not convey much land. He is a Monsieur Schurch and his work lies more in the courts. What is inexcusable is that the Land Registry also failed to perceive this flaw. But twice in the year, in January and July, all registrations of sales are sent to the Head Office, Paris, from all over France. And there they are scrutinized, before they are filed. This registration went up to Paris last month, and only ten days ago an order came down to Pau that it must be revoked. And so, of course, must the sale. The money will be handed back. But now the trouble is this—that Monsieur Schurch has not Monsieur Shapely's address. On the Deed he is entered as of an hotel in Pau. But there he left no address.

Yet, he must, of course, be informed. And his signature is required."

"I think," said Jonah, "that I can help you there."

"Ah."

"But, before I do that, I have a story to tell. It deeply concerns the purchase of this particular field. We shall have to go to the police, but we'd like to do that through you. I mean, this mustn't be bungled, if they are to get their man."

De Moulin sat back in his chair.

"I will see that nothing is bungled. The *Procurateur Général* is a personal friend of mine."

"What could be better?" said Jonah. "Well, here we go."

He told the whole tale very well, and de Moulin sat and listened with half-closed eyes.

When it was done, the lawyer got to his feet and put out his hands.

"I felicitate you, my friends. A beautiful piece of work. It is like a story one reads. But in the stories, right at the last, the villain is always brought low. And so it must be this time. *Mon Dieu*, but it is a mercy that you did not go to the police. They can shoot an assassin or trace a motor-car. But this business requires finesse. This murder is old. And the man who did it is rich. He will have the very finest advice. And let me tell you this—that if you arrest him in England and if he employs a French lawyer with half as good a brain as my own, he will never come to be tried. . . .

"You see, you can prove so little. Do not think that I do not believe you : but courts require proof. Consider this only, Messieurs. That Customs official who thought that Shapely was Tass . . . and gave him Tass's passport . . . and helped him to take the 'bus. That official, you know, is paid *not* to make mistakes like that. And when it comes to making a statement— well, he will think of his pension and he will insist upon oath that he made no mistake and that it was Tass that went by, and no other man. And if it was Tass that went by, but did not come back, then it cannot be Tass's body that lies in the barn. So this monster, Shapely, must not be arrested in England.

" ' What, then ? ' you say. I will tell you."

He set a foot on a chair, an elbow upon his knee and cupped his chin in a palm.

" He will be arrested here—at the scene of his crime.

" You see, it is very simple. The stars have fought against him, and no one can stand against the stars. You will give me his English address, and Schurch will write to him and tell him that the sale of the meadow must be revoked. That will bring him here hot-foot. At least, it would me. And if he is told, when he comes, that in forty-eight hours the meadow will cease to be his, I think that, if I were he, I should seek to use that time . . . by trying to remove or destroy the evidence of my crime.

" So he may be caught red-handed . . ."

" I congratulate you," said Jonah. " That is a brilliant idea."

" We will try to bring it off," said de Moulin. " I shall see the *Procurateur* this afternoon. He will, of course, wish to see you—and the English Inspector. And there is a happy chance— that he should be arriving to-morrow." An eye-lid flicked. " A bad combination for Shapely—you and the stars."

* * * * *

We afterwards learned that Shapely had been in Scotland when Schurch's letter arrived. He had rented a deer-forest there, and a very mixed bag of guests was having fun and games at a castle which had made history in days gone by. The letter had reached him on Sunday—and Shapely had left for London within the hour.

The next day he left for Paris, and early on Tuesday morning he came to Pau.

When the French police like, they can put up a lovely show. Red tape goes by the board, and the scene becomes a stage. In Shapely's case, of course, they had only to spread the net. But it was a very fine net, and they spread it extremely well.

Shapely's appointment with Schurch had been fixed for ten o'clock. Schurch would receive him, of course, in his private room. This had two doors. One had been taken away and a curtain had been hung in its place. And Schurch had moved his table, so that when he was facing his client, the curtain would be at his back.

R

At half past nine that morning, six people took their seats in the office the curtain hid. Jonah and I made two, and a short-hand-writer, a third. Falcon stood by the curtain, with his back to the wall. . . .

Though I never saw Shapely's face, I knew that his nerves were ragged the moment I heard his voice. I am sure that he knew that he had been mad to come : I am equally sure that he came, because he would have gone mad if he had stayed away. So it was with Eugéne Aram. Be that as it may, the man was beside himself.

Only a man of iron nerve could have done what he had done. Having murdered one man, he had set out to murder another, bearing his victim's passport and wearing his victim's clothes. Apart from obtaining the passport, four several times he had to produce that passport and meet men's scrutiny. Had he fallen at but one of those fences, he must have lost his life. But because he never faltered, he did not fall. Then again, in the train, with me . . . He took the count, when, with my tale of Crippen, I hit him between the eyes : but long before we parted, he had me where I belonged, and, but for the chance which sent Carson to fetch the lime, that he had put Tass to death would never have entered my head.

But now that iron nerve was broken, and, but for what he had done, I could have pitied him.

In that dingy lawyer's office, I heard him put the rope round his neck. He refused to accept the revocation. He shouted and raved. He swore to raise the matter in Parliament. He spoke of international complications—the man was mad. Then he tried bribery. He gave the lawyer instructions to offer the Registrar five hundred pounds. And then, after forty minutes, he threw in his hand.

"All right," he said. "I'll sign. But not to-day. Have the papers ready on Thursday. Till then, the meadow is mine. I've a right to go up and enjoy it. Besides, I've left some gear there."

"But, Monsieur, of course. So long as——"

"And get this—and pass it on. You're a treacherous race of blackguards. The glorious French Republic goes back on its solemn word."

With that, he flung out of the room.

But he did not wait till the morrow. He hired a car at a garage and drove alone to Echelle that afternoon.

But we were there before him—we and the police.

He was shadowed wherever he went. And at four o'clock that day a message came through to Cluny to say that he had left Pau, and was driving south.

We took our respective positions before he came.

It was half past six before his approach was signalled. He was driving leisurely, to allow the dusk to come in. And he stopped at Bielle, to purchase a pick and shovel—and a blacksmith's hammer, with which to smash the skull.

Concealed in the bushes with Jonah, I saw his car steal out of the tunnel of leaves and come to rest by the bridge. I saw him alight and look round. Then he took the tools from the car and hastened over the water and up to the silent barn. . . .

I found it rather dreadful—watching a fellow creature walk into so deadly a trap.

I have said that the police were thorough. They actually had a camera set in the roof of the barn. . . .

The sun was gone and the shadows were coming in, so I saw the flare of the flash-light under the eaves. And I knew what Shapely must have looked like, with the pick in his hand and his mouth a little bit open and his eyes all wide and staring— and the ground broken up at his feet.

And then I heard a sound which I prefer not to describe. A ghoul made it—a ghoul about its business, caught in the act.

A moment later, I heard a rush and a crash and two or three cries in French . . . and then Shapely was in the meadow and was running as hard as he could.

And then I heard the roar of an automatic . . .

Shapely staggered and stopped. Then he seemed to draw himself up. And then he swung slowly round and fell flat on his back.

I was the first to reach him.

He was trying to raise himself, and I put an arm about him and lifted his shoulders up.

For a moment he stared at me.

Then—

"By God," he said, "it's Pleydell. You're always turning up." Then he seemed to forget I was there and to talk to himself. "Silly to fall down on Tass. Now if it had been Old Rowley . . . But that's the way it goes. You win The National, and then you break your neck in some —— point-to-point."

And I think he would have said more, but a rush of blood choked his utterance, and, when it was over, he died.

As I laid his body back in the long, sweet grass—

"Better so," said Jonah. He turned to the Superintendent. "Your men do you credit, Monsieur. That was a beautiful shot. Can you keep this out of the papers?"

"Why not, Monsieur?" said the other. "What good will a scandal do?"

"That's how I see it," said Jonah. "I'll lay that none of his relatives know where he is. And all they need ever know is that his body was found and shoved under the sod. We'll pay his funeral expenses."

"And his passport, Monsieur?"

"Is not to be found," said Jonah. He felt in Shapely's breast-pocket, picked the passport out and slipped it into his own. "An unknown man is found dead. We can settle the details later. Don't you agree, Falcon?"

"Whole-heartedly," said Falcon. "France has done the justice that England could not do. A formal letter will be written, expressing our great admiration and grateful thanks. But what has that to do with the public? It is not for us to feed a sensational Press."

"Rely upon me," said the other. "The matter is closed."

* * * * *

They can do these things in France.

Except to make sure that the body was that of Tass, the remains that lay in the barn were not disturbed.

Shapely's body was officially 'found' the next day.

When Shapely failed to keep his appointment with Schurch, the latter 'got in touch with' the police. Schurch identified the body, which was then buried forthwith. Shapely's passport was found in a suit-case at his hotel. The British Consul was informed of what had occurred. And he reported to London ' the facts of the case.'

The following paragraph appeared in some of the papers in France.

STRANGER LOSES HIS LIFE IN THE PYRENEES.

M. F. C. Shapely of London is the latest victim of the folly of venturing alone into unfrequented parts of the Pyrenees. He had left his car, presumably to explore some valley. He lost his way and was overtaken by night. When found the following day, he was already dead. Exhaustion and exposure had done their work.

After a little, Shapely's obituary notice appeared in *The Times*.

By de Moulin's advice, the purchase-money was repaid to the peasant from whom Shapely had bought the land, and meadow and barn were presumed to belong to the State.

*　　*　　*　　*　　*

As we said goodbye to Falcon—

" Your hunch was right," said Jonah. " You always insisted that Tass was somewhere down here."

Falcon smiled.

" It didn't help much," he said. He turned to look up at the mountains, bathed in the evening sun. " Shapely was, of course, that, happily, very rare thing—the murderer born. His work was brilliant—you can't get away from that. But he had the misfortune to run into you and Captain Pleydell. Your powers of deduction were as brilliant, as had been his work."

" I can't allow that," said I. " We had at least three slices of the most astonishing luck—the train conversation, the lime and the meeting with Caratib."

" No man," said Falcon, " no man can make bricks without straw. But very few men I know would have made such bricks. To go back to Shapely. What was so very clever was the way in which he convinced us that he had conspired with Tass and that, if we could only find Tass, Tass would make some statement which let him, Shapely, in. And all the time, Tass was dead. Curious the way he lost his nerve at the last."

" Schurch's letter," said I, " must have been a terrible shock. It showed that the stars were against him, just as de Moulin said."

" They were—all along," said Falcon. " If you hadn't built up here . . . Oh, well, it's all over now. And I'm really more than thankful he died as he did. What things the French can get away with. Now if we had powers like that, what couldn't we do ? "

" I know," said Jonah. " I know. They've been very helpful here. But I have known cases . . ."

" Oh, yes," said Falcon. " You're right. The English Coroner's Inquest has saved a great many lives."

*   *   *   *   *

My sister was reading the paper.

" Hullo," she said. " Shapely's dead. ' In France, very suddenly.' "

" Oh, is he ? " said I. " Well, I decline to mourn him."

Daphne laid down the paper and looked at me.

" You were sure he had something to do with Old Rowley's death."

" I shall always think that," I said.

" You and Jonah suspected his alibi. I've seen you come in all thoughtful. Did you ever find anything out ? "

I shrugged my shoulders.

" Odds and ends," I said. " But it doesn't matter now."

My sister sat back in her chair and a hand went up to her mouth.

" ' In France, very suddenly.' And you were out all day . . . and Falcon was here."

" My sweet," I said, " now don't go getting ideas. And please don't talk like this to anyone else."

" I won't. But tell me this. Did you know he was dead ? "

" Yes."

" I may form my own conclusions ? "

" Of course. But please don't hand them on."

" You are provoking," said Daphne. " I'm sure you know everything."

" Indeed, I don't," said I.

" Well, you know a good deal." She moved to the arm of

my chair. " Tell me one thing, darling. Was it he that put out Old Rowley ? "

" That's my belief," said I. " Let's talk about something else."

Daphne laid her cheek against mine.

" I'm very discreet. I'll never say a word to a soul. But you were there, weren't you ? "

" I don't know where you mean."

" Oh, yes, you do. You and Jonah did it."

" I don't know what you mean. We never did anything."

" I mean, brought it home. And when he saw he was done, he took his life."

" That's near enough," I said. " Please leave it there."

" I will. Does Berry know ? "

" Something. But he won't talk."

" Oh, well," said Daphne. And then, " Poor Shapely. If his father had lived, it wouldn't have come to this."

She was probably right.

All the same, I could not forget the words I had heard a Judge use, when he was about to sentence a convict to death.

' In your hungry lust for gold, you had no pity for the victim whom you slew.'

Poor Tass.

CHAPTER XVIII

IN WHICH JONAH TELLS US THE TRUTH, AND BERRY HAS CAUSE
FOR COMPLAINT

THE garden was taking shape.

Before Jonah had left for England, the lawn had been levelled and sown ; and now, in mid-September, the grass was coming up well. Soon it could be rolled and then, very carefully, scythed. And in the spring the turf would be firm enough to employ a lawn-mower. With unremitting care, we should have a lawn worth having in two or three years.

Berry, Jonah and I had paved the paths ; this had been easy

work, but it gave us great satisfaction : men, I suppose, have a weakness for things that are built to last. All things considered, the display of flowers which Daphne and Jill had contrived, did them, I think, great credit : but they, of course, were looking to years to come. Ulysse had commended one Olim, as a builder of dry stone walls, and Olim worked with us for day after day. An elegant bay of dry wall about the base of that hazel, retaining a violet-bed . . . a curling flight of steps that led from a meadow below to a meadow above . . . fair standing about the grotto—we did them all. We could not have done them without him, for building without any mortar is expert work. Any fool can pile stones in a line to make a fence ; but to build a wall so well that it looks like masonry, to round your curves or to hang half a dozen steps—these things can be done by a craftsman, but not by anyone else. Olim had a wonderful eye ; but all his tools were three hammers of varying size and shape. He had a small ball of very ragged string, and now and again he would ask for a straight piece of wood. And with that equipment he did his beautiful work. But he had no part in the rock-garden. That was our own affair. Berry and I did that—in the sweat of our face. Daphne and Jill gave the orders : we carried them out.

The thing was this.

Long years ago, between the house and the *ruisseau*, there must have been a very slight fall of earth. All traces of this occasion had disappeared, and the turf was as good and as firm as anywhere else : but, at that point, the rise of the meadows had been broken : for some fourteen feet the ground rose much more gently and then stood up in a little cliff of turf, as though to regain all at once the height it had lost. This little sloping dip was roughly square and, since it lay close to the *ruisseau*, it was easy to school some water to tumble along its length. In the course of the excavation behind the house, some substantial rocks had been found ; these had been carefully saved and carried along to the dip ; so there we had our site and material. All that we had to do was so to arrange the rocks that the dip should become the garden which Daphne and Jill desired. All. The girls were merciless. It was the Waterloo balusters over again. The slope was not so steep, but some of the rocks must have weighed three times what the balusters weighed. We managed with levers and wedges. So perhaps Stonehenge was built. Twice we had to call upon peasants, working in neighbouring fields. It was a question of man-power, and nothing else. But exacting as was the labour, we worked six hours a day with grateful hearts. Munich was on.

Each evening we spoke with Jonah . . .

When the rocks were all in order, we settled the line of the rill ; and when that work was done, we piped the water in and we piped it out. Daphne and Jill were ravished. Here they would plant such a garden as never was seen. Then they withdrew to the house, for the stuffs for the curtains had come. But Berry and I had our hands full. Creepers had to be planted at the foot of Hadrian's Wall ; wistaria shoots, the length of the terrace walls ; daffodil bulbs in the meadows ; planes by the side of the *ruisseau* ; firs in the scarecrow field . . .

And then, on October the fifth, my cousin, Jonah, returned.

I shall always remember that night in the library.

Daphne and Jill had retired, and the logs, which had been flaring, had sunk to a winking glow.

" For better or for worse," said Jonah, " the date of the coming deluge has been postponed. For six months or a year. I'm inclined to think for a year. The Boche has always meant business : but this time the business he means is going to be very big. We're going to have our backs to the wall as never before."

" And we ? "

Jonah looked down.

" Our services are not required. The war to come is to be a young man's war."

" But——"

" I said it all," said Jonah. " I said it very loud and clear. I indicated the obvious. But all in vain. And then, at last, Roderick appeared. He dined with me on Sunday at Cleveland Row." He paused there, to set a match to his pipe. " You won't expect me to tell you all he said. But I like to think that he didn't leave anything out. I mean that. He says he can bear being starved, because he has always been starved ; but what's breaking his heart is this—that, because his news is bad, it is considered unfit for human consumption and, apparently, thrown away. Well, that's all right with fish. But this isn't fish. It's the truth—from Germany."

" Great God ! " said Berry. " And Roderick, too. What the devil's the matter with people ? "

Jonah leaned forward.

" A disease called ' wishful thinking.' Things are going so well that, though they are shown the spanner, they decline to contemplate the possibility of its being thrown into the works. Spanner ? Monkey-wrench. And it damned near went in last month."

" Can he help us ? " said I.

" Not now. He's tied and bound—with the chain of other men's sins. But his hour is certain to come. It will come with the crash. Then they will turn to him, and he will make his own terms. In that case, I shall go back and he will look after you. Berry, he says, must stay here, because he has a way with the French. That is perfectly true. Berry changes hats with the Mayor, while we are shaking hands."

" And in the meantime ? "

" We are to do our utmost to make the Entente a real thing. He was very pleased when I told him about the house. ' Nothing could have been better. You have paid well for your land, you've employed a lot of labour ; better still, you've worked with the men and, if I know you, you've made a lot of good friends. Would you like to build another ? Say, Orleans way ? ' I said no, we couldn't do that, but I've ordered a cinema-van and a packet of films. ' The King and Queen in Paris ' and less emotional stuff. If we tour the Department, and Berry would lecture a bit . . . I mean, it's better than nothing, and the sands are running out."

* * * * *

The curtains were up. The rooms were secured against the winter blasts. And all was very well. The servants were content with their lot. Eugène was insane about the electric range. Thérèse would let no washing go out of the house. The heating worked like a dream. Madame Martigny's clock kept beautiful time. The chimneys drew to perfection. The daffodil bulbs went in. The Waterloo balusters turned from black to gray. I think we were, all of us, fitter than we had ever been. Our ivory tower had proved an immense success.

Four nights a week we took out the cinema-van. Three of us always went with it : Daphne and Jill took it in turns to come. We always went by appointment—each time to a different place. Very soon we had a waiting-list. We had to limit our range to seventy miles, but people beyond that radius used to come in. We never advertised, but the word went round. As commentator or *compère*, Berry was simply superb. On the nights when he did not go, I tried to use his thunder and take his place. The enthusiasm was marked, wherever we went, and the poor people crowded about us, shaking hands and begging us to return. We never went to a town, but only to villages. Once I found that money was being taken. I was in charge that night and I waited until the show was about to begin. Then I rose and said that there had been a mistake, that this entertainment was free and that it would not take place until every penny paid had been handed back. It was handed back under my eyes, while gramophone records were played. We were not invited to drink with the Mayor that night, but word went round and the English stock went·up.

Any way we had a good time.

* * * * *

Berry was writing his reminiscences.

" Listen to this," he said. " D'you think it's all right ? "

I laid down my pen.

" Look here," I said. " You'll simply have to sit in the morning room. If you're going on like this, I cannot possibly work. I've been here for nearly two hours, and I've written a page and a half."

" Just this one," said Berry. " I want your expert advice."

" Well, this is the last. I have to have a table, but you can lie on your back in any room in the house. Besides, you don't look things up. I must work in here, for I need the books."

" I must work here," said Berry. " I need the atmosphere."

" Then work in silence, as I do. The only peace I get is when you're out with the van."

"Now don't be ungracious," said Berry, "or I shan't give you any ideas. Now listen to this.

"*I well remember the General Election of ——. Both in its conduct and its results, it presented what was probably the finest argument for dictatorship that the world has ever seen. That day were set before the English, the blessing and the curse. They chose the curse—thanks to the false pretences made by the winning side. For months before the day, a rising flood of misrepresentation had been skilfully directed into the system which had been surreptitiously prepared. The truth was swamped. Evil begets evil. Four years later, the Cabinet included more than one member who would not have qualified for the reference traditionally accorded to the incompetent charwoman.*"

I fingered my chin.

"It's on the warm side," I said. "If you leave out the date of the election . . ."

"But that would spoil it," said Berry.

"Well, if you don't," said I, "the publisher will." I picked up my pen. "Never mind. And now——"

"Wait a minute," said Berry. "Then, just to ease the tension, I take the reader back to Montmartre."

I covered my face. Berry's memories of Montmartre were—well, arresting.

"First, I thought I'd put in a short monograph on the nomenclature of the cafés. That'll have to wait, for I can't remember them all."

"I shouldn't try," said I.

"Don't be silly," said Berry. "Besides, it's never been done."

"It never will be," said I. "By you or anyone else."

Berry frowned.

"The omission must be repaired. Who knows what history lies behind those names. One, I remember, was called *The Seat of the Clergyman's Trousers.* Well, there must have been some reason for that."

"No doubt," said I. "But I tremble to think what it was. And if you propose to indulge your powers of surmise . . ."

"After the monograph," said Berry, "I return for a moment to London.

"*From time to time, in London, efforts were made to capture the spirit and manners of Montmartre. Such an endeavour was commendable, but hopeless. Naturally reserved, the English must drink to get going. The French require no such stimulus. They can become uproarious over a grenadine. Still, with the aid of liquor the old —— in —— Street did contrive to reproduce some of the less attractive features of the cafés of the Latin Quarter. It says much for the conduct of this establishment that, while it was condemned by the kill-joys, it was approved by the police. As a house of call, shortly before mid-night, it did more than serve its turn ; and I must confess that I find it engaging to remark how many of its habitués have made good, as pillars of Church or State. There were occasions, such as ' Boatrace Night,' when the clientèle unbent, and I have had the privilege of seeing a future Bishop follow a future Cabinet Minister into the dock at Marlborough Street Police Court as a result. The point is that youth was served. But my most elevating memory of the ——, was the arrival in its hall of a German and his wife, who, attracted by its name, had decided to stay there during their English holiday. It is, of course, just possible that before now some English Vicar's Warden has been set down with his family and luggage at the doors of* The Red Nose *in Montmartre, but I cannot believe that his welcome was more enthusiastic than that accorded to two of the most objectionable Teutons that I have ever seen. While their luggage was being unpacked, a* table d'hôte *was hastily improvised and ten minutes later four of us took our seats, attired in the changes of raiment the man and his wife had brought. It takes a lot to put a Boche off his food. . . . They looked pretty hard at me—in a morning coat and plus-fours and a celluloid dickey and a pair of banana boots ; but when their eyes settled on Sibyl, who was wearing a Mannheim model as no Mannheim model was ever meant to be worn, the woman endeavoured to rise and the man wrung his soup from his beard with a gesture I shall never forget. . . . The things they said about England. But then, you see, on arrival they should not have spat in the hall. One of my collaborators is now a member of the House Committee at* The

Athenœum ; but I sometimes wonder if his something ponderous responsibilities afford him one tenth of the pleasure which that one did. After all, as the poet says, ' One crowded hour without a name Is worth an age of public life.' "

" Very good indeed," said I. " I suppose you'll get someone to print it. You'll have to cut out that bit about Marlborough Street."

" That just shows," said Berry, " how much you know. Why, everyone will be asking which of the Lords Spiritual it is. And *The Glass* will have an article—THOU ART THE MAN. I tell you, the public will eat it."

" The Church and State won't," said I. " And publishers have to live."

" The trouble with you," said Berry, " is that you have lost what sense of proportion you had. Just to show you what I mean, I'm going to read you my appreciation of The League of Nations."

He did so faithfully.

When he had finished, I took a stroll on the terrace, to let my emotions cool down. I knew of no case in which the submission of a manuscript had constituted the publication of a libel ; but I could see no reason why it should not. If it did . . .

* * * * *

We spent Christmas and the New Year in England, as we had done before. But, happy as everyone made us, the world seemed gross after Gracedieu, and we were relieved to return to the meadows and hanging forests and the unspoiled beauty that waited upon the topless hills.

As Berry had foretold, the change of scene was effected in less than nineteen hours, and the great cry of London seemed scarce to have died away, when I heard the song of the Columbine down in the valley below.

That night we all went to bed early, but we had brought back some new films, and the following evening we showed them off at Lescar, a short eight miles from Pau.

Spring came in in glory. Standing on the terrace one morning at seven o'clock, I watched the miracle. The sun was lacing with splendour a lovely world. Beneath his wand, the emerald pile of the meadows was standing up, pale green and gilt was stealing into the mountain's cloaks, the diamond snows were trembling against the blue. Magic was being made before my eyes.

A footfall, and Jill was beside me, finger to lip.

Then she slid her arm through mine, and the two of us stood in silence before a royalty of ritual that Milton might have sung. Only an organ-voice could have caught its majesty and rendered unto mankind a thing that was God's.

When at last we turned away—

" And all this for nothing," said Jill. " Boy, you know, we're so many millionaires."

To my mind we were far richer than anyone that I knew.

Then the daffodils which we had planted began to peer . . .

By now the lawn was being mown twice a week, and all the pains which Daphne and Jill had taken, began to shew forth a promise for which they had hardly hoped. It was clear that the garden would be a lovely sight. The creepers were taking hold of the base of Hadrian's Wall, undismayed by the height of the bastion they were to clothe ; and all that we had planted was finding its pretty feet. Still, because they were young, all had to be cosseted, and every hour we could spare went into ' the property.'

June came in, and spring began to pass into summer—I think, the fairest transition I ever saw.

* * * * *

" Well, why not do it ? " said Berry. " Now is the time. It'll take us two full days. We leave on Tuesday morning and get back on Wednesday night. We can go to Carcassonne in the autumn. That'll need three."

" All right, I'll see Eugène," said Daphne. " Will you telephone to Goursy and take the rooms ? "

" Yes, he will," said Berry. " I've got to translate some slugs. I'm going to weigh them this time. If it takes three quarters of an hour to pass two pounds of slugs into Paradise, how many years will it take to clear Evergreen ? You know they concentrate on this place. The order has gone out to rally at Gracedieu. There are millions still on the way. But they'd all turn round and go back, if they knew what was waiting for them. Fancy taking a couple of months to crawl to your doom. Why the 'nine o'clock walk' isn't in it." He rose to his feet. "Nine o'clock. It always used to be eight. Another sign of decadence. Never mind. What'll you bet I don't get three pounds to-night? Of course, if you'd rather I didn't . . ."

"Oh, no," said my sister, quickly. "It's got to be done. But I do so wish it hadn't."

"It won't," said Berry, "one day. Every night I turn two round and tell them to make their way back and say what they've seen. Between propaganda and attrition, I think the rush should subside in two or three years."

As the door closed behind him—

"Tuesday then," said Daphne. "I do hope the weather holds."

"Ulysse says it will," said I. "And he's always right."

To the east of us lay four passes—the Col de Fer and his fellows, cheek by jowl. We proposed to drive over two and to sleep the night between the second and third : then we planned to drive over the third and fourth and so return to Lally by way of the plain. It was the fairest season at which to make such a run, for the snows were over and gone and the uplands would be in flower ; and though, of course, we could have covered the ground in one day, that would have meant that we had no time to linger ; yet a journey so handsome as that should never be rushed.

So I took the rooms at Goursy for Tuesday night, and early that day we set out, with luncheon for Tuesday and Wednesday bestowed in the back of the cars. Carson made one of us, for, though we all could drive, neither Berry nor Daphne nor Jill were accustomed to roads like these ; and Jonah and I would be glad of some relief, for the way we were going was long and the man at the wheel must keep his eyes on the road. Sometimes I drove the Andret and sometimes I drove the Rolls, and sometimes I did not drive, but took my rest. Indeed, we kept no places, but constantly changed our seats, for the cars kept close together the whole of the time. And that was, of course, how it happened.

At five o'clock on Wednesday, we slipped down the eastern slopes of the exquisite Col des Pins after two flawless days on the top of the world.   Each day we had broken our fast five thousand or more feet up.   Each day we had stopped and gone strolling, to prove the promise of some view-point or taste the sweet of some dell.   In a word, we had let time slip and had gone as we pleased.   The forests through which we had climbed ; the thunderous falls of water that wet the cars with their spray ; the hamlets, looking like toys, three thousand feet below our incredulous eyes ; the peerless peaks, wearing their snow like jewels instead of garments ; above all, the flower-starred meadows, rising and falling and scenting the scented air—all these we had enjoyed at our leisure for two long, glorious days. And not only at our leisure, but all to ourselves.   What is called ' the tourist season ' had not begun.   I never remember an excursion of which I had so much.

As we swung into Castelet—

" Do they look like stopping ? " I said.

Jill slewed herself round, to keep an eye on the Rolls.

After a moment—

" No, they're coming," she said.

She and I were alone in the Andret ; Berry had left us nearly an hour before, " for," he said, " my hams are not what they were, and, after two days, I'd rather have English coachwork to help them out."   The truth was, of course, that he was drowsy, and for one who desired to sleep, the back of the Andret was less convenient than even the front of the Rolls.

I turned to the left and on to the road to Pau.

Once I was sure they were coming, I let the Andret out.   We had eighty miles to cover, and if we ' popped along,' we should be back at Gracedieu before night fell.   The Rolls, of course, could do ninety ; still, we could do seventy-five.

" Boy," said Jill quietly, " all this is too good to be true. We've no right to be so happy in such a world."

" Damn it," I said, " we've had our whack of misfortune.   For year after year it pursued us.   It never let up at all, till we came out here."

" I know.   We'd a rotten time.   But look at the last two days."

s

"A fellow called Herrick," said I, "once gave some damned good advice."

"You're an Epicure," said Jill. "Or isn't that what I mean?"

"It's near enough, sweetheart. But you must admit that gathering rosebuds is rather fun. And if you gather the right ones, they never fade."

"That's quite true," said Jill. "And they keep their scent. Jars of *pot-pourri*. And when everything is hellish, you just go and take off the lid."

"That's how I see it," I said. "And, taking it by and large, we've got quite a lot of jars. All full of stuff worth having, that can't be pinched. We're living in difficult times, and he's a wise fellow who knows what the following day will bring forth; but I often think that, if one day, I'm shoved up against a wall, I'll be able to laugh in the face of the firing squad. They can take my fortune and they can take my life: but they can't take my jars of *pot-pourri* . . ."

"What dreadful things you do think of. But these two days have been so full, they'll have to have a jar of their own. Darling Boy, will you mind if I go to sleep? Just for five minutes? It's only the pace we're going, after the mountain air."

She laid her head on my shoulder, as she had so often done. . . .

Not until we had passed through Pau, did she open her eyes.

I must say, we came very well. We entered Gracedieu's drive at half past seven o'clock.

As I brought the car to rest on the apron, Thérèse and Felix were descending the last of the ninety-three steps. . . .

Jill and I emerged from opposite sides of the car.

"Miladi has enjoyed her excursion?"

"Thérèse, it was wonderful. The very loveliest thing. You'll have to come next time."

"Miladi is kindness itself, but I have had a great time. I have cut out Miladi's step-ins. They will look ravishing."

Here the Rolls slid alongside, and Felix opened her door.

"My God," said Jonah, "that little fellow can move. Carson had his work cut out to keep on your tail."

With that, he followed my sister out of the Rolls.

"And where is Monsieur?" said Thérèse.

There was a horror-struck silence.

Daphne looked wildly round.

" But isn't he here ? " she said faintly, " I thought he was in the Andret."

" He said," said I, " he was going to ride in the Rolls."

" God in heaven," said Jonah. " When was the last time we stopped ? "

We all knew the answer to that. It was some twelve miles from Castelet, up on the Col des Pins.

*   *   *   *   *

At half past eleven that night, four miles beyond Castelet, a familiar figure stepped into our headlight's beam.

" At last," murmured Jonah, and brought the car to rest.

Carson and I alighted. The air was more than fresh, and Carson had with him Berry's camel-hair coat.

No one said anything.

In silence Berry turned his back upon Carson and put out his arms. Tenderly Carson slid him into his coat.

As Berry buttoned it up—

" Should you desire," he said, " to turn your automobile, there's a spot higher up the mountain conducive to such a manoeuvre. I passed it—some years ago. Funny how these trifles stick in your mind . . . But then I was always observant."

With a fearful effort I maintained my gravity.

" We have here," I said, " a collation. If you'd like to start right away, Jonah and Carson will leave us and turn the car, and——"

" Not on your life," said Berry, getting into the Rolls. " I'm through with treachery. They might lose their way or something. And strangely enough, I have an urge to sit down. It's very peculiar. I've only been on my feet for seven hours. Marvellous dews, they have here. Two minutes after sundown the whole of this pass is drenched. Of course you *can* sit down. You *can* sit down in a basin which you have previously filled : but I've always understood that, unless you've a change of raiment, such action is apt to be productive of most distressing results. I did think of taking off my trousers and relaxing for a minute or two ; but I felt the bears mightn't get it, so I hung from a branch, instead. I believe that's very healthy. They say it lengthens the arms."

We were under way now, but I dared not trust my voice. Berry proceeded quietly.

" Of course you won't be forgiven. I've seen to that. You won't even be admitted. I've put St. Peter wise. I've laid the facts before him. A blasted, cold-blooded outrage—that's what it was. Ferdinand and Isabella aren't in it." He regarded my open cigarette-case. " Perhaps, I will. I've gone off smoking lately. Astonishing how easy it is, when you've got no cigarettes." He took a cigarette and accepted a light. " I've given up food, too, really."

" We haven't," said I. " We haven't eaten since lunch."

" If I had my way," said Berry, " you wouldn't eat for a month. That'd learn you to take out your betters and leave them in desert places without a word."

" You declared," said I, " you were going to change to the Rolls. When I heard them shut their doors, of course I assumed you'd done it. And as I was leading the way, I started off. And the Rolls followed on."

" There is," said Berry, " no need to tell me that. I left the car, to round a small eminence or knoll, because I surmised that such perambulation would afford me the prospect I desired. In this, my judgment was good. Before me, I found a very remarkable view. This took me some time to observe, because the hag I protect had seen fit to alter the focus of my binocular—a vile and selfish practice which I have, too often, condemned. On my return to the road, I supposed at first that I had mistaken my way, and that I had struck the thoroughfare either above or below where the cars had stood. Yet, the place seemed familiar ; and upon closer inspection I perceived the very beautiful specimen of a decayed sheep's head which I had remembered observing, as I had emerged from the car. In a state bordering upon frenzy, I ran to the nearest brink, from which I knew I could see the road below ; and there, about two miles distant, I saw two cars. With shaking hands, I employed the binocular—only to make assurance obscenely sure. Of course I shouted. I screamed. I made arresting gestures—some of which, I fear, the bears may have misinterpreted. I might as well have spat at the moon. Returning to the binocular, I had the infinite privilege of watching the cars disappear. . . .

"The next few minutes I frankly prefer to forget. Indeed, I have reason to believe that I had a slight mental seizure, for, when I came to, I was running—a procedure, as you will agree, even more vain and unprofitable than that of addressing companions some three miles off. Then I practised wishful thinking. I convinced myself that my absence could not long remain undetected. My presence would be demanded. You would want some money to pay for a drink. Jill would want to know if I had remembered to efface what some fowl of the air had done to the Bunker's Hill totem-poles. Daphne would want to know if I felt my throat. I mean, that's been going on hourly for forty years. . . . So I started working out mileage and watched the clock. And then at last I knew that Fate had put a spoke in my wheel. For once in my life, no demands would be made upon me. For once in my life, I was to be left in peace, and it would be left to my servants, nearly a hundred miles distant, to notice the absence of their lord. Without prejudice, am I right ? "

" I think Thérèse was the first. But——"

" There you are," said Berry. " The widow's mite. But for that faithful soul——"

" Don't be absurd," said I. " Jill and I assumed you were in the Rolls. Daphne and Jonah assumed you were in the Andret. Thérèse——"

" — observed my absence," said Berry. " If only Thérèse had been here, I should not have been marooned in a desert place. You're a poisonous lot of jackals—that's what you are. What harm have I ever done you ? And not a human being, much less a vehicle. The blasted world to myself. I never felt so utterly gregarious. If I'd seen a verminous nigger, I'd have put my arms round his neck. And then night fell. Damned well fell. I saw it. And that was the last thing I did see—till moonrise, at half past ten. Talk about darkness . . . I was afraid to move. You know, it isn't funny—being marooned by night on the edge of a bottomless pit. The natural lust for movement becomes less marked. At last I entered the forest, in the hope of finding a staff, with which I could tap what I hoped was the ground before me, as blind men do. . . ." He sighed. " The coppice in question seemed to be out of staves. Plenty of roots, you know. I—found them all right : but, as I kept on pointing out, I wanted something detached. And then, at last, I fell over something that moved. . . . I returned to the road with a branch which must have weighed seventy pounds, but, you know, you soon get tired of handling a cane like that. Besides, it wanted lopping. A lot of minor branches, so to speak, confused the issue : and when I'd tripped over them twice, I screamed like a madman and cast it into the draught. At least, I thought I had, but I never heard it fall, so I thought I must have made a mistake. And then, two minutes later, I heard a very faint crash. . . . You know, that sort of thing is bad for the heart. After that, I proceeded in the ditch. I confess I've known better going, but at least I ran no risk of walking over the edge. Culverts, of course, don't count. If you strike one of them, you only fall thirty feet. At the foot of the second one I found myself screaming aloud. I thought of my bath and the soapniche, of the pleasant change and a cocktail with my back to the fire, and then one of Eugène's dinners . . . I suppose I'm in my right mind. I've had so many brain-storms, I don't know what to think."

Here the road bellied out, and Jonah, with Carson to guide him, began to turn the car.

" We're all very sorry," said I. " But it was nobody's fault. So long as you haven't caught cold. . . . And now what about a snack ? We've some soup in a thermos-flask, and two of Eugène's pâtés, and beer and champagne on ice."

" A glass of champagne," said Berry, " would help me up. Supposing we stopped about here. But I won't get out of the car. How much champagne have you got ? "

" Three bottles," said I. " Of the Roederer '21."

" Only three bottles ? " said Berry. " That was very short-sighted. Well, you and Jonah and Carson will have to get home on beer."

In fact, we got home on brandy—at half past four.

As we alighted on the apron, Daphne, Jill and Thérèse appeared at the head of the steps.

" They must be in heaven," said Berry. " Ring for the lift."

" There's a great gulf fixed," said I, " of ninety-three steps."

Berry leapt into the air and began to run down the drive.

" I'm a nymph," he yelled. " They caught me up in the mountains. They've got designs upon me. Where's Uncle Pan ? "

Daphne and Jill were scathing ; but I had a feeling that Herrick would have approved.

CHAPTER XIX

IN WHICH WE GAIN A SPARE ROOM, AND JILL TURNS THE FOUNTAIN OFF

JUNE slid into July, and Lally was full.

Visitors drank the waters and strolled up the road to Besse : the little Casino was crowded—sometimes a slant of its music would reach our ears. All day long, on the farther side of the valley, cars snaked up to Lally and on to the Col de Fer. None of the world of fashion were staying in Lally itself : many, of course, passed through, but those who stayed were quiet men and women of the upper shop-keeping class.

Berry had a word with the Mayor—our very good friend. And very soon word went round that on the Fourteenth of July, the terrace and the gardens of Gracedieu would be open to visitors from two o'clock until five.

That day the flags flew from the terrace, the Union Jack and the Tricolour, hoisted at either end, lazily floating in the sunshine which filled a cloudless sky.

At noon we drove out for a picnic, and Carson, Thérèse and Eugène were left in charge.

We passed through Cluny and Jules, climbed three thousand feet and lunched at the foot of the famous Pic des Loups. Here was meadow and beechwood and, if I may be believed, a lazy stream—that might have come out of the English countryside. We made good friends with a herdsman, aged sixty-five. He had been born at Jules and had never been further than Nareth, except to fight. Yet he was well-informed and his judgment was good. What is almost more to the point, he was clearly content with his lot. His words have stuck in my mind.

" I would not change places, Monsieur, with any man that I know. Two years ago my brother left me his fortune—more than enough to have bought a substantial farm. But how would that profit me ? I earn a decent living, I have my cottage at Jules and an excellent wife. Be sure, we talked it over ; but we did not think that we could improve our portion. I think much unhappiness comes to people who strive to do that. Consider only the Boche. He has a fat country, but he is not content. He desires to rob his neighbours and rule what is theirs. The maggot of domination has eaten into his brain. And if he gained his end—which he will not do—would he be any happier ? I do not think so, Monsieur. If I am wrong, and he would, then he must be put to death. Such men endanger the well-being of other folk."

We were back at Gracedieu that evening at half past six. Carson's report afforded us very great pleasure.

" We closed the house at one, sir—shut all the ground-floor shutters : we thought it best. And sharp at two I went down to open the gates. There were forty waiting there, and I think we had more than five hundred during the afternoon. The peasants came in, as well as the visitors ; but every one had put on his Sunday best. They were all of them most respectful : I'm sure not a flower was picked. They could teach us something there. They left no litter at all, and the Mayor had ordered ' No smoking,' so they threw down their cigarettes before they entered the drive. No one set foot on the lawn, but I think they liked the fountain best of all. Kept on coming back to that. And the ladies loved the grotto ; but the men just raved about the terrace—as well they might. A lot of the Besse people came. Ulysse was there, and Olim, and Pernot and Madame Pernot and both the Mayors. Thérèse and Eugène—I've never seen them so pleased, and every one was laughing and shaking hands. And nobody went away without saying goodbye, and every one asked us to thank you for letting them come. The Mayors stayed on, as arranged, and we took them over the house. They were very pleased about

that, and I can't begin to tell you the things they said.   But
Therèse will do that, Madam."

Remembering what Joseph had told us, that night we opened
all shutters and turned on every light.   Then Jill and Jonah and
I drove round through Lally and on to the Nareth road.

The highway was like a fair.   All Lally was out, and car after
car, which was passing, had come to rest.   And when I saw
Gracedieu lit up, I was not surprised.   Two crow's miles away,
above and beyond the gulf which lay between, a fairy castle
seemed to be hung in the air.   I could not believe that we lived
there.   It was too good to be true.

*   *   *   *   *

Jonah left for London the following night.

From that time on, he spoke with us three times a week; but
he could not say all that he would on the telephone.

Besse held its *fête-champêtre* on August the sixth.   (This is a
pretty custom.   The French peasant works very hard, but on
one day in every year his village keeps holiday.   It is always a
summer day, when men and girls can dance on the village green.
And all make merry that day, from dawn to dusk.   Many
peasants wear ' national dress ' : this is not made to-day, but is
handed from mother to daughter and father to son.)   At nine
o'clock that day representatives came to ask us to come to the
fête.   They brought two bouquets of flowers for Daphne and Jill.
We asked them on to the terrace, and there the fiddlers struck up,
while the others danced.   In their black and white and scarlet,
they made the bravest show.   And that afternoon, of course,
we attended the *fête*.

That evening brought a letter from Jonah.

August 4th.

Dear Boy,

*It won't be long now.   Yesterday one of our ' statesmen '
declared, ' War to-day is not only not inevitable but is unlikely.
The Government have good reason for saying that.'   Both statements are false.   Roderick would like you to do liaison in France.
That means that you will go out with the first lot they send.   I'm
afraid it's the best we can do.   For every reason, Berry must stay*

*where he is, as must Daphne and Jill.   Roderick insists upon
that, and I know he's right.   For God's sake, ram this home.   A
man is as old as he feels, till it comes to the test.   He'd that go
of bronchitis in London, and after that show in the mountains
he was in bed for two days.   He might, perhaps, get a job of
filling up forms ; but a close-up of things without any active job
would send him out of his mind.   I sometimes think that everyone
here is insane.   They are obsessed with the idea that the German
people is a bullock propelled by a Nazi goad.   Bullock ?   Gorilla.
Goad ?   A dangling gobbet of human flesh.   One day, perhaps
they will learn : but Baldwin's Soothing Syrup has got a hell of
a grip.   My work may lie here for the present.   Thousands of
German spies are being comforted here as refugees.   What a mercy
White Ladies is safe !   If we had tried to hang on, the place
would have gone.   Conceive evacuees in those time-honoured
rooms.   But now it is safe—except, of course, from the air.   I'll
let you know when to leave, but I think I should send your big
baggage down to the cloak-room at Pau.   If I had to bet, I'd say
the end of August.   But nothing can stop it this time.   I'll lay
five million pounds that before September is old, we shall be at
war.*

Yours ever,
Jonah.

I had a tussle with Berry, but in the end he gave way.   I think
that he wrote to Roderick and I think that Roderick wrote back.
And Roderick was no traitor.   He had a little girl, and she had
been blind from birth.   To say that he worshipped her means
nothing at all.   But he would have slain that child, if that
would have profited England.   And that, without hesitation.
So when Roderick said that Berry and Jill and Daphne must stay
where they were. . . .

Three gorgeous weeks went by, and all of us worked in the
garden all day long.   Manual labour, we found, relieved the
mind.   And at night we went out with the van, and gave
our show.

And then, on the last day of August, Jonah talked to Daphne,
and then asked to speak to me.

" That you, Jonah ? " I said.

"It is. I should leave to-morrow. I don't like the look of things, and you don't want to get stuck."

"Without fail," said I, for Daphne was by my side.

*   *   *   *   *

Carson, of course, was with Jonah, and I had ordered a taxi for eight o'clock. That would give me plenty of time. My train did not leave Pau until ten that night.

I was in my bedroom at five, frowning upon the suitcases, which had already been packed, and wondering how to make room for three or four books, when the door was whipped open and shut, and there was Jill standing against it, with a stricken look in her eyes.

"Daphne's told me," she breathed. "First Jonah, and now you, Boy. And I thought—I believed we were going to be happy here."

"So we are, sweetheart." I put my arm about her, drew her into a chair and then kneeled down by her side. "These things happen, you know. But we're going to finish it this time. And then, for the rest of our lives——"

"I've told myself all that, but it doesn't help. We went from five to six, and from six to nine. And then we came back to six, and then to five. But we were the original five, and that tempered the wind. And the old, old days came back, as if they'd been waiting for us. And now . . ."

Her great, gray eyes were brimming, and she put up an arm, like a child, to hide her tears.

As I had done since she was two, I picked her up in my arms and held her close.

Then I told her the fairy-tale which she and I had shared for so many years, the tale I had always told her whenever she cried.

The absurdity of the position made her smile. Jill looked twenty-five, but she was older than that.

She wiped her tears away, and laid her cheek against mine.

"See how I need you," she said. "That's always been our secret."

Feeling rather as robbers feel—

"I can't help it," I said wildly. "Sacrilegist or no, when I come back on leave, will you marry me, Jill beloved, my blessed queen ? "

She sat up at that. Then she took my head in her hands.

" Of course. I'd love to. I've been longing for you to say that for more than a year. What's a sacrilegist ? "

Then her arms went round my neck, and I kissed her beautiful lips. . . .

As we were going downstairs—

" I don't know how to tell them," I said.

" You silly darling," said Jill.

She danced before me into the library.

" We're going to have a spare room," she cried. " Boy's going to share mine."

* * * * *

We were married very quietly in Pau, on New Years' Eve. Jonah was my best man, and Berry gave Jill away. Our honeymoon was spent at Gracedieu. The great thing was we were all together again. After five glorious days, Jonah and I withdrew, he to an unknown destination and I to the north of France. We were to do our best to get leave again in July—July, 1940. Even Roderick, for all his wisdom, never foresaw that horror—the fall of France.

* * * * *

Berry wrote to me from Oporto.

I was lying in Hertfordshire, with a splintered knee.

June 25th, 1940.

DEAR BOY,

Sic transit gloria mundi. *White Ladies, and now Gracedieu. I suppose one survives these things. We are all three safe and well—in body, if not in mind. Myself, I still feel dazed, and Daphne is very quiet. Your darling keeps us going, but then she is not of this world.*

Our departure was of the stuff of which nightmares are made. Eugène cursing his country and clinging to Daphne's knees. Thérése—a Medusa in tears. The poor people swarming about us, catching and kissing our hands and imploring us not to go. Of that, there was no question ; but the mayor sent up a message by dead of night. '*Leave immediately, Monsieur. I know what I know. Your names are high on the list. You have done too much good.*' *That drive to the frontier! Jill drove and I sat beside her, pistol in hand. I never knew what a bend in the road would bring forth. The girls stood up very well to a very exacting time. One goes on somehow, but I am too old for these things. France. Sixty million decent souls betrayed by a handful of maggots—Judases all. Foch must be whirling round and round in his grave. There's a special hell for traitors—so Dante says. If I get nothing better, let me be a stoker there. Those poor, bewildered peasants, with the tears running down their cheeks.* '*Nous avons été vendus, Madame.*' *I think that terrible cry will always ring in my ears.*

We have next to nothing with us. There was no room and no time. But Portugal is kindness itself, from bottom to top.

Your cable has just arrived, in reply to mine.

Rest assured, I will do as you say—as Roderick says.

'*Daphne and Jill are not to return to England.*' *Well and good. Yet we are not to stay here for more than two or three months. I see the wisdom of that, for, if anything were to happen, we shouldn't have time to get out. Whither, then? I wish to God you'd get well and come out and take my place. Jill is mad to be with you, but makes an obedient wife. I tell her you will be invalided and then will come to her. I see I've never said how sorry I am. The knee, too. It must have been damned painful. That strip of coast was always unhealthy for you. Remember when the cab-horse kicked you, years ago, at Boulogne?*

Well, there we are. I never thought to write a letter like this. But then I never thought to see a lot that I've seen and do a lot that I've done in the last eight days. Days? Years. The last week seems like a life-time, and that's the truth.

We shall win, of course. You can't weight the English out. But the fall of France will add two years to the war. More, if Japan comes in. It's dreadful to stand aside, but if they won't use me in England, it's better to be away. A close-up with my hands in my pockets would send me mad. I will not go to America, come what may. But if I can contrive to get East, I might pick up something there. But I won't leave Daphne and Jill, unless and until you come.

I find it hard to look at things as I should. The personal element is obtrusive.   After all, we did build Gracedieu, to be our home. And, wonderful as the girls were, there was a look in their eyes which I shall never forget.   The last thing Jill did was to turn the fountain off.   ' Put out the light, and then put out the light.' And yet I have a feeling that we shall see it again . . . and that one day we shall stand upon the terrace and once more lift up our eyes unto the hills.

Well, here we go.

BERRY.

THE END

NOVELS BY DORNFORD YATES

BERRY AND CO.
" Berry is one of Heaven's best gifts to man."—*News Chronicle.*

JONAH AND CO.
" Mirth-provoking upon every page."—*Irish Times.*

ADÈLE AND CO.
" It is, indeed, great fun all the way."—*Daily Telegraph.*

AND BERRY CAME TOO
" Mr. Yates describes as well as ever the hair-raising adventures and idiotic situations in which the *Pleydell* family are embroiled. I could go on reading about them for a very long time."—*Punch.*

THE BROTHER OF DAPHNE
" Like a cream puff—very light, but vastly delectable."—*Glasgow Herald.*

THE COURTS OF IDLENESS
" To give Mr. Yates his due, he is expert in light banter. He can be strongly recommended to anyone who thinks that the British take themselves too seriously."—*Punch.*

ANTHONY LYVEDEN
" Behind Mr. Yates's grace of style is real power. Successive scenes of real comedy and tragedy show an equal mastery."—*Sheffield Independent.*

VALERIE FRENCH
" An unusual story marked by considerable powers of imagination."—*Liverpool Post.*

AND FIVE WERE FOOLISH
" The book deserves a host of readers. Extraordinarily powerful and intriguing."—*Daily Telegraph.*

AS OTHER MEN ARE
" Be sure of this, there is a ' Yates ' touch, an unexpected vivid phrase, a wonderful adjective, that gives colour to page after page."—*The Sketch.*

THE STOLEN MARCH
" The author is in his most humorous vein, the dialogue is brilliantly witty and clever, and humorous happenings and situations abound."—*Time and Tide.*

MAIDEN STAKES
" Mr. Yates is an extraordinarily pleasant novelist. His flair for dramatic thrills and clever dialogue is extraordinary."—*Liverpool Courier.*

BLIND CORNER
" There is not a dull page in the book."—*The Times.*

WARD, LOCK & CO., LTD., LONDON AND MELBOURNE

NOVELS BY DORNFORD YATES

PERISHABLE GOODS

" Dornford Yates holds his reader enthralled from cover to cover."—*Daily Mail.*

BLOOD ROYAL

" The story goes with dash and brilliance."—*Daily Telegraph.*

FIRE BELOW

" It is tremendously competent, exciting and quick moving."—Frank Swinnerton in the *Evening News.*

SAFE CUSTODY

" Amazing and breathless incidents . . . Mr. Yates at the top of his form . . . a most capital yarn."—*The Sphere.*

STORM MUSIC

" Dornford Yates is a clever story-teller, and his skill is cleverly revealed in this adventurous romance."—*Punch.*

SHE FELL AMONG THIEVES

" For speed of action, ingenuity of situation and breathless excitement, I do not believe Mr. Yates has an equal to-day."—*Punch.*

SHE PAINTED HER FACE

" A tale of strife and cunning, wild adventure and sweet romance, in his best style . . . Thank goodness for Mr. Dornford Yates."—*Nottingham Guardian.*

THIS PUBLICAN

" Mr. Yates tells his story in his usual entertaining, witty way, and brilliantly succeeds in making his somewhat difficult characters appear real."—*Liverpool Daily Post.*

GALE WARNING

" ' Gale Warning ' has every attribute a novel of this type should possess. Most refreshing entertainment from first to last."—*Daily Mail.*

SHOAL WATER

" Worked out with Mr. Yates's accustomed ingenuity. The action is quick and the dialogue in his best vein."—*Sunday Times.*

PERIOD STUFF

" ' Period Stuff ' is the chocolate-cream of fiction, and very enjoyable in these rationed days."—*Punch.*

AN EYE FOR A TOOTH

" Mr. Yates is as successful as ever. The opening is ingenious, the middle portion of the book sensational, the close a climax worthy of Mr. Yates."—*Birmingham Post.*

WARD, LOCK & CO., LTD., LONDON AND MELBOURNE